*To Christine,
a good fries.*

Renate

NITSCHEWO

"You are only a plennie"

Wilhelm Max Rose

Translated by Renate Butler

NITSCHEWO
Copyright © 2020 Renate Butler

All rights reserved, including the right to reproduce this book, or portions thereof in any form. No part of this text may be reproduced, transmitted, downloaded, decompiled, reverse engineered, or stored, in any form or introduced into any information storage and retrieval system, in any form or by any means, whether electronic or mechanical without the express written permission of the author.

ISBN: 978-0-244-57489-5

Wilhelm Max Rose was born in April 1905 in Patschkau, Silesia, Germany. Silesia is a historical region of Europe located mostly in Poland with parts in the Czech Republic and Germany.

His grandfather was named Schmitt and he uses his name in these memoirs.

Before World War II, he studied Theology, married Charlotte, and they had five children.

Early in the war, he volunteered as a combatant. In 1945 when he was a Captain Adjutant, he was captured in Konigsberg [East Prussia] and became a 'plennie' – a prisoner of war in Stalin's Soviet Russia until 1953.

This is his personal graphic account of imprisonment written by him in the 1960s, but was never published due to being considered 'too Russian friendly' in the then Cold War atmosphere.

His original has been translated by his daughter Renate Butler, now residing in Scotland.

NITSCHEWO translated from Russian means "Whatever"

Yea, though I walk through the valley of the shadow of death I will fear no evil; for thou art with me; thy rod and thy staff they comfort me.

Psalm 23 Verse 4

A sketch of Wilhelm Max Rose
A prisoner of war in Stalin's Soviet Russia
1945–1953, drawn by a fellow
prisoner of war in March 1949.

Prologue

The sky in the west is a wild orgy of colour in red and ochre. None of the most delicate nuances of the colours are missing. Slowly the colours fade and change to a bright shining green which darkens toward the zenith. It then turns to a light blue which takes on the night colours towards the east.

Here and there a bright star flickers. The colourful display comes down to earth from space. How often do I feel captivated by the sheer magic of the hour when day departs and night takes over? The rejoicing of the last glow of light and then it's passing into the oppressive secret darkness. It is this moment which turns into silent worship for me.

Words from the psalms come into my thoughts. "The heavens display the Lord's praise and the many wonderful feats of his hands," and the other verse which proclaims: "Light is the robe that you wear: you spread it across the sky like a carpet."

A rough hand destroys the mystery of this moment. The floodlighting is switched on and lights up the area, which until now was covered by the merciful darkness, in a brash cruel light. The watchtowers stretch towards the sky. Barbed wire fences, the dead area; the dogs with their clinking chains – everything is here again. Only for a short while it was hidden from view by the velvet darkness of the night. The other reminder was there too – the smell of crude oil and dust, all there to bring me back to my status as a prisoner of war in Russia – a plennie.

This hour is of special importance to me now that I know my wife and children are alive. During the war years we always had this time between night and day wherever we were – when we thought of each other. Maybe she now thinks of me, as she knows for certain that I am alive.

PART ONE

1

**Russian Prisoner of War Camp
Kazan, Tatarstan, Soviet Union
1947**

The voice of Hans Schubert draws me back into reality. "You certainly are far away in your dreams, time I brought you back down to earth, your soup is getting cold. I brought it for you from the kitchen."
"What is it?"
"The usual cabbage soup."
"Let it get cold. It tastes horrid anyway. This evening atmosphere is extra nourishment for the soul."
"Sentimental slop! That you can be moved by that, you should turn it into cash. Paint it! In really lurid colours, the Russians will happily pay for that; the brighter the better!"
"Hans, your mood is very dour tonight. Usually you are quite social in the evening hours, who rattled your cage today?"
"These bastards tricked me out of my extra bread ration! I worked like a madman to get the extra bread and what do I get? Nothing! They can kiss my arse!"
"I doubt if they will, but you shouldn't let them upset you. You have had time and opportunity since 1943 to get used to this sort of thing. It really isn't worth it to allow it to spoil such a beautiful summer evening. Just let yourself be distracted through something beautiful and enjoy it."
"That's what I'm trying to do – but today is one of those days when everything goes wrong. I keep thinking of my wife – it's so

hopeless! Then the thing with the bread. I am entitled to it and they are not letting me have it – I get so mad!"

"OK then, but please find some other object to take your temper out on!"

"I see things as they are. I can't live in cloud cuckoo land."

"Nobody expects you to. But it's pointless to get angry about things that are beyond your control. Nothing changes, it just becomes even more oppressive."

"Do you not get riled by obvious injustice?"

"Of course I do – but I will never give the Russians the chance to see it! That's his whole aim. Instead I try to think of something beautiful, my wife, my children, then they can...."

"I noticed earlier on how far away you were. I am beginning to know you very well."

"Well then. Do the same. It lifts you out of the dark grind and makes life a little easier."

"It's easy for you to talk. You have been married for years. You know the joys of looking after a family. You have memories which will carry you through many difficult hours. I have nothing."

"But you have memories of a kind, you were married."

"Exactly three days, that is not enough for memories!"

"Bullshit, you are wealthy because of it!"

"I am concerned as my wife lives in the Russian zone of Germany. She was only in her last year at school, not trained in anything. You don't have those worries. Your family lives in the west – the American zone. I know they were refugees but now they live in relative security and have more food than the people in the eastern zone."

"You should trust in the Lord to look after your wife."

"Please spare me the pious twaddle! I don't have your faith."

"I can only pity you. I get comfort through my faith and the certainty that God will protect my own."

"Oh no. I want to take care of my wife, just me. I am young, healthy – I can work. What I wouldn't do to make her life more tolerable. My life here is totally useless – I build houses for Russians while my own wife is exposed to all kinds of deprivations. I am sick of staring longingly towards home. I need to see her – I have to get out of here!"

"You'll have to speak to the Russians about it, that's their responsibility. I only want to warn you urgently – change your attitude. Life will become intolerable for you if you don't. You may come to a decision which will have awful repercussions for both you and your wife."

"You are right of course – keep pouring oil on troubled waters. I know I have to be patient, but you are usually quite a decent chap. But when you are wearing your parson's hat, I've had it. In the Bible there is a quote somewhere about being either hot or cold, but not luke-warm. I translate that in my way, I have come to a decision and then use up all my energy to effect its fulfilment."

"You do surprise me with your knowledge, more so with your personal interpretation of the Holy words. You always told me you had no truck with the Bible."

"To be in frequent contact affects even the strongest. You will be pleased to know that now I have had it. It just paralyses the thoughts and makes me unable to act. From today onwards life is going to change."

"But I still want to urge you to be cautious."

"Stop giving me advice and warnings."

"If I didn't care I wouldn't do it!"

"Oh I know that albeit reluctantly. I just don't understand how you, as an ordinary plennie who appreciates stolen potatoes as much as the next man, suddenly, when life itself is up for grabs, he refuses to act."

"You are quite right. I had no problems to steal potatoes when there was a chance. It's the impossible way of life which forces you to do things you couldn't normally do. A theft like that doesn't give me any moral scruples. It would be against plain common sense to rather starve than steal when I have the opportunity without hurting anyone else."

"Alright, we agree as far as this. What I can't understand is your reluctance to organize our way home?"

"You quite rightly accuse me of not being brave enough. But my objection to your present plan are different. I cannot be responsible for everyone's living standards in this camp to be reduced because I have decided to try to get home. You know how cruel the Russians can be in their retaliations if one plennie tries to escape."

"Never mind that. In our situation everyone is responsible for their own skin."

"My conscience stops me from thinking like that. I am trying to find a way where I alone have to pay the price of such an undertaking. I have thought and thought but so far with no solution."

"You are just too afraid to make such a decision."

"If other people have to pay with their lives for my action because the Russians are altering the living and working conditions to such an extent, then it's not a question of courage but pure egotism."

Hans shook his head angrily. He cannot agree with me. He is of course much younger than I and it is also the adventure that appeals to him. He probably already dreams of a gloriously successful escape.

That the Germans were kept prisoner after the unconditional surrender without hope of a date of repatriation, in fact without certain knowledge that the Russians plan to let us go at all is a violation of the Geneva Convention, it is also sheer brutality. Against this I can only use my reasoning that if through my escape only one man dies – it would be too high a price to pay.

Poor Hans has a bad day today, he is temporarily stir crazy.

The best thing to do is just to let it run its course and in a while he is back to his usual self. And then I suppose he has a point – one should do something to speed up the journey home. I often think about it but never discuss it with anybody. Toying with the idea of escape has become a familiar pastime since I know that my family is alive, have a roof over their head and that they are waiting for me. Life now looks totally different to me. It's worth the effort to stay healthy and to look for the best in every situation. Hans has observed this change in me and with intuitive feeling found my tender spot and now he picks at it at every opportunity.

In the past he has paid dearly for his impatience. He had the border within eyesight, he could see the Turkish border patrol but a dog barked! The Russian border police didn't touch him, but when the guards of his camp collected him, hell on earth started for him. The guards on duty at the time of his escape too had to pay dearly for his attempt by doing time. When he arrived at our camp a few months later he had to spend time in hospital.

I want to protect him from a repeat version – it could finish off much worse. It took him a long time to trust me, both of us had unfortunate experiences with our own compatriots.

We return to the barrack and eat our soup. Usually we sit and talk together but this evening he just sits and stares at the ceiling.

I lie down on my bunk and follow the smoke of my cigarette. It takes on the shape of my loved ones who follow me in my thoughts throughout the day and night. They are of course pictures of my past, as I know nothing of their present life.

The air in the barrack is gradually getting unbearable. The heat of the day lingers on added to that the smoke of 200 smokers and the usual human odours – breathing is difficult. Still, I am just about to drift off to sleep when Hans sits down on the end of my bunk. He is puffing away on his homemade pipe and he appears calmer. He has come to collect me for our constitutional evening stroll before we finally go to sleep.

We go out into the cool night air. Every night the miracle of the night sky touches me and never do I feel closer to the Almighty and his creation. Why did I never feel like this in my earlier days? Did I have to be humbled to see it in all its glory?

Hans must feel the same. Even he is caught up in the mystery of the moment. I suspect that he thinks of any emotional feeling as unmanly and shameful. We walk to our favourite place somewhere hidden by the shadow of big storerooms. We are protected there from the harsh glare of the floodlighting.

This is a good viewpoint, way beyond the restrictions of the prison camp. The railway lines of the Trans-Siberian Railway is open to see as it turns into a huge bend, about 400 metres from the camp. In about 15 minutes we will once more witness the exciting spectacle of trains arriving from Vladivostok, Omsk, Sverdlovsk and Kazan on their way to Moscow. We can see the red light flickering.

We often wonder why the railway line took an unusual turn. A teacher had explained to me how it came about when the then reigning Tsar gave the order to build the line from Kazan to Sverdlovsk. According to the story he drew a straight line but he had his finger on the drawing and drew round it. Who would dare to question the Tsar? So, there for all time is the massive arc of the line.

If the Tsar only knew how many travellers unable to pay for a ticket, use this time to jump off and get away scot free when the train slows down.

We see the lights of the approaching train and hear the roar of the engine getting louder and louder. The signal is still at red, the train slows down, and we hear the squeal of the brakes and the sound of the banging of the pistons. The engine looks like a prehistoric monster in the darkness. No doubt the engine driver is swearing like mad as he is losing time. The stoker is feeding the monster with loads of coal and bright sparks burst into the darkness. With a massive sigh the engine stops.

We watch as a great number of the non-paying customers jump off. It looks as if there are more of them than actual ticket holders! No doubt someone had been well bribed to stop there every night. Suddenly the green light flares up, the train gathers speed again and the engine is hidden from view in a white cloud of steam. The train glides past us and we see the lit-up carriages, still divided into 'soft' and 'hard' class with white gathered curtains for the soft – so much for equality!

The illegals can take their time as the train stops in the station to take on water. They just have to watch out for the militia. When the train slowly leaves the station they can remain on the train.

"Oh Max," Hans says. "Wouldn't it be wonderful to get to the West?"

Now my apprehensions are realized. This has to be the way Hans wants to escape. How do I explain the futility of such a venture to him? He must realize even amongst the poorest of the passengers we would stick out. We speak very little Russian, our heads aren't shaved and our state of health is such that we could not compete for a safe place. The next tunnel would see the end of our journey. Hans can't see it my way, his need to get back to his Hilde obscures all common sense.

Maybe God has put me in his way so I can protect him from going into certain painful death.

Hans is a bit ashamed, he bites right through the mouthpiece of his pipe in anger. That has calmed him a little and I know his love for his wife is pulling at him with 1000 strings.

He had fought in Stalingrad and had been reported as missing, presumed dead at home. Hilde and Hans grew up together and gradually realized they were in love. Hans finished his secondary education and has lots of war experience. In a very short time after joining up he rose to the rank of Captain, their future secure. In his last home leave in 1942 they got married. Three days was all they had when the telegram arrived to call him to Stalingrad. Since then they have had no contact. This silence nearly drives the poor man demented. He lives off the memory of those three days. He may have had other sexual encounters, but nothing touched him. He gives the impression of a pure simpleton.

"Max, it's easier for you. You have lived, known love, have memories no one can take away. But what about me, I only started to live and it came to a sudden end."

"You are confusing love and living. What you describe as love is only temporary and is not the only basis of a good marriage."

"Oh shut up, I've had enough. I have got to get home to my Hilde, the longing is driving me crazy. I can hear her calling for me every night. She needs me: she is suffering as much as I am. I have got to get home."

Of course I understand him. I too miss my wife and children. The balance of my life had become somewhat uneven since I learned that they are alive. Hans has nothing to support him, his philosophy of life totally collapsed with the downfall of the third Reich. He is like a reed in the wind. I want to help him but he just withdraws into himself. I wish he would abstain from his crazy plans and ideas.

"Even if your escape succeeds," I tell him. "It would put your wife in danger. You can't hide yourself in Jena, you need ration cards. And always remember our national character. Many an officer shed his backbone with his boots, decorations and uniform. Just remember that Tank Major who sold all his trusting men to the Russians for a promise of a quick repatriation. But the Russians first had a good laugh, took all his men prisoner then sent him to our camp! He had the misfortune to meet up with one of his Corporals and his body was found head down in the latrines. Remember all that and also at home that people are no different. It just needs one of those former bosses to find out about you and he would use the knowledge to buy extra privileges with the new masters. Do you really want your wife to end up in a Russian work camp?"

"Do you think I don't know all that? But I still have to get home." If only he knew how often I dream the same dream.

"Come Hans it's late. Tomorrow is another day. It's Saturday and with any luck Sunday might be a day off. Let us look forward to something within our sights."

The worry with Hans stays with me. I must try to get more of a hold over him, to protect him from himself. It's not easy. I have to listen to all sorts of insults and accusations. But he is always sorry afterwards and looks totally beaten.

The prevailing heat augurs a bad night. I toss and turn in my sleep. An odd dream keeps recurring. I see my mother surrounded by my children. She has Bernd the youngest whom I baptized on my last home visit sitting on her lap. She looks at me with a very sad expression just like she used to when I was a youngster and had been up to some mischief. Then she waved to me and I can clearly hear her deep voice *'You must come home soon'*. I wake up and the picture dissolves. For hours I lie awake and try to interpret the dream. It's so different from the usual plennie dream. We dream of wonderful restaurants, mountains of meat, sausages and bread are stacked in front of me. *'And they lifted their hands to start their delicious meal'* as Homer put it. A real debauchery in eating and drinking begins. But this dream was different.

My fellow inmate in the upper bunk no doubt had one of the latter dreams and continued with the digestion of his dream meal right to the bitter end and the almost foul air became unbearable as my sheet is overrun with fleas, they seem to be intent on jumping and biting me for all they are worth.

I almost prefer bedbugs, they only seem to march up and down my body without biting me. I just hate it when they are next to my nose, it smells of marzipan. In my rush to get into the fresh air I forgot to get dressed. Much as I enjoy the clean air I have to return for my underpants. The soldier on guard duty is full of disgust and as a sign of his disapproval he spits in my direction. I return suitably covered with my underwear and he relaxes.

It's amazing how prudish the Russians can be. There is a statue of a young huntress in the 'place of culture' surrounded by flowerbeds and benches. The bronze statue is unclothed apart from a bra and short skirt. And I don't think the clothes were put on because of any sexual feelings she might arouse amongst the captured men. Hunger is a total depressant of any sexual impulses. In full contrast to this modesty is the fact that there are only female nurses and in general also young female doctors. That took a bit of getting used to for most of us.

The guard has got over his attack of modesty and lost interest in me. Maybe he is too captivated by the spectacle that begins to take place in the sky. It is about 3.30am. The horizon in the east is clear as glass and a reversal of last evening's sunset begins.

It looks as if the night is shedding its dark coat towards home in the west. It must be a sunrise like this which prompted Homer to talk about Eros with fingers made of roses. I keep thinking of this poet as I managed to exchange some tobacco for the Iliad and Odyssey some time ago.

But suddenly I feel cold. I must get back to catch just a few hours more sleep before work begins. The working day is quite long enough. I quickly get back to sleep and in my dream I travel on the Siberian Express. But before I can get really involved the gong sounds. Time to get up.

It is awful to be dragged back into the reality of life as a plennie.

But I suddenly remember that it is Saturday and tomorrow may be a day off. Providing some quota obsessed lunatic does not decide that we have to load wagons full of coal and bricks. But even here in Russia we have the odd miracle and I want to believe in them.

Hans is just on his return trip to the washroom as he whacks me across the shoulders with his wet towel. Very funny. I have a hard job to keep my temper in check. I still have a lot to learn. But being a plennie gives you lots of occasions to do this.

Soon I join Hans in the morning queue for our soup and 600g of bread. In a tin are 40g of sugar, in another 20g of lard. 15 cigarettes are given to us at the same time. We breakfast together as we do every morning.

In normal times I never had visits in the early hours, I am still not a morning person. I still think of my dreams of the previous night.

Hans, irrespective of my silence asks: "Well, have you thought of my suggestion last night?"

First I am speechless. I thought I had made my reaction quite clear! And then I kicked his leg and said:

"Did the birds crap in your brain?"

I don't usually express myself in such a fashion, but it finally got through to him that it was a highly dangerous project within a room. There is always someone ready to sell a comrade for extra rations of bread.

Even a mere hint of suspicion is sufficient for the MWD to effect a transfer to another camp and I have to keep him close to me for a while to make sure he doesn't attempt to escape from captivity. Of course I understand his longing. I listen to him when he talks about Hilde in the tender hearted of ways. And if I didn't know that the only books he probably ever read were '*Mein Kampf* 'and technical books about guns. I would compare his style to Frank Thiess, '*Paradise Lost*' and '*Door to the World*.' However there is no danger of that. I just have to prevent him from committing an absolute blinder.

We continue with our breakfast and it is an awful temptation to eat the lot in one go. But it has to last until this evening and it's good to have something to look forward to. And it's Saturday – a double excuse to have prannick (a feast) in the evening. We will just have to fool our stomachs with cigarettes.

At the sound of the gong we line up for the morning muster. A group of workers remains in the camp.

The rest march to the gate where we are met by young Ali. He had been working in the factory for six months, originally was meant to learn carpentry, but as he was as skinny as a rake the powers that be decided he should be in charge of three plennie brigades to give him a chance to put on a bit of weight.

Ali has his rifle over his shoulder – his status symbol as being one of the men. He is grinning from ear to ear and heads off at the head of the gang towards our place of work. As he sees a group of others approaching he decides to go through the motions of a recount. He takes it all deadly seriously and basks in the admiration of his mates. Our job at the moment is to rebuild a big garage. We had to build it during the winter when it was down to minus 40 degrees, against all warnings by building experts. When Spring came it collapsed one night, luckily no one was hurt.

Young Ali is fond of us. As he is a Tatar he has a deep-seated dislike and mistrust of the Russians. He is the oldest of 5 children, and his father was killed early on in the war. My Russian is not up to much but Ali's is equally limited so we sign and use body language and get on like a house on fire. He often scrounges a cigarette and he just loves to talk. Unfortunately I understand only a fraction. I just throw in the odd 'da-da' and nod my head. He is happy with that and I am pleased to win his affection.

He had heard what monsters the Germans were but through knowing us he has revised his opinion. I once helped him in a very awkward situation. Usually after loading coal we go to the showers before returning to camp.

This evening however he decided we were going straight back. He yelled and shouted, started prodding us with the gun and generally gave the impression of a dancing bear. To add insult to injury he found that his gun is jammed. By now he is surrounded by a large group of laughing men. He felt very embarrassed and tears of frustration rolled down his face.

I took the gun from him, rectified the jammed breach and returned it to him. He quickly checked that none of the other youngsters had witnessed the debacle. As quickly as his temper flared up it subsided when he found out that none of us had talked about the incident, he was our friend for life. As a sign of his appreciation he gave me a few semilchkis.

We all know our place in the big cog, we work well together. Until midday Hans and I will carry bricks. He never mentions last night's conversation. Maybe my unusual burst of temper persuaded him to shelve his plans for the time being.

It's getting very hot, we strip off to shoes and trousers and do very little. I still pursue the dreams of the previous evening. No doubt they were triggered by our conversation and sight of the Express.

But I had hoped too early for a change in his thoughts. When he once more starts talking about the futility of our daily life and work I try to explain how I am trying to find a meaning to our lives.

Just look at me in my previous existence. I never had to work with my hands, I never appreciated the monotony and thoughts of a labourer. I sometimes feel that being a plennie is a way of life showing me the other side of the fence. So many times I preached and theorized about the Lord's Prayer, especially the part where we ask for our daily bread!

But I never knew what hunger was, real hunger which is with you day and night. Hunger which can turn an honest man into a thief, a murderer even. I take hope this episode in my life will come to an end one day. But I feel I may learn something new every day in my journey of discovery. I see this life, miserable as it may be at present as a means of coming to terms with myself.

"Oh Max I envy you your philosophy, you can still see a positive side to our situation. I just can't cope with this. I was brought up to think that my fate was in my hands only. That it was up to me to change things, not ever refer to a higher authority."

How limited the frontiers for some individuals were became painfully obvious in the long years of imprisonment. We are totally in the hands of our guards. If they don't feel like it they can deny you your most basic needs. I often feel that we have to do penance for our past deeds of the German people. Maybe we weren't personally an active party but we kept quiet.

"But wasn't it you Max, who told me of the horror you witnessed by the Russians. Sheer brutality against defenceless women and children? And you talk of atonement."

"There has to be an end to it somewhere and a new beginning has to be found. We have to decide that we actively want to contribute to a lasting peace."

2

The sudden screech of the sirens interrupts our talk. A proper plennie should just drop his tools where he stands, but being orderly Germans we put everything away neatly. Ali collects his men, he too is in a hurry to get back so we quickly line up in a row of five and off we go towards the camp. As we approach we notice signs of excitement. The Commandant is rushing about as well as the operativnik and the Quartermaster. As we come closer we see a new Lieutenant Colonel is there having a go at the Quartermaster. They are obviously looking for someone. One group of plennies has already gone through the gate and now it's our turn.

The Lieutenant Colonel comes towards us. He is quite a sight for sore eyes. Tall, slim build with wide shoulders – a chest full of medals, a well-tailored uniform and beautiful soft boots to round it off. Behind him are most of the camp officers plus a few Sergeants. He reads from a paper.

"Schmitt Max," and I reply automatically.

"Wilhelm, Null (=1905) pjat."

"Over there, the rest can go," all in good German. I am right in front of him and something in his demeanour makes me stand to attention. He notices and smiled. "Right, follow me to the admin office."

Now I notice all the other Russians are grinning as they notice my inner excitement.

Once we are in the office the Lt Colonel informs me that I am off to Moscow next day accompanied by a Sergeant. "You will be ready to leave at 9.45pm with the Siberian Express. You will be informed of all the other details."

My knees are shaking but I make an effort, salute, turn about and leave the office. I pass the Sergeant who gives me a well-meant pat on my shoulder and then I enter my barrack. Everyone wants to know what is happening. Hans has collected our lunch, the usual soup.

"I am off to Moscow tomorrow evening."

"You lucky bastard!"

"That remains to be seen. You remember my last post was in counter espionage. My General is in Moscow awaiting his sentence. But before that they are collecting all the remaining men of his staff. I have a very uneasy feeling about it. You know the plennie saying: Nothing is impossible, everything is probable, especially the least expected! I have no hope of a sudden repatriation."

We were interrupted by Herman Klug who assists the German camp leader. He found out from the Russian operativnik that I am to join a group of parsons ready for home! The Soviet was trying to show they were 'church friendly". At the moment I don't care what the reason is, but Moscow is a few 100km closer to home. Any change in my plennie life is positive.

A runner from head office informs me that I am off work this afternoon to give me time to collect my things. Such thoughtfulness!

But I have been a plennie too long. I know how their minds work. Butter him up, make him feel relaxed – and wallop we've got him! It's a rare pleasure not to have to join up for the afternoon shift. I take stock of my time here, and incredible as it seems there were good moments here too.

Now all these years later I can reminisce, cast my mind back to moments for ever in my memory.

One evening in February 1947 for example, the German senior officer brought me the news that my family were still alive. I was totally speechless – all I could do was press his hand gratefully. I am one of the last three in the camp who had had no news from home. That night I barely slept. Wherever they were, however they managed to survive there will be a *Wiedersehen* one day! I never prayed so intensely as that night to thank my maker for the gift of my family.

In the morning everyone is pleased for me I can read their faces. They offer me cigarettes, the plennie's most precious possession. At lunchtime a Sergeant takes me to the operativnik who is sitting grinning behind his desk. My goodness, he is offering me a chair. In his hands he was holding a postcard. Even the interpreter, who is known as the 'icicle' because of her normal attitude towards the prisoners, looks almost animated. Usually she looks pale and cold. Her eyes look suspiciously damp.

"Schmitt, you post have of wife and children."

The operativnik has learned this sentence off by heart. He passes the card over to the interpreter who reads it to me. She has to repeat for him in Russian, and I can see the tears running down her face. Oh Russia, Oh Russia! This is the same man who beat me within an inch of my life a few months earlier because I wouldn't admit to having been a spy. This man who had brandished my only picture of my family in front of me and shouted: "We'll shoot the lot of them unless you confess!"

The same man sits in front of me, grabs my hand and we both cry our eyes out for joy. Time seemed to have hardened all our hearts – but even 40 years of Bolshevism couldn't erase all traces of humanity.

Suddenly Grisha the Sergeant arrives and I'm back to the here and now.

"Come Schmitt, off to the supply depot. New clothes for the journey. We go to Moscow."

I can tell by his face how pleased he is to be chosen for this escort duty.

My clothes are more or less a bundle of rags, mended and stitched together as best I could. Joseph's coat of many colours must have looked a bit like it. All but my shoes, I have them under my head every night, I even sacrificed my leather belt to have them resoled.

The clothes offered to me are not a vast improvement, but I couldn't care less. In the kitchen we collect our travelling rations for six days: 3600gr bread, 120gr butter, 240gr sugar and nearly a kilo of pickled herrings. I am absolutely flabbergasted by such riches. I sign the receipt and then ask the kitchen boss to store my supplies until the morning, to stop me from eating them during the night.

It's beyond Grisha's understanding that I am prepared to leave my goods here – won't it be 'shrunk' a bit by morning, but then he just shakes his head.

'Nitschewo. I'll come and collect you tomorrow at 4 o'clock.'

It turns out to be a very long afternoon. Everyone makes an effort to be nice to me. Only now I find out how many good friends I have here. They have talked of nothing else all afternoon. In a way they feel sorry for me. No one believes in my repatriation story. It would be against all previous experiences. How often have we met up with others who officially were going home? In reality they often had been transferred to other harder prisons in an attempt to wear them down to confess to whatever crazy crimes they had or had not committed.

But I had seen my discharge papers, I am prepared to go through hell providing home is at the other end of the tunnel. What I do notice is that none of the other plennies give me their families' addresses. Just no one believes in the idea, they all know how much the Russians suspect me of war crimes. They remember in what state I returned from some of the questioning sessions.

As it gets dark Hans and I once more watch our train.

I implore him to let events take their course. I remind him of comrade Ulbricht's speech.

"If it were up to me, none of you would ever return. You would obstruct the democratic rebuilding of Germany."

Hans agreed with me in principle but because of his youth he just felt he owed it to his wife to do something, anything.

I tell him about my dreams the previous night. He gives me his wife's address, just in case, and we watch the train arriving and departing. We have said it all, there was nothing more to say.

This was to be my last night amongst this group of men whom I have known for just about a year. I know of many of their life stories. So many found it hard to adjust to prison life again once they had had their first news from home. Sometimes it helps just to have someone who can listen. I was not officially permitted to act as a chaplain but I could still look after their souls.

I am glad when night turns into day. Sunday work has been arranged in a nearby kolchose (farm) as there was some sort of emergency. I went to the barber to shave off my beard and my hair. Then I checked out my rucksack, the few bits of clothing and my travel rations are hardly going to fill it up.

It was a bit of a shock when I saw my face in the barber's mirror. I looked as if I was in the advanced stage of TB. The rest of my body looked similar. Where once I had a stomach there is now a hollow. A well-nourished clothes stand would describe me aptly.

As I expect to be body searched on my exit I will have to remember to hide my pocketknife. Usually I hold it in my hand, as they just don't think I would dare to do that. As for my wedding ring, I used to put it over one of my fly buttons. Later I saved it under the sweatband of my cap. Filthy looking old thing that it is, even the Russians don't like touching it. What else can I put in my rucksack? I nearly forgot my overcoat, which I have had since 1945. It's just as well that I was never very vain. When I got this coat I never thought it would do me such good service in Russia.

Lunchtime is here at last. Theoretically I am off the roster but there was a bit to spare. Then off for a few goodbyes. Especially from the senior officer and his aides. They try to be pleased for me, but I can guess at their hidden apprehension, that things might turn out quite differently. The senior officer looks at me as if he were to make a long speech, instead he shakes my hand and just wishes me all the very best.

Now I have to wait a while for Grisha. I must have dozed off on my bunk because suddenly he is here.

"Schmitt. Wake up, we go to Moscow!"

There is nothing I can do to affect my fate one way or another. My fear and uncertainty have left me, I am in God's hands and I feel safe.

I put on my rucksack. Grisha checks me over and seems satisfied.

"You very thin," he says pointing to a lamp post. A quick goodbye to the German officials then into the guardroom. 'Otkritj' (take off) he says pointing to my rucksack. He gives it a quick once over and that's it.

Now just the usual report to remove my name off the register and it's goodbye to this place. He presses the lever to open the door, I grab my cap and believe it or not he wishes me 'Wojo chareschewo' (all the very best). Wonders will never cease, he must have a soul after all.

Grisha crosses the yard with me to get to the main guardhouse. Everyone has to go through there, not just the plennies. Otherwise the locals employed here would acquire bits and pieces of machinery.

The soldier on duty no doubt feels very important as he gives me a rub-down search, but then he is about to check my trouser pockets and Grisha says something to him which I don't understand. The Russian language had a wealth of descriptive oaths and swearwords and the two of them curse and shout at each other, but when the guard takes my rucksack Grisha lands him one, and his knees buckle. Grisha pushed me out of the door. The guard on the next gate along the perimeter fence has heard some of the shouting and joins in the chorus. As it happens to be a female guard it sounds particularly bad. No doubt it's the highlight of today's shift for her.

The other guard has recovered sufficiently to get to the door and starts to shout again. Grisha grabs a broken piece of metal and flings it with some accuracy at the man.

Luckily he took cover behind the door, so only a bit of the door took a battering. His head would not have been able to withstand it as well. Grisha and I quickly make our way up to the railway lines.

Alongside is a dirt road which turns into a proper road after 500 metres. As we are coming closer to a town a lorry passes us, Grisha flags it down and we have a lift to the railway station.

Only now do I get a chance to have a good look at Grisha. He only wears his belt over his uniform – no sign of a gun. The Nagan is too large to put in his pocket. Very odd. Maybe I will be in luck after all.

I remember the road to the station from previous occasions when we were ordered to help with the unloading of freighters. The docks are just a bit past the station. On one occasion we have to unload a freighter containing barrels of butter. We had been allowed to take spoons with us, a broken barrel was bound to come our way. But no bread. But it turned out to be a mixed pleasure. We were allowed to let nature take its course straight into the Volga as our bodies couldn't cope with the influx of real food. But we had an hour long march through the town where many of the men were doubled up in pain and the pressure got too much – it went straight into their trousers!

The guard post wouldn't let us in initially and to the delighted grins of the whole mob we had to crawl to our barracks. It took ages to get rid of the stink.

As Grisha and I pass by the railway station we turn away and after many little alleyways we arrive in front of a one-storey building. We go up to the first floor, all is in darkness. Grisha kicks against a door and when it opens a babuschka (old lady) invites us in. A friendly pair of eyes in a face marked by time and hard life examines me. I give a hint of a bow. At this moment the young wife of Grisha comes in and talks nineteen to the dozen. She is very young but her hands show that she is used to hard labour. She is barefoot and wears one of the brightly coloured dresses mass-produced in Russia.

She is not a Tatar – her face is too European – she has beautiful white teeth and she wears her long hair in a plait like a crown.

Now it's her turn to check me out. I am most likely the first plennie she has ever seen. After the inspection she shakes my hand. It's been three years since I shook hands with a woman. She relieves me of my rucksack and asks me to sit down.

I can't understand a word they say, they speak to me in an unknown dialect. The old lady speaks to Grisha who tells me to take my coat off. She has seen a button that is loose and quick as anything sews it on.

Now I have the opportunity to inspect my surroundings a bit closer. So, this is how a Russian and his family live. He is a soldier and his wife works too, but there isn't a single item in the flat which could vaguely be described as a luxury. The room is spotlessly clean and about 3.5 x 4.5 metres. There is a small tiled stove plus cooker and a door leads into a tiny eaves room with just a fanlight. In the main room there is a table, one chair and added to that is a chest. No doubt used to store clothes and linen. The cooking utensils consist of 2 mess tins of German origin and the cutlery to go with it, plus a few homemade carved wooden spoons and whisks, and a few glasses.

The family ablutions take place in a small metal bowl with a snow-white towel hanging above it. Next to it is a bright pink piece of soap in a vivid plastic soap dish. The marital bed is a simple army bed. A jug and a bucket complete the list of contents apart from a demijohn filled with cloudy liquid.

Suddenly we hear the angry shouts of a small child. The babuschka puts down her sewing and goes to fetch the child. Grisha proudly points to the baby, a bin (boy) who is being breast-fed by his mum.

After Grisha junior has been fed he gets changed and his nappies go in the bucket. His mother returns the baby to his bedroom where he happily gurgles and smiles. The room is lit by a single bulb suspended from the ceiling.

There are many signs that Grisha works with German plennies. Empty tins used for storage and the star item, a homemade electric hotplate. Cost to the plennie 7 roubles for materials from the local workmen. Cost to Grisha: 12 roubles – good business.

The old lady takes a few potatoes from a sack under the bed and goes down into the courtyard to wash them at the communal pump. I quickly pick up the water jug and the bucket to fetch some water but Grisha takes the bucket and by clear signs I realize that is not for clean water. When I help the old lady she looks quite surprised, that a man helps her carry her load is a bit of a novelty. Equality is not the order of the day in Russia.

Before we eat, Grisha has to have a top-to-toe wash, which is just as well as he takes his boots off. Everything is laid out for him. A snow-white shirt, cleaned uniform trousers and the Russian loose jacket held together by a leather belt.

Only when I see him point to his boots I see his wife looking none too pleased. His mother quickly takes the boots away for a major clean and shine.

I get the definite impression the young woman is not very happy about her husband's forthcoming trip to the fleshpots of the big city.

The babuschka returns with the shiny boots and Grisha puts them on and goes down to the communal toilet in the yard.

In his absence his spouse quickly removes a few roubles from his rubaschka (uniform) pocket and sticks them down her cleavage!

In the meantime the potatoes are cooked, what a lovely smell and only now do I realize how hungry I am. The table is moved to the centre of the room, 3 metal plates and a mess tin are put on the table.

A pickled gherkin is put on each plate and a bit of salt.

Here we go, I thought, but no. the three of them stand in front of an icon in one of the corners. Grisha gives me a glance so I stand next to them and make the sign of the cross. Grisha seems to be a bit embarrassed.

Then we do sit at the table - what a joy to sit with a family, and the potatoes taste wonderful. The babouschka fills our glasses with the cloudy liquid from the demijohn, it is Quas. A very refreshing drink in the prevailing heat. Both Grisha and I get served more potatoes and a gherkin and I have to loosen my belt.

After the meal Grisha gives me a wink. "Davei, Max, kuritj," (cigarettes). I pass him the packet, which he passes to his mother and then to his wife. We are enjoying our smoke when I remember I still have a packet of Grusinskaja tea. I give it to the young woman who seems to be reluctant to take a gift from a poor plennie but then she puts it with her other meagre supplies and I can see how pleased she is. She boils water and brews the tea. As they don't seem to have any sugar I contribute some of mine and we enjoy a peaceful atmosphere.

By then it is 8pm when Grisha points to his prehistoric pocket watch. He has a quick check that everything is in order and his wife no doubt tells him to behave himself in the big city and just smiles. No doubt he is thinking of the roubles, now a few less, in his pocket. His wife prepared his travel rations. The potatoes get mashed with a bit of salt and gets squashed into a mess tin. To that she adds a three pound loaf. What a sparse ration for a Sergeant in the victorious army.

It all gets put into my rucksack and we are ready to begin our big adventure. When I want to say goodbye to the women I realize we are getting an escort to the station. I am somewhat curious what weapon Grisha will carry on him. But no, nothing. However I see him putting a thick blue folder into his wide trouser pocket. I know that folder well. I saw it first in the Lieutenant Colonel's hand when he gave me the good news. There is just that bit of hope, that it may be just that – good news, homeward journey? Why shouldn't I be lucky this time? But 'posmotrim'? We will see.

The women had dressed the little boy for his outing. He had one more feed, a nappy change and now was tucked up securely in a pillowcase and fast asleep.

We take off in formation. First grandma with her grandson, then me and behind the young couple. No doubt Grisha is getting his last orders to behave himself in Moscow. I suppose he is promising to be a model of decorum with the alas mistaken belief in his hidden wealth. We cause a bit of a stir on the street, but Grisha isn't bothered. Even when we pass an officer he just gives him a casual salute. Once we get to the station we still have an hour's wait.

The station platform looks like an eastern market, bright and colourful. The tatars with their embroidered caps and their womenfolk in those multi-coloured skirts. We once more pass the cigarettes around. The baby is sleeping peacefully.

Grisha asks me to come with him. He takes me to the soft waiting room, just to have a look. Soft carpets, beautifully set tables, waiters done up in frock coats and black tie, each one looks like a duke.

The waitresses wear black tight fitting satin dresses with a frilly white lace apron, even nail polish and lipstick are in evidence. Crystal glitters on the tables and silverware is there too. The things you see in Potemkin's country. Even Grisha looks longingly at this different world. It is as close to him as it is to me.

By now it is 9.30 and Grisha says farewell to his little family. He doesn't want them to come with us to the actual platform. I shake their hands and say "Bolschor spacia."

The platform is full of commotion, outside the compartments are signs with numbers which correspond with numbers on the railway tickets. We are walking about and I am surprised we are not stopping at any of the signs. I hope we are not travelling with the freight. Suddenly he drags me into a dark corner of the station, undoes his trousers and produces a Nagan!

"Max, no fear. I get us seats."

With a big grin he pushes me back to send me flying into a group of travellers. Before they have time to gather their wits they see the Nagan pointed at me and recognize the red band of the MWD (Military Security Branch) on Grisha's cap. That's enough and they clear a space. The usually calm Grisha has turned into a devil. He curses his family way back to the Stone Age as he had been picked to escort this cursed Nemek (German) to Moscow.

He is a war criminal and no doubt they will hang him there. He pushes the barrel of the gun in my neck and gives me repeated shoves with his newly polished boots. Every time I get propelled forward closer towards the edge of the platform.

The other travellers open a path for us. Grisha explains in a loud voice that it is his unchosen duty to escort this despicable object to Moscow to his deserved fate. I get the impression that Grisha's behaviour doesn't meet with general approval but one spectator decides to join in and wants to give me a good smack. Luckily his aim is none too good and he hits the Nagan instead. The barrel recoils and hits him on the head and a few of the onlookers give a subdued cheer.

A military policeman has come over to find out what is going on. With my limited knowledge of Russian I can work out that he is telling Grisha off for allowing a prisoner of war to be mistreated. He grabs hold of the foiled attacker and drags him off to the delight of the other travellers. Ah well, one less on the train.

3

The train arrives and everyone pushes towards the doors. The train official on the lookout for the new travellers looks straight into the barrel of the Nagan and his hands are above his head before he can take another breath.

My escort tells him short and sharp to clear a compartment for the war criminal. The conductor returns within seconds and we climb aboard and everyone watches fascinated as Grisha pushes me along the passage. What excitement to see a candidate for a death sentence, it's certainly something to relieve the monotony of the long journey.

The conductor shows us into a hastily vacated compartment. Grisha collapses onto one of the seats with tears running down his face. I too am close to tears; his pantomime was just a bit too close for comfort at times. He pats me on the shoulder and locks the door from the inside, only a conductor can open it with a special key. Grisha undoes his trousers and exchanges the Nagan for his blue folder.

I produce my cigarettes, we both have to calm down a bit after all the excitement. He goes to the window and the astonished audience sees two peacefully smoking men – a total transformation from the ranting soldier and the cowering plennie. To really confuse everyone, Grisha puts his arm around my shoulder. His family instead of going home have watched the whole charade and are highly amused. The old lady gently strokes my face with her work worn hand. The military policeman joins the group and accepts a cigarette. It was all a pre-arranged performance. Grisha once more gets last minute instructions. I can read his thoughts, *'out of sight, out of mind.'*

In the meantime the train has taken on board water and other supplies, the signal sounds twice and we are off. We wave until everyone has disappeared from view and close the window.

My escort takes the window seat and I have one of the upper bunks. I use my coat as matting and my rucksack as a pillow. Grisha takes off his uniform blouse and his wallet falls out. He quickly counts his money and once more turns into a raging madman and almost pulls the emergency cord. He discovered what his wife had done. So much for Moscow and nights on the tiles. But after a while he calmed down once again and puts his uniform back on.

There is a knock on the door. I just understood the word 'police' as Grisha opens the door at once to be faced by two men who without even having to show their shield are typical detectives. They study my blue folder and our tickets, give me a friendly smile, say goodbye and leave.

Grisha however is more concerned with the hole in his funds than the detectives visit. Suddenly he has a bright idea. He points to the empty seats in our compartment and says "Sell." He makes his way along the passage and returns with a young air force captain. This man shakes my hand – it's the first time a Russian officer has done that. He gives me a nudge and indicates that I should follow him. When we appear in the passage, quickly every door is shut. When we do get to the end of the wagon we find a well-dressed young woman who is sitting on her own hugging her crying child. Obviously a victim of Grisha's clearance operation. Politely the officer takes some of her luggage and asks her to return to the compartment. There are two more huge cases and a smaller one. The officer takes the larger cases and points for me to take the smaller one.

Once we are back in the compartment everything is stashed away and I am back in my bunk and I can watch the woman and the child. It is a long time since I have seen a woman in modern European dress.

She knows that I am watching her and after a few moments she returns my gaze. She has beautiful large blue eyes. She is of slim build and with her straight eyebrows she looks very intent. Her long hair is plaited and worn in coils over her ears. A beautiful mouth with white glistening teeth complete the picture. She knows that I admire her and she enjoys it. The little girl is just the opposite of her mother. She has long blonde hair and sparkling blue eyes and she watches me full of curiosity. Suddenly she reaches up to me to touch my hand and her mother follows her example. Another barrier is overcome.

But Grisha had suddenly disappeared and returns accompanied by a gypsy girl. She too had contributed to Grisha's travel fund in her own way.

I suppose she is there to cheer up Grisha and make up for not having his wife with him. He allocates her a space above the door which is considerably more comfortable than her original mode of transport, she had been travelling on the footplates.

She is dressed in a white blouse and a full brightly coloured skirt – otherwise she doesn't seem to wear anything. Grisha must have checked her over carefully before pulling her into the train through the window of the wagon door. He looks full of admiration at his acquisition. His wife's warnings didn't last for long!

The air force Captain asks me to sit next to him. He speaks good German. He is on his way to Leipzig from Siberia where he visited his parents. The young woman is a doctor who is travelling from Vladivostok to Moscow to join her husband there.

The airman greatly admires Germany. He loves the town of Leipzig, the beer and the girls.

"I live with babushka and beautiful daughter; will soon get married."

He looks at me thoughtfully, asks my age and whether I have a wife and children. He also wants to know my rank. When I tell him that I too am a Captain he seems very pleased. But then he is back to the favourite topic of conversation of all soldiers: girls! He seems to have worked out that a woman's role in Germany is somewhat different to her sisters in the Soviet Union. No doubt his girlfriend has given him this positive impression of German women. I can imagine that it's often hunger that forces a lot of women to sell their body to feed their children. I try to deflect him from his subject of conversation by showing him the few pictures that I still have.

They are snaps of my family, my house and my church. He passes them on to the young doctor who is called Alexandrova.

The more I listen to the young officer, the more I have the suspicion that he is not exactly a good advert for Papa Stalin. He is too full of admiration for the vanquished and their way of life. Once again he looks at the photos.

"Beautiful wife, lovely children." He understands that I am longing to get home, but he looks very concerned when I tell him that my family live in the American zone. "Americans nix good," he says with a frown. I try to find out the reason for his answer but he avoids my questions. Could it be that the allies no longer are *one heart and one soul.*' Now I am beginning to understand the repeated question: 'Why did you Germans fight against Russia?' at many of my interrogations as a plennie.

I obviously didn't feel qualified to give a satisfactory answer then or now. I could not explain to him Hitler's plans for the extension of *Lebensraum* of the German people, even less the role he had in mind for the mission "Untermensch." But the airman doesn't expect an answer, he thinks all Germans are capitalists. To prove a point he looks at the photos. It just depicts the living room of an average German family. Settee and chairs, standard lamp and a piano – blatant examples of a capitalist way of life. He points to the radio which is a model which cost about 3,500 roubles (£10) before the war. It's quite beyond him that a person can live like that.

He is honest enough to admit that workers in Germany have different living standards than Russian workers. It took him a while to come to terms with the fact that the German proletariat differed vastly from the Russian – but they all had one thing in common, they worked with their hands.

The way that every German housewife likes to have some sort of supply of stores and goods is totally alien to him.

His answer to it all is that the workers are corrupted by the capitalists but it lacks a bit of conviction. The other travellers listened to our conversation full of interest as the captain translated as he went along. I can see they all think the same old question. "Why make war on Russia?" People who live in such a paradise as Germany appears to them to have no need to attack other countries. And I suppose they are quite right really.

Alexandrova has prepared her bed for the night with the aid of the conductor who brought her a pillow, a cotton wadding pad and a sheet.

Irina, her daughter, has had her night time wash and both return from the washroom smelling sweet and clean. Soon the little one settles down to sleep and the night-light is turned on in the compartment.

Her mother sits and chats with us for a while. She produces little sweets and cakes out of her suitcase. She invites me to join them. She asks the young Captain lots of questions about me and she asks once more to see my photos and turns the light up for a while to see them properly. No doubt she too finds it difficult to find a bond between the snapshots and me in my present getup and situation.

She regards Grisha disapprovingly, he is busy getting very friendly with the gypsy girl on his bunk. He is blind to everything else.

"Duschinka," he keeps whispering into her ear. "Duschinka." The full light disturbs him so he switches it off.

The young Captain too is trying his luck with Alexandrova but when the light once more is turned down I hear a sudden smack and a few angry words from the doctor, so I take that to be a "No" for the Captain's amorous advances. When the atmosphere has quietened down once again Alexandrova leaves the compartment to get changed into her night attire. On her return she is dressed in a bright red dressing gown and her hair is hanging down her back in two long plaits. She moves the little girl over a bit in their bunk and with a general "spokoinij notsche" she too settles down to sleep.

The Captain had left the compartment to regain his composure. When he returns he stretches out on his bunk and tries to sleep. The night-light is extinguished, very much to Grisha's delight. As we are in the midst of summer the Russian nights remain light, a ghostly shimmer of light extends across the sky.

Suddenly a bottle of pure vodka appears next to me, no doubt the Captain's attempt to drown his sorrows. I only take a small sip, it's like pure fire trickling down my throat. To restore the night's peace Alexandrova too has a drink and after a few long swallows the Captain passes the vodka onto Grisha. Peace settles on our compartment apart from Grisha who is busy stripping the gypsy of her clothes. After years of not having seen a woman in the nude it was beautiful to observe. There was nothing repellent, indecent in this picture. It was for my eyes only and gave me pleasure.

My heart travelled ahead of me towards my wife who is longing to see me. I can hear the noise of the pistons, every stroke brings me closer to home. When I finally doze off I have the dream of my mother once more. I am so sure I am going home, in spite of all I know about the Russian way of going about things. There is always hope. I regret not to meet up with Schubert again, we were good comrades in adversity.

When I wake up bright daylight floods the compartment. Irina is the next person to wake up and shortly after her, her mother too opens her eyes. I would like to say *'good morning'*, but I just can't recall the Russian word, so I just say "drastuitje" (good day).

Little Irina jumps up and bounces about on her bunk and the Captain too joins the land of the living. He stretches his hand up to "Dawai Fritz dai zigarette" (Hurry up Fritz give me a cigarette).

I take this as a sign of approval and I pass the cigarettes around. Grisha is still fast asleep as is the gypsy girl in her bunk above the door. I can just see a bit of her bare leg sticking out.

I open the window just a little and a welcome breath of fresh air floats through the carriage. I really savour the morning, no appell, no work! Only 24 hours and I shall be in Moscow, hopefully a free man once more. No shouting by guards, no barbed wire. I suddenly remember young Ali. He will miss me for a while, as I will him, but life moves on. I am on my way to Germany!

The airman picks up his toiletries and I ask him whether I can go with him. After the way the passengers reacted to me yesterday I am not certain of his response. However he nods.

But before we leave the cabin the cleaner appears dressed in a grey dress and big white apron. She carries her tools of the trade with her – a feather duster, a cloth and a brush and shovel. She does a thorough job and we will see her again several times during the day. Every wagon has a cleaner who travels with the train who is responsible for the cleanliness of the whole wagon. After a thorough inspection she departs, but she had obviously seen our unofficial traveller, the gypsy girl who is still fast asleep in the luggage rack.

Everyone seems to be still asleep or busy with their affairs and the passage is still empty. The toilets and washrooms are at the end of the wagon. Luckily there are two hand washbasins. In the absence of a toothbrush I have a good gargle but when I produce my plennie soap the Captain takes one sniff of it and throws it out of the window. I am a bit startled as the piece of soap was my only one and a treasured possession. However he hands me a new piece of elegant toilet soap.

"There, you keep it." To really make use of this sudden windfall I take off my vest and have a thorough scrub. When I am dressed again and I am ready to leave, the Captain stops me. "You shave now." He points to his shaving gear, good German makes both the razor and the blades. I try to reuse his blade but he insists I take a new one.

In the camps we were shaved by German barbers (plennies were officially forbidden to have sharp instruments of any kind in their possession). We were only allowed to line up for a shave if our stubble was at least an inch in length. The barbers considered themselves part of the camp bourgeoisie; when the Russians were around 'brown nosing' was developed into a new art form. Another group with special privileges by the very nature of their job were the chefs. Germans are not slow in coming forward to improve their own lot even if it's at the expense of fellow Germans – another dark chapter in our history.

In the meantime the Captain has completed his toilet, he looks like a newly laid egg – clean, bright and cheerful. No doubt Alexandrova will regret having turned him down last night, or so he hopes.

As he is about to leave the washroom we are faced by a huge man in uniform, a Colonel. The Captain swiftly disappears and leaves me to cope with my fate. I bow and try for a quick exit, as this is usually the best way with senior officers whether German or Russian. I can tell from the colour of his braid that he is not a political officer, which makes him a bit more likeable. He starts talking at me but I just want to get away especially as I can't understand a word, so I put together my few words of Russian.

"Ja woina plennie, ja goworja tolko odschin plocho po Russki." (I am a PoW, I speak only very poor Russian). He views me like an apparition and then he roars with laughter, pats my shoulder and exclaims in excellent German.

"Please stay here, I am delighted to meet you."

Had he been a political officer his greeting would have sounded very different. The Colonel took off his uniform blouson and I look at him; a fine figure of a man, well fed but not fat. When I compare my shape with his I look rather like a walking stick clothes stand.

The Colonel must have had similar thoughts and he asks me whether I had to endure a lot of hunger. The question is so sudden that I hesitate and the Colonel assures me that if I say the truth it won't be to my detriment. He is in the army, a commander of an artillery regiment. I explain to him that as a plennie I have been hungry more or less all the time.

The rations are sufficient to keep us alive and working but never enough to satisfy a man fully. He asks me about my rank in the army and what I was doing when I was taken prisoner. He is surprised when I tell him that I was a Reservist no longer in active service due to repeated stays in army hospitals after being wounded. He is not too sure when I try to explain that I am a parson in civilian life. But I suddenly remember the word 'pope' and he is totally amazed.

As by now I have finished my shave and I feel I ought to leave he points to his jacket pocket and tells me to help myself to Papyros and matches. He is interested to find out my views on Russia as a country. I try to explain that I only see Russia from a prisoner's point of view, from within the barbed wire encampment.

He acknowledges that but still feels I must have formed some lasting impression firstly as a soldier then as a PoW. I had to think this one out carefully but then came up with a satisfactory reply. If I could, I would like to be able to travel the length and breadth of Russia as a civilian. I would be able to get to know its many different people. No doubt the immenseness of this country must affect the Russian character? I have met great kindness but also great cruelty.

Whilst the Colonel completed his ablutions I have finished off half a packet of Papyros. Out in the passage wait two more candidates for their morning wash. The sight of the Colonel's uniform jacket had persuaded them to quietly wait their turn.

The officer accompanies me to my compartment. He mentions his compartment but decides it is better for him to visit me later. As a farewell gift he hands over the remaining Papyros. Grisha has just woken up and automatically helps himself to my Papyros.

"Very good," he says with a pleased grin. He throws the empty vodka bottle out of the window, stretches and yawns. A bit of a hangover no doubt, too much forbidden fruit in more ways than one.

At this moment the two detectives from the previous night once more enter our carriage. Grisha and I are already known to them and the Captain and the doctor and her little one quickly pass muster. One of the policemen tickles Irina's toes and she giggles delightedly.

The two men are about to leave when the gypsy girl wakes up no doubt roused by Irina's giggles. One of the policemen climbs up on the bunk and demands.

"Ticket, passport, papers!"

But of course the girl can't come up with any of them and as such her fate is sealed. She is ordered to leave at once. Unfortunately she tries to use her seduction technique on the policemen, with no effect whatsoever. After flashing every bit of her anatomy she is confronted by a shout by one of the men.

"Kurval!" (Whore)

Now she has to face facts. The illusion is now ruined, we all know that she earns her keep in the horizontal position. The language coming out of her mouth would remove any possible doubt as she demands her fare from Grisha plus extras for services rendered!

Grisha has lost interest the minute he hears money and refunds. One of the policemen hits her in the face as she is attacking Grisha and the other one fits on the handcuffs. These men are used to dealing with women. Poor girl, she is sure to end up in a labour camp.

Grisha now stands with his back to us, as no doubt he is ashamed. He then takes off for the washroom and when he returns he seems to have washed the whole anecdote out of his mind.

After Alexandrova and Irina have had their turn in the washroom we all settle down to our breakfast. I contribute bread and herring after being shown by the Captain how to cut it up properly – after he rips the head off and chucks it out of the window. Grisha is very keen on my herrings but he is very careful with his cold mashed potatoes. I only get offered a bit. Alexandrova willingly shares her goodies with all of us.

The train travels through a densely populated area. We will soon reach Gorky. The dirty tenement houses of the suburbs come into view. Washing hangs in front of the windows. We are gradually slowing down to the railway goods yard. On the roofs we can hear the stampede of the illegal travellers.

I have to think of Hans Schubert. How would he have coped with all this?

Many of the men must surely fall off and get badly hurt if not worse when they try to get off quickly before they are discovered. No one cares here, one dead person more or less makes no difference.

The train stops, we are in Gorky. Many of the travellers have reached the end of their journey. As has the gypsy girl as she passes our window she pulls a face at Grisha. She is trying to improve on this gesture but her rear meets up with the boot of the policeman.

4

Whilst the engine is being exchanged and the water supplies are being replenished Grisha and I are walking along the platform to stretch our legs.

It is absolutely amazing to see how much luggage some people carry with them. But I think a lot of them are not travelling for pleasure – that luggage contains all their worldly goods.

Grisha soon gets bored and climbs into the train – he doesn't seem to be concerned about me and my whereabouts. He just looks out of the window then he disappears.

Suddenly a little old lady stands in front of me and gives me a white roll. She looks around just to be on the safe side and before long a lot of people follow her example. My pockets are filled with gifts of food and even some papyros (cigarettes). In Kazan they shun this frightening plennie but he seems no longer an object of their fear but rather one for their pity. Unknowingly I had also placed myself in a very opportune spot next to the little hut where all the travellers came with their water containers to get hot water for their tea.

Two young officers take me to a kiosk where they treat me to lemonade and ice cream. I can only say "bolschoi spaciva" (thank you) again and again. The man who had appeared to be a frightening criminal has to them become a poor sod with no human rights; in short, a plennie!

Alexandrova watches the proceedings and collects all my gifts from the window then puts them on my bunk. Grisha tries to help himself but Alexandrova sharply smacks his hand and shouts at him. As usual I can only understand some of it. but it seems to have a resounding effect and Grisha's face turns bright red.

I continue walking along the train until I reach the 'soft' class. My Colonel shares his compartment with an MWD. Now I understand why he did not invite me. To show a friendly gesture towards a PoW was definitely politically incorrect.

As I return to our wagon the Colonel appears at the entrance. He presents me with a loaf of white bread, a packet of papyros (cigarettes) and something I have only dreamt of over the past three years – a large piece of smoked bacon. I hide the bacon in my trousers with Grisha in mind. If this hiding place is good enough for Grisha's gun it's good enough for my side of bacon. As I am about to board the train a little girl turns up with a piece of smoked fish for me. What a day of unexpected riches!

Grisha checks me over as I enter the carriage and with a careful look at the doctor he quickly grabs the smoked fish and eats it. If only he knew about the bacon! She realizes that greedy Grisha has to have something that's why she allowed him the smoked fish. But he is still my guard and I am dependent on his goodwill so I divide everything and Grisha pockets his half with a big grin. Out of the window goes his wife's mashed potato – he now has better fare. He gets me to clean his mess tin and carefully puts his newly acquired rations away in the dish.

Alexandrova and her little girl have gone to the next compartment for a visit. At the exit of the station we observe the illegal ticketless travellers rejoining the train. Nobody stops them.

As we are on our way the detectives come to speak to Grisha. As always I can only understand part of the conversation but what I do pick up is "Syphilis." Grisha's face changes from green to grey! Poor old Grisha. Now I can understand the behaviour of the Russian soldiers who came to our camp as guards from other placements.

Not only did they treat us well, they offered goods and money in exchange for sulphonamides which we might obtain from the camp's sickbay. Compared to the way Russians treat their own if they are infected with a venereal disease makes our experience in PoW camps seem a holiday.

Grisha has become very quiet, no doubt trying to find a way out of his dilemma. I have a rest on my bunk, have a smoke and think of tomorrow. This uncertainty is very draining. But I am ready to see it as a good omen. Why shouldn't I be lucky? I interpret this individual transport to be a positive sign as usually arrests look quite different, having had occasion to observe them so many times.

Hans Schubert and the other inmates will be able to talk about my fate for many weeks. I sleep well past lunchtime; I am not even hungry. The decision that awaits me robs me of my appetite.

Grisha continues to be a worried man. He has taken several trips to the toilet, no doubt to check for early signs of the dreaded lurgy. Finally he comes to a decision. He stands next to my bunk.

"Max. You Sulphonamide!"

He is close to tears and tries to hide his worry behind a mask like grin. I have decided to play with him for a bit by pretending I don't understand. I give him a chunk of white bread as for now I have to gain time, I can't afford to disappoint him. But where on earth am I supposed to get that medication here and now? But it's typical of the faith the Russian guard has in his German plennie who can turn his hand to most things, and now it's my turn to provide Sulphonamide!

Alexandrova is relaxing on her bunk and quietly hums a tune in a lovely deep voice. She reaches over to squeeze my hand as if to show sympathy and understanding for my state of uncertainty.

But then she switches on the full light and the magic and the intimacy of the moment is broken. I notice the hard lines on her face, life is hard for a woman in Soviet Russia.

With the light Grisha once more joins the land of the living and demands medication. This time I give him a sore throat pill, and promise him immediate positive effect.

We all pass the evening in the carriage thrown together by fate, and an affinity of a sort has been created. But already there is a hint of *goodbye* to the atmosphere, all our thoughts are straining towards the tomorrow – what will it bring, what will it hold in store for us?

Alexandrova is very moved by the confusion of this plennie's life, and her look of compassion tells me so.

We are just about ready to settle down for the night when Grisha returns from the washroom absolutely shaking with anxiety. I know straight away what has happened. The pill I had given him, Atebrin is inclined to change any urine passed to a blueish colour! He talked himself into quite a state but lost me quite early on in this torrent of words. I quickly spoke to the airman who explained the details to Grisha after first having a good laugh at his expense. Alexandrova gives him two tablets from her medical supplies, with any luck these pills might be the real McCoy.

This incident more than anything has managed to destroy our feeling of security and belonging, once more we are separate travellers following our own paths. Only Alexandrova once more looks up at me and tells me "skoia buditlutsche" (everything will get better soon).

As I am drifting off to sleep I wonder where I will sleep tomorrow. I don't care as long as it is on the way home.

Next morning I waken early. Today is a special day. My eldest son is 12 years old today, I recall saying to him that he would have to stand in for me while I was away. I didn't realize then for quite how long he would have to be the 'old man' as the other children call him. It is a beautiful bright day and I take it as a portent of things to come, but unasked the prayer of our Lord comes into my mind. *'Not as I want but as you decide for me. Your will be done.'*

The houses are more plentiful on both sides of the track. Instead of the straw covered farmhouses I see dated country holiday houses surrounded by beautiful gardens. But more and more of the woods and fields disappear and make way for the ugly grey suburbs. Even on a lovely day like today the houses look dirty, neglected and bleak. We can hear the rattle of passing ancient trams.

Everyone is busy getting their bits and pieces together. I have used up all my supplies apart from a few pieces of ancient underwear, my new toiletries and my drivers coat, I have no further luggage. Everything fits neatly into my rucksack.

Grisha as usual takes life easy, he quickly pats his hair into place, puts on his uniform hat, and hey presto, he is ready! The train slows down. The many illegals have reached their goal: Moscow, with a few sad exceptions. A militiaman watches the people jumping off the train, there is nothing in his job description about their existence. However, had they got off 100 yards later his colleagues would have arrested the lot.

In spite of the revolution and its horrors Moscow remains a city with a skyline of turrets and church spires - an awe inspiring sight. The magic of this spectacle floods my mind. The charm of this city, the breadth of her history may it be written in blood, surrounds me. For a short moment we see the walls and the towers of the Kremlin. The centre of the other side of the divided world. One half looks here full of hope and the other half sees the Kremlin as a symbol of oppression and misery.

I too am full of hope, I long for the greatest gift of all mankind, my freedom. This is why I see everything in a golden light. All my hopes and fears are tied up in the heart of this city.

5

**Moscow
1947**

This is my second trip to Moscow. The first time was in 1945. The hours of that Whitsun will always stay with me. We were made to stand in line for 24 hours squashed together like sardines. Amongst us were people who had died, as they couldn't cope with the hardships of the transport.
But today I try to banish these thoughts.
I am going home.
The Captain has completed his packing, he says his goodbyes to Alexandrova and Irina. I help to carry his luggage into the passage. He shakes my hand and wishes me a good journey home. Oh, how positive we all felt!
Except that is for Alexandrova who has tears in her eyes as she blesses me. Irina climbs on my bench, puts her arms around my neck and gives me a kiss. The train enters the station, we have arrived at our destination: Moscow. Good or bad, here we come!
Irina anxiously looks out of the opened window. Ah, there he is, a tall handsome officer.
"Daddy, daddy."
I hand her through the window to her father and the suitcases follow. A somewhat astonished looking man accepts both child and luggage. Her mother had disappeared in the passage to join up with them at the door of the wagon.
Grisha and I are the last to leave the train, in the happy confusion of family and friends reunion we are the odd ones out. Nobody waits for us, we just make our way through the throng of people when suddenly a heavy hand falls on my shoulder.
"Schto ta koi? Schto solkelaeso scljes?" (What have we here, what do you think you're up to?)

He probably thought he had the catch of the day, an escaped plennie.

Grisha was nowhere to be seen and I seemed to have lost the power of speech. Luckily my escort catches up with us just as I am about to be taken into custody.

No doubt one of Moscow's "flowers" caught his eye making him forget his duties.

He has to produce all my papers before the policeman is prepared to relinquish his hold on me, only now do I get a chance to look at him properly.

He wears a dark navy jacket with a long coat-tail, snow white belt and a bandolier across his chest. His Nagan is suspended on a blue and white cord. He also wears a long sabre in a leather sheath with beautifully carved handle. On his head he wears the usual flat uniform hat.

As usual everyone has to show their papers before they are allowed to leave the station.

A group of apprehended illicit travellers are ahead of us in a corner of the station. Women in tears, men shouting and swearing.

The station is a collection of Russians from every corner of this vast country. Amongst lots of people patiently waiting for their trains there is also a group of young people who are busy checking out a map for a town in Siberia. Volunteers no doubt to settle in that newly opened area, how many of them will ever return?

The first signs of excitement have the same effect on Grisha and I, we need a toilet. When we find it we are utterly amazed by the utter cleanliness of the place.

As we leave we are surrounded by a group of young boys with little boxes. The Russian shoe-shine boys.

They direct us to a nearby bench and attack our footwear. Grisha's lad has a good pair of boots to work on, but my chap only now realizes that he has landed a plennie.

"Djengi jest?" (Have you got any money?)

"Yes," puts his mind at rest and he falls over my footwear with gusto. I never managed to create that sort of shine, even so I did try my best with what little I had to work with in the past.

It's just a shame that my shabby *uniform* is in such a contrast to my shoes, but 'Nitschewo!'

The boy expects three roubles and when I give him four that brings a deep bow and a gratefully doffed cap. As we leave the station it is just 7am and the adventure can begin.

There is a wonderful smell of flowers from the recently watered flowerbeds.

I got caught up in the surge of the city. I forget that I am a plennie. Grisha and I exchange roles, he suddenly turned into a shy provincial in awe of the big city who is glad to be looked after by me. But he can relax, I have no plans to leave him, after all I am going home.

We take a seat on a bench and watch as the city comes to life. People rush to their places of work, women walk past wearing floaty summer frocks and high heels. This is a totally different type of people compared with the folk in Kazan. Grisha is impressed, he checks that his uniform is all in order and we are off to take our chance in the big city.

Opposite us is a huge building, we take a look through the big glass doors. The stairs are wide and made from shining marble. We then enter a main street which is being swept and sprayed. We see lots of buses and lorries. People at the bus stops stand in disciplined queues, no pushing and shoving here.

Grisha is totally moved by all these big city pictures and needs to recharge his batteries at a nearby Stolowa (small inn selling beer). He orders a vodka for both of us, maybe not such a good idea in the heat, especially as we haven't eaten anything yet. But Grisha seems to have had the same idea as he orders a roll with fish for both of us.

The vodka quickly takes effect and I too am ready for anything. The cool beer which followed the spirit is a welcome change. I drink it slowly whilst Grisha tips it down in a few gulps, Russian style. I drink to Michael, the birthday boy and to my journey home.

A civilian joins us and starts talking to the Sergeant. He observes me full of curiosity and then informs me in broken German that he too was a PoW in Schleswig Holstein (North Germany). He thought it was a beautiful country. What luck I have with my new acquaintances, he obviously had been treated well. He wants to show us Moscow and Grisha is all for it, he dreams of a long pub crawl. I have to pay 50 roubles; I only have 40 left and that's my lot. Grisha adds 10 roubles to the bill. Moscow seems to be an expensive place but I also seem to have lost the know-how of dealing with real money, barter has been a way of life for three years. So far we have spent 2 hours in Moscow and all my money has gone, not an auspicious start.

When we try to move on we both feel the effect of the alcohol, everything is moving in front of my eyes. Accompanied by the civilian we sit on the kerbstone. Before long we are surrounded by a group of well-meaning onlookers who hand out free advice to Grisha. But so far it's falling on deaf ears with him. For me however things are gradually getting clearer and I can study the group in more detail. The men are casually dressed, just shirts and trousers, there are a few in uniform and the women brighten up the picture in their colourful summer dresses.

Grisha too has regained his faculties and he comments on the charm of the Moscow ladies very much to the delight of the crowd. But Grisha had to chance his luck by grabbing a young girl's leg in an attempt to get her to sit on his lap. But instead he earned himself a good smack and a caution that this kind of behaviour is not tolerated in Moscow.

I would dearly love to just disappear just now as I notice a policeman has joined the circle. He seems to have grasped the situation quickly, he views us with some amusement and shakes his head. Once he has checked our papers we are asked to move on. Easier said than done. However, we link arms and just about manage to get to the next street corner where we run straight into the arms of yet another policeman and Grisha has to once more produce our papers (which he keeps tucked away in his underpants) to the cheers of the onlookers.

Just as well we have our trusted civilian, Grisha is beginning to be scared to cross the road and added to that is in urgent need once more to empty his bladder. We turn off into an alleyway and once we are used to the twilight after the bright sunshine we note that many people before us had the same ideas, as we are standing in it! Then an old lady joins us, no doubt driven by the same need.

After this short moment of relief we return to Gorkistreet. We are heading for Red Square. Whilst the main roads are tarmacked, the side streets and alleyways are inches deep in dust and rubbish. No more high buildings, just many, many small wooden houses right in the centre of the big city, all 300 metres of Gorkistreet.

I manage to actually look into one of the little houses. The walls are covered in newspaper and there are clear signs that bedbugs are regular occupants. The furniture is old, shabby and neglected all covered in lacy doilies and other tasteless knick-knacks.

I am glad to be back on proper pavements again as we go up a narrow street and suddenly we are in Red Square.

About 200 metres away is the Kremlin, the living quarters and the spires and onion dome towers over the broad massive walls. So this is where Stalin lives. Here is the nerve centre of this enormous country.

Both Grisha and I are equally impressed. We face the wide front of the Kremlin wall and right in the centre we see the red and black Lenin Mausoleum. On the left and right side the grandstands are erected where the high ranking dignitaries sit during the annual parade.

The Red Square also contains Saint Basil's Basilica and historical museum.

There is a long slow moving queue in front of Lenin's tomb. A policeman points out to Grisha that he should move me elsewhere and quickly. So I gather that a visit to Lenin is not an option. I would like to see the Tredjakowgalerie but Grisha refused to come, and we both suddenly realize how tired we are. Not only physically but also overloaded by the impact of all we have done.

The civilian guide takes us to another stolowa. Before we enter I point out that my funds have run out. But apart from Grisha's 'Nitchewo' we find a seat and we are glad to rest our weary legs.

We spend some time enjoying the rest and a cool bottle of beer when the civilian once more invites us to join him on his tour. The metro is our next destination, and when we reach our goal I am impressed as is every tourist.

Grisha buys two tickets for us as he is eager to find out about this Metro, something to talk about to the folks back home. We go down an escalator and it is amazing how deep the shafts are.

The effect of the first stop 'Plostschadj Rewoljwzie' is simply overwhelming. Sculptures depict the road the Soviet Union has gone down since October 1917. It is all a very good quality and very tasteful. Grisha checks with his fingernail whether it is real marble. The floor is covered in clear black marble which reflects the light of the wonderful chandeliers. It is difficult to decide where to look first. I am torn between the magnificent lights and the majestic mosaic on the ceiling. It is difficult for me to take in such beauty and splendour. It all stands in such contrast to all that I have seen in the Soviet Union until now. The cleanliness too was awe inspiring, not a single cigarette butt or sunflower kernel in sight.

A train approaches and we decide to continue our journey of discovery. People leave and enter carriages in an orderly fashion. I am a bit slow and my rucksack gets caught in the doors. But it was noticed by the stationmaster who arranged for the doors to re-open and I was pulled inside by a helpful Moscow citizen. A young girl even offers me her seat.

Wherever we stop, it's a new picture of wonderful statues, beautiful crystal lights and stunning mosaics.

I just wonder what the people who use this mode of transport daily must think. Their lives are lived in such contrast to this effusive wealth and splendour. But the citizens are very proud of their Metro and look after it like a jewel.

One can see how a thirty year long propaganda can afford to produce such magnificence.

We are taking it easy on a bench in one of the stations, we are both very weary. I was not really set to do the whole tourist bit. I just wanted to put off the final moment when the decision for my future would be made.

Grisha understands that the day has come to an end. He is prepared to take me to the Ministry of the Interior as it says in his orders. After a lot of questions we finally find it. We have to pass the usual police control and then we enter the building through big revolving doors. My feet sink into the deep plush carpet, but alas, this was the door for the big boys, other mortals had to enter by the side entrance. However we weren't to know this, but when I found myself lifted by the seat of my pants and propelled back out onto the street I soon saw the error of my ways. One of the policemen helped me back on my feet.

"Nitschewo, comrade."

This word encompasses the philosophy of the nation, it consoles and cheers and more or less covers everything you want to say:
Never mind. Who Cares? Whatever.

In this so-called classless society there was bound to be a separate entrance for the *haves* and *have nots*.

The poky side entrance leads along a smelly passage poorly lit by a bulb suspended on a wire. No signs of luxury here! Typical MWD atmosphere. At the end of the corridor I notice a lieutenant behind a glass window busy picking his nose who is trying hard to ignore me. Grisha waits patiently for a few minutes then gives a few cautious knocks in an attempt to try and attract his attention.

This lieutenant obviously sees us as an unwanted interruption of his peaceful evening. He shouts at Sergeant Grisha until he finally manages to produce the famous blue folder. After a short study he picks up a phone and spends some minutes shouting through to various other departments. We are asked to take a seat until a decision has been made.

I have reached the stage where I no longer care, and fall asleep. Grisha is just about to nod off too when the door flies open and two MWD soldiers enter, both armed.

That's enough to wake anyone.

Their arrival concerns me as the two men look anything but friendly and they treat Grisha with disdain. I am beginning to fear the worst. I cease to exist for him, wiped out are the memories of our sightseeing tour of Moscow.

The MWD soldiers point to the door and I note the arrival of a policeman. I try to tell myself that they are just taking me somewhere to spend the night before my trip home, but it is looking more and more unlikely. A short journey brings me to a big building. I get hassled through one entrance after another, all big heavy locked gates and with each door shutting one behind the other a little bit more hope dies.

At last I get pushed into a large empty and lightly lit room. There is only a table and chair, no window, nothing. Through a side door a MWD officer enters accompanied by a prison warder who carries a torch and some equipment. I am told to remove all my clothes, every seam and pocket is carefully checked, the contents of my rucksack are itemized and written down. I manage to hide my pocketknife but my hat is put under scrutiny and my wedding ring is discovered. I expect to see it disappear in the warder's pocket but it is just added to the list of possessions. No one talks to me, I get completely ignored, just an object to be dealt with. All is done by sign language. My fingerprints and my photo are taken. They shave my head totally bald and then I am led to a shower room. The freezing cold water does away with the last of my illusions. On my return to the large room I get handed a jacket and a pair of trousers made from indestructible brown material, some washed used underwear and a pair of rubber shoes. The officer has disappeared and any attempts to start a conversation with the warder are a wasted effort.

I have to sign the inventory of all my worldly goods and I am off to face whatever is now my future. I am led to another big door, which is opened by another warder armed with a machine pistol. There might as well have been a sign over the door. *'Forsake all hope whoever enter here.'*

I am told to face the wall whilst the warder rang a bell. After a while loud footsteps approach and I get handed over to yet another warder. We go through many doors which are opened on demand and up and down several sets of iron steps. At long last we come to a passage with many small steel doors. Each one has an inspection hole covered by a flap. We stop in front of one of them and two bolts are pushed back. The door is unlocked and I am in my cell.

**Prison
Moscow
1947**

It is 2m wide and 4.3m long. On the right wall is a metal folding bed with some cotton padding. On the facing wall is a small opening near the ceiling covered with tin. A stinking bucket completes the furnishings of my new habitat. The light of the strong bulb in a wire cage over the door floods the room with a cold light.

As the door gets locked and the bolts are pulled across, I am totally alone and locked in. Farewell home, hello prison.

Just now I really can't think about my present situation. I feel dreadfully tired after the exertion of the day and the experience of the last two hours; I sit down in the typical plennie fashion with my knees drawn up to my chest and I fall asleep.

Someone opens the door and pushes in my supper in a metal bowl with a wooden spoon. The soup stinks of fish but I am ravenous and eat the lot. When the door is opened once more, the warder shows me how to erect my bed and points out that I have to sleep with my face towards the inspection hole and that my hands always have to be visible. I barely stretch out before sleep has overtaken me.

My body is unfortunately not yet used to the new sleeping regulations, loud shouting and swearing reminds me of the rules. But finally I seem to have the hang of it and drift off into deep sleep only to be woken by the warder. I have to empty my bucket – nobody is in the passage. I am told to have a quick wash in the washroom and before long I am back in my cell with my bucket.

Breakfast is the same fish soup with the addition of a piece of black bread, and then I wait. There is still that tiny bit of hope that this is all a big mistake, just time for me to await my transport home.

The noise of the keys announces the arrival of the warder.

"Idi" (Go)

Shaking his keys he walks behind me. It seems to be a sign for any other prisoners to stand with their faces to the wall as we pass. I am led to a small walled courtyard. I am told to "Gilijati." Exercise time. I can just see a small bit of clear blue sky above the tall forbidding walls. I walk around the walls for 250 rounds and then I am taken back to my cell.

The warders must have strict orders not to speak to inmates as yet another attempt at communication fails. I now have ample time to contemplate my fate. What real or imagined crimes am I being punished for? When I think of my past life there is many a corner that may not quite muster an in-depth inspection, but nothing to warrant incarceration. Am I being used as a sacrifice for others' misdeeds? But I pull myself together, I have to be mentally on the ball.

In the last PoW camp I learned Rainer Maria Rilke's Elegies (German poet) off by heart, that will do to overcome oppressive silence. My recitations seem to have caused some confusion in the passage. I hear a noisy altercation which is followed by a loud crack, screams and yelling and terrible cries turn into pitiful whimpering. Once more silence reigns.

But I have to do something to keep my mind active. I will set up a Russian dictionary. I still have to use German script, as I have not yet mastered the Cyrillic alphabet. Next day in the washroom I find a few red tile shards. I hide my precious find carefully.

Once back in my cell I can produce 43 words from memory. After a few days' work I am up to 182 words. I even included a few swear words, the Russian language contains a wealth of these. Some of them are simply untranslatable. Lunch interrupts my studies, it is not sufficient but it keeps me alive, as I don't have to do any physical work.

The warder so far has not noticed my literary efforts. In the all-pervading silence I quickly move to my accustomed plennie stance when I can hear him go past my cell.

One day he surprises me and discovers my handiwork. At first he gives me the usual mouthful of abuse, then changes tactics and hits me in the face. Blood spurts – oh, how well I could use that for my writing. I had managed to hide the tile shards under my collar and in spite of a detailed search he could not find them.

Next day when I go to the washroom I find a bucket of hot water waiting for me. I also get given a minute piece of soap and when I am finished with my ablutions I receive a piece of towel to dry myself. It is customary in Russian jails to provide inmates with a facility to wash properly once every ten days. So, that's how long I have been here, and I am still none the wiser. Which gives me an idea. I must write down a calendar to register the days of my stay in this Moscow jail, except for the fact I have nearly run out of writing implements.

But on my next exercise I find a piece of coal which I manage to secrete in my rubber shoe. It makes walking back to my cell a bit awkward but anything to put one over on my warder is a challenge.

I draw the calendar on the other wall between the top end of my bed and the rear wall. That's how the days pass, how I remind myself of all the poetry and songs I know by heart. I even remember the context of a piece of French literature I had to learn by rote in high school. Aided and abetted by many a clip around the ear when I faltered! I add that to my writings and once more get a good hiding from the guard.

Alas the next day he has found a solution, he presents me with a brush and a bucket of whitewash and all my efforts are despatched.

After supper I suddenly hear a very cautious knocking, the tone remains the same but the frequency alters. It's not Morse Code, I understand that.

I detect that there are at least two people involved. Maybe they are Russians using their own version of a code. My hearing by now is supersensitive to any noise but I cannot work out their secret.

Twice I have been for a bath which brings my stay to 30 days. It is amazing how man can get used to anything. I have totally given up any thoughts of home. My mental energy is aimed towards one goal only. Why am I here and where am I?

I think on my first walk to my cell I was deliberately led on a false path in an effort to confuse me, all those stairs up and down just mixed up my sense of direction. I can frequently hear footsteps passing above me so I presume it's a corridor, not a cell.

One evening just after the warder has brought my soup, I sit with my back against the wall when I once more hear the knocking. Just for fun I knock a few Morse signs with the palm and knuckles of my hand. 'I'm calling I'm calling.' But initially I receive no reply, but suddenly to my utter joy I hear 'Please come! Please come!' I just cannot believe it, the cell next to me is another German inmate. We quickly agree to chat every morning after breakfast as the guard is busy at that time, and we don't want to stop the conversation of the other two in the evening.

During our talks I find out my neighbour is Captain Werner Berg. He had been given the death penalty by a tribunal for war criminals. He has appealed for clemency to Stalin himself and now awaits his fate. We talk about our families and exchange addresses.

Suddenly I remember Grisha's behaviour and what he said before we boarded the train in Kazan. Maybe he hadn't been fooling around, maybe he actually knew what was in store for me. I refuse to be depressed and try to think of Werner Berg. I so want to help him to give him some inner strength to cope with whatever fate has in store for him. I recall the words from the scriptures which gave me strength when I faced horrendous interrogations. *"Do not fear the enemy who wants to kill your body, fear instead Satan who wants to ruin your soul in hell!"* He acknowledges my message with "Thank you."

Bath time has come round again and I have learned how to sleep according to regulations and I am almost resigned to my fate of not knowing when footsteps approach and I hear them stop outside Werner's cell. I hear voices and understand his appeal for mercy has been turned down. They came to take him away for his execution!

I feel as if the walls of my cell are pressing in on me. The ceiling is coming down to squash me and I scream and cry in utter terror. It's the basic creature instinct, the fear of dying. The only consolation for me is that the Russians shoot in the back of the neck, a mercifully quick death.

When I regain my composure I find I am lying on my bed surrounded by two warders and a female doctor. She is in the process of pushing a syringe in my arm. Everything dissolves in front of my eyes and I begin to float weightlessly and drift into healing sleep.

I don't know how long I slept but when I recover consciousness I look into the face of the doctor. She is taking my pulse. I am too tired to speak and I vaguely hear her saying "spatsch" (sleep).

When the medication has fully worn off I get up and drag myself around my cell to restore some sort of circulation. I try to contact my neighbour, just in case it was all a nightmare, but no it stays quiet. Instead of going with him in my mind on his trip to Golgotha I so sadly let him down and was busy with my own fears.

By now it is 40 days since I arrived here. Maybe Hans Schubert was right when he said you have to take your fate into your own hands. Why did I never request to be taken for an interview? I still hanker after my dream of going home and I don't want to do anything which might jeopardise it.

Decision time is here. I knock on my cell door and it's opened at once and what do I see? The warder who refused to speak to me all this time, who gave me two heavy beatings, he smiles at me!

"Nu schto?" (What's the matter?)

I think I must have heard wrong. Has the prison changed into a sanitorium?

I utter "Officernacks." (An officer is required)

He pats me on the shoulder and assures me that everything will be better soon. How often have I heard that?

At night I once more dream of my family, I am full of determination to do whatever I can to speed up my trip home.

In the morning my warder wishes me "good morning". I get presented with a piece of soap and a whole towel and the guard informs me that I shall be leaving soon. With him are a civilian and behind him a MWD soldier, with his machine pistol slung over his shoulder. All three watch me with great curiosity. The MWD Captain who has also arrived opens the conversation.

"Schmitt," and it takes me some effort to answer with the required response.

"Wilhelm, Max 1905."

He informed me that I would be returned to a PoW camp and replied to my questions about the 45 days I had spent in prison, that it had been a mistake!

I am to be taken at once after having acknowledged the receipt of my rucksack and clothes. I also had to sign the protocol again. I even find my pocketknife, which I quickly hide amongst a couple of handkerchiefs without anyone noticing.

As I get handed my wedding ring I attempt to put it in my pocket. The civilian informs me that I am now allowed to wear it. As on my arrival here I go through many doors and clanging gates producing my discharge papers every time and giving my name and year of birth.

At long last we are on the street. It is an August day full of light, sun and warmth. A lorry awaits me, the guards help me to climb in and we are off.

I still cannot take it in that my life has been given back to me. What is to happen next is totally out of my control and frankly, right now I don't care. I am alive.

"Posmotrin." (we shall see).

We pass through Red Square, pass the river Moskva where mothers take their children for a walk.

Oh God thank you, life is wonderful.

We quickly drive through the city and suburbs, I can see a factory building in the distance and close to it an airport.

Ah there it is; barbed wire fence, watchtowers, the familiar picture. The lorry stops in front of the Budka (Guardroom).

PART TWO

1

Russian Prisoner of War Camp
Moscow area
August 1947

Once inside the Budka we went through the usual formalities, my luggage was checked and then I was told to wait inside the camp.

After a while a young chap comes towards me. A very unpleasant type, long blonde hair, close shaved neck and when he walks he swings his hips in a certain way which makes me wonder about his sexual preferences! His clothes are equally startling for a plennie. He wears riding trousers with leather patches and shiny riding boots. He turns to me and says in a snotty way:

"So, you are the new boy then?"

In all the officers' camps I have been everyone uses the third person 'thou' as is customary in Germany. It is primarily polite to do so and it also protects one's privacy. I feel I must take a stand right from the beginning.

"As you can clearly see I am the only person here, please take me to the senior PoW officer," being careful to use the 'thou' as I speak to him. He looks at me as if I am not too bright and asks me where I have come from. I could just lose my temper and give him a good smacking, but that's probably not the best introduction into a new camp. I once more point out to him that we neither are, nor ever shall be *bosom buddies*.

An evil grin spreads over his face and he tells me not to worry.

"Darling, we've had your type here before! Where on earth have you come from?"

I told him I had been discharged from prison.

"Ah well," he said "They are all a bit mad when they've done time."

I give him my rucksack to carry and we move on, but not before he has made some comment to the Russian sergeant.

"Your days of having a batman are over."

Without a word I pick up my rucksack and follow him. We pass the usual bleak barracks and bunkers. The camp street looks clean, but there is a lot of rubbish on the verges. The camp hospital is on the right marked by the usual red cross. Opposite there is a large work hall and close to that a somewhat more cheerful barrack. There is a big blackboard with news items cut out of Pravda (Russian daily paper). I seem to have arrived in a camp that's flying the red flag, to go by first impressions. There is one door with a sign "Camp Elder" and my young escort enters the room. He cautions me to wait with a casual wave, but as soon as the door is shut I hear the sound of a ringing slap and loud squealing followed by the young man flying backwards through the door and landing at my feet. Five fingers are clearly outlined on his cheek. Harsh customs in this place, but well deserved.

A grey-haired man of stocky build invites me to join him.

"I am sorry that your arrival has caused such a stir, but I can assure you that this camp is run in an orderly fashion. Such behaviour is not tolerated or encouraged. Unfortunately you will find that you are the only German officer in this place and life will not be easy for you. But it you try to fit in and not expect to be treated differently things should be okay. My name is Sepp Pszybilla. I am the camp elder and senior activist." (Communist)

From his accent I could tell his origin – Upper Silesia. I introduced myself and apologize for the commotion and hoped that I had not caused any inconvenience. I just felt I had to make a point with the young yokel. He replied that from time to time he had to put the young lad in his place.

He asks me to take a seat whilst he gets all my particulars, he looks puzzled when he sees my wife's maiden name Wonneberger. He wants to know whether she comes from Oppeln (now Opole) but adds nothing further.

The camp holds 2,000 men, 800 of which are from Hungary. The remainder are Germans. The Hungarians are getting the worst of it as most of them are originally farmers and as PoWs they are now working as labourers on a building site where the monetary rewards are very small. Most of the Germans work as specialists in factories in Moscow where the pay is considerably higher.

My quarters for the time being are with twelve Hungarian officers. When we discuss work allocation he wants to know my previous work and my previous profession. When I tell him that I am a parson and my skills so far only suffice for basic labouring.

He will have his work cut out to find financially productive employment, but he promises to try. He admonishes me to keep a low profile, and then takes me across to meet my new companions.

It's time for all the workers to return to camp – drawn and tired groups of Hungarians walk past me in their brown torn uniforms. It's a long time since I have seen such beaten and careworn men.

A big factory hall is their home. Three tiered bunks fill part of the space divided by passages. In one corner of the hall is the officers' accommodation. Unlike the German PoWs they still wear their rank insignia. In totally correct manner (using the 'thou') Sepp introduces me to their senior officer who welcomes me on their behalf.

Word has obviously got round about 'my reception' and he assured me that he and his fellow officers would do their utmost to make my stay a tolerable one. He pointed out that any serious problems with German PoWs were dealt with in conjunction with the Russians and should anyone ask, 'we are all activists for obvious reasons.'

Captain Kovacs accompanies me to the stores to get some bedding and guess who is waiting for us, but the rascal with attitude!

In a taunting voice he asks the Quartermaster to pick out an especially soft mattress and blanket and the Quartermaster selects a torn blanket and a mattress where the padding is torn and spoiled. The young lout watches full of satisfaction as I inspect my handouts, but he hasn't counted on Captain Kovacs. When conversing with me he had spoken in a soft Viennese accent, but now his voice was clear and cutting.

"Give the Captain decent bedding or you will have had your cosy post, you stupid oaf!"

He adds a few words in Hungarian to a Hungarian PoW who seems to be employed in the stores.

At first it looks as if the German Quartermaster is going to put up some resistance, but then he decides that caution is a better option. I feel very embarrassed to witness this appalling behaviour of my countrymen with a foreigner present. Would you believe it he stands to attention and hands over a good quality mattress and blanket. My compatriots always seem to fall into two categories – either they are the best friends a man could wish to have or they are the most despicable people who would sell their own flesh and blood if they could benefit from it. No points for guessing into which group the Quartermaster fits. Needless to say, my young friend has made a quick escape.

I am allocated a two-tier bunk close to Captain Kovacs. The youngest of the Hungarians presents me with a carved pipe, a welcome gift from all the Hungarians.

It is satisfying to be welcomed after the very negative response of my own people. I find out that the young Hungarian is the nephew of Cardinal Mindzsenty.

I am informed that the officers receive their daily food rations from the Infirmary to make it appear to be of better quality. In a German setting this would have caused a riot, but here the privates first checked out if there actually was a difference and when they found none, it was no longer of any importance.

It had been a long day full of new impressions. Last night I was still sleeping in a prison – figures glide through my thoughts. Werner Berg, where are you? Was it just a figment of my imagination? Only the detailed address of his wife in my memory tells me it is not so.

The first camp seems a lifetime away as do Hans Schubert and my mother, wife and children. Sleep quickly overtook me until I was wakened in the usual camp fashion – two pieces of iron bashed together, all the same anywhere in Russia.

I go and collect my morning soup – hot water tasting of soya beans, at least it is a change from the taste of fish. I am still eating my soup when a runner arrives from the German camp elder. I am to report to the laundry as I am still not allowed out of camp.

Nitschewo! Nobody has died of overwork in the laundry and it's also a bit of promotion for me. Camp jobs are popular and are usually only handed out to a select few who are in favour with the camp elder, but it hadn't been through my efforts that I have got this job. The ordinary PoWs normally despise people who have wangled such jobs.

At 6.45am its line-up for the roll call. All lined up in groups of one hundred. I am with the Hungarian officers in their group when I hear:

"Gdjehemsky officer?" (where is the German officer?) I step forward and the Sergeant salutes smartly and asks me how I am? (kak poschiwajete).

I return his salute and reply "Spasibo charascho," (thank you, fine).

The whole camp is witness to this unusual sign of respect from both sides, I don't suppose this will cut much slack with my fellow Germans. Now everyone will know me. It was the same Sergeant who was present when I first entered the camp and showed his disapproval then.

The Russian Sergeant has a good face and I read from his face that he feels some compassion for my present situation. Whatever his motivation, he repeats the salute at every roll call.

While we are still lined-up I hear a buzzing going through the lines of men. The doctor – Dr Rachmanova.

"She gets her daily kicks out of the inspection of two thousand men," Captain Kovacs informs me.

She is certainly an eyeful as she takes a leisurely stroll past all these men. She laps up the admiration of these poor souls as she shows off her feminine charms. This performance is quite a regular occurrence apparently. Many of the Germans earn sufficient roubles to supplement their diet so they don't have to exist just on the camp food, so all they need is access to a woman to feel complete – as this Doctor knows that she revels in the longing of the plennies. By now she has reached my level and I get a moment to see her close-up. She has a very slavic face, high cheek bones, beautifully large grey eyes and a full red sinuous mouth. The dark eyebrows are in contrast to the blonde hair, tied in a knot in the nape of her neck. I found out later that a lot of plennies look forward to this display – the only bit of excitement in a plennie's life.

I report to the Starski in the laundry. He is not pleased to have me in his working team. As usual he is suspicious that I receive better supplies and rations. This sort of attitude can be explained as a result of the Russian system where soldiers are fed according to their rank. The German army doesn't work like that, so whether real or imagined this difference causes ill feeling.

When I first enter the laundry I can't see a thing. All is shrouded in big clouds of steam. It takes a while for me to discern nine big cauldrons. A man works at each of them, while another is folding sheets. All eye me full of curiosity. The Starski introduces me to them as their new workmate and I go round the group shaking their hands. I am to man the nine washing tubs, a piece of soap and a washboard are my tools. The daily norm is twenty-five pairs of underpants and twenty-four vests with the two hundred gram bar of soap. That works out at four grams per item. But a lot of the underwear belongs to men who work in the blacksmiths as their gear is black. One of my new workmates explains that it's impossible to get them white, just basic cleaning is all that is expected. The washboards were made by Germans, the metal had been acquired from a nearby factory which manufactures aeroplanes. The wash tubs seem to have very similar origins. There is plenty of hot and cold water. The experienced workers manage their quota in three hours – it takes me four and a half. It is not only the actual washing, it is also the hanging up, folding and checking by the Starski. He inspects for cleanliness and keeps the numbers right.

After a few days I am accepted. The others have carefully checked me out and found that I am not so different – a former officer but just now only a plennie who dreams of home and family. After a while I find that one or the other chooses me to speak to about their worries and problems. I have no pet solutions, neither do I loosely quote excerpts from the Bible. Sometimes it is just good to talk.

They were relieved to find that a parson was just an ordinary bloke. In their regiment they originally had a very genuine man, but he was killed and replaced by a clergyman who wanted to use his post as a means to obtain promotion and to add to his useless collection of military medals.

Dealing with soap and water all the time not only cleans the outer man, it also seems to effect a cleansing of the soul. I shall never forget Werner Berg and his lonely death. It shook me up and made me realize that I had to do something to get home. Just what, I did not yet know. However, escape was not an option. My Russian is still in its infancy and I haven't just got what it takes for such an undertaking.

From time to time we hear about a failed attempt. It is certain that the Russian people on the western side of Moscow have had bad memories of the German soldiers and will not aid and abet any escape.

There has been no news of any repatriations of any plennies from here either. I am under no illusion re my part in any future transports. Firstly, having been an officer and added to that the odium of the Abwehr (secret service) are enough to put me right at the back of the queue. I must appear a complete hooligan to them, as they try to put my place in the Abwehr and my profession on a common footing and then to add to all my troubles it becomes known that my last boss had been Admiral Canaris's aide during peacetime. It brought me the undeserved reputation of being a 'Bolshoi specialist' (big expert). Countless questions did not dispel the notion in spite of all my appeals that it was due to a war wound that I found myself in this dark corner of the German army.

By now August is just about over, the days are pleasantly warm and life could be almost bearable, were it not for being a plennie. I found a private corner for myself in the midst of a pile of scrap metal. I come here once I have completed my work in the afternoons. The hideaway can't easily be seen, whilst from it I have a vantage point over both the camp and the airport in preparations for the 'Day of the Air Force'.

The airmen are practicing their descent by parachute, unfortunately not without incident. It is horrifying to watch a dark bundle attached to an unopened chute falling to the ground and worse to hear the resounding thud as it hits the tarmac. Another poor airman's fate!

Another display involves a group of fighter bombers who fly in a formation so that the word *Stalin* is printed by the contrails. Two planes come into close contact, one gets away but the other loses control and lands upside down on the tarmac. A burst of flames, followed by an explosion is all that is left. Ambulances and fire brigades can only clear away the debris.

All in honour of Papa Stalin, all so expendable.

Sepp Pszybilla the Camp Starski has soon discovered my hideout. Quite accidentally he turns up one day.

This quiet feared man is quite sociable. Normally I only see him when I attend the compulsory meetings. He talks fluently, giving us the old spiel we have heard so many times. He talks about the gratitude we owe Stalin for liberating us from Hitler's tyranny. He talks of the terrible guilt we all have to carry and have to do penance for. There is also frequent mention of the re-education programme and our political responsibility towards the 'New Germany.'

The amazing thing is however, that I, who have heard all this so many times before, feel that coming from this man it's not just something he does because he has to. A genuine depth of conviction becomes evident in contrast to so many others who quickly jumped on the bandwagon. Where yesterday they were shouting 'Heil Hitler", today it's "Heil Stalin!". With disgust I recall how the senior officer in an earlier camp, a survivor from Stalingrad, addressed us as 'war extenders and criminals'. It was a known fact that this old man, a captain, was the owner of a big factory in West Germany and has certainly never been a 'drawing-room socialist.' Pure egotism persuaded him to make that speech hoping that it would gain some Brownie points with the Russians. Little did he know that they despised him as much as we did. Treason is welcomed but the traitor is despised.

Sepp Pszybilla barely takes any notice of me within the camp, but here in my special place he seems to be able to open up. The signs of his hard life are etched into his face. Words about his personal life and thoughts don't come easy. He appears to be the prototype of the German workman – his feelings for justice, his honesty and his diligence. He is a Communist as he genuinely believes in its ideals and principles. He has made sacrifices aplenty for his convictions and he should be happy now. Living in the promised land, where life is free. Only the tight lines around his mouth betray the daily disappointments he has to overcome in the country of his dreams and his fellowmen. There are many "cash bolsheviks" (cash = food) who only spout the political slogans for the extra helping of food. Most of them come from middle class secure backgrounds who are busy trying to prove their proletarian roots and who will sell anyone for an extra plate of food.

2

During one of our talks we discuss that young chap who was my first introduction to this camp. He works as a kind of batman to Sepp. I was curious how he coped having him with him all the time; but in his usual quiet way he explained that the lad had been taken by the Russians when he was only 15 years old. His father fell quite early on in the war and his mother had no time for him – too busy with a succession of boyfriends, so he really was quite alone. An ideal candidate for the Hitler Youth.

He spent his time as a messenger until the Russians nobbled him. He had a relationship with a camp leader and where others died of starvation, he thrived. Conscience never came into it, he just wanted to survive and people can get used to most things. He also did a bit of informing on his own people to improve his living standards.

When he turned up in his particular camp Sepp took him under his wing in the hope that he might effect some change in the boy. Before long he realized his efforts were all in vain, the boy was damaged goods and unable to change. He only kept him close by to avoid him causing more harm to others in the camp.

I did wonder whether due to Sepp's position as a camp leader he wasn't expected to inform on the rest of us to the Russians. He must have read my thoughts because he said: 'No doubt you think I too am selling my countrymen for that extra bowl of soup. I can nip a lot of things in the bud though, I know who the informers are and just for the record someone informs on me as well.'

He showed me how easy it was to point out the spies. Anyone suspicious was transferred to another workplace and the Russians wanted to know why.

My work colleagues had quite a unique way of showing me that I was now one of them, that I was accepted. I was allowed part of their lunch rations! Only if you have been really hungry can you appreciate such generosity.

No one bothers me with political matters, my profession makes me a sort of apolitical being and I also think that I am being protected by Sepp.

Today I am covering the evening shift; I have just prepared all the laundry for the morning by giving it a good boil and then it gets divided into two big tubs from where the workers collect their quota in the morning. I am just having a quick breather and a smoke when Sepp once more pays me a visit. He makes quite a to do about cleaning his pipe and I begin to worry what's on his mind. He is not often seen out and about at this late hour. It is after 10pm and the Russian Dejourni had done his late check. I remembered that on my admission papers I had given my wife's maiden name. Maybe that was the connection? I was right. He told me that he had worked in the railway repair yard at Oppeln, where my father-in-law had been one of the managers.

Sepp had actually worked in his department as a foreman. My wife's father had insisted that he kept his job when others were keen to throw him on the street, because of his activities as a functionary in a workers union which had been very politically incorrect in a Germany governed by Nazis. He had to give up his senior position but had stayed in the department. With ten children under 21 his family would have suffered greatly as his wife had lost her job in the works baths as well. He names a few more of the senior employees to correlate his statement, I had believed him anyway, his gratitude to my father-in-law had been repaid in his many acts of kindness to me.

Sepp watched me as I prepared my evening bath – one of the perks of the late shift. He noted how very thin I was, but remarked that he couldn't provide me with extra rations as someone would find out and it would be considered favouritism.

Again we discussed internal politics and how he had found out how very interested the camp's MWD officer was in my case. He was sure there was an informer about, especially for me. Sepp's job as camp leader was to sift through informants reports. In a word he was the chief informant. Only by agreeing to do this was he able to sift through all the reports to be able to water them down and often prevent real damage.

His lot was one of the German Communists who had actively worked in the Resistance and had gone to the Russians in 1943 which gave him somewhat of a counter weight with the Russians. He also helped to overcome the many intrigues by others within the camp. It also gave him the opportunity to dissuade any new informers.

"Not an easy life," I said expectantly as I could feel he had more to say. He waited for me to finish my bath and once I was dressed he told me he would point out the man who was on my case.

It was a cold, wet and windy night and Autumn was approaching. You wouldn't send a dog out in this weather. The laundry is connected to the shower-rooms, with some effort he climbs up on the roof and as we both lie on our stomachs, we move carefully along the roof. All is in darkness, only one window throws bright light across the area just in front of the laundry. Then we get to the end of our night-time excursion we have a perfect view into the washroom through a small opening and what do we see but our doctor having a shower! She is totally uninhibited and seems to have a great time. She appears to be talking to someone. Sepp knows my feelings regarding women – the prison food is enough to subdue any feelings of that kind. However after we've both had a good eyeful I am still in the dark as to the purpose of our mission.

"Wait," he says. "We are both a bit early."

As he speaks a fairly young man comes into the picture and he drapes his arms around the showering beauty. I have recognized him instantly and we carefully climb down from our vantage point.

Sepp must have had good reason to have taken me on this trip. He points back to the laundry. As we are sitting in the warmth of the laundry once more, we both have a smoke.

"This young chap will suddenly show a lot of interest in you, you are his pigeon! He has been appointed to shadow you and if he can't find anything he will make it up."

This chap went by the name of Schneider. Dr Schneider.

The knowledge of his affair with the lady doctor could cause him no end of problems with the other plennies. The Russians were a different story as the Camp Commandant was another of the doctor's amours.

The day would come when I needed to defend myself, so it would be useful to know that Sepp knew of their carrying-on too. Dr Schneider was a known coward so to have an associate was useful to me.

I was curious how Sepp had found out about Iwanow and he told me he had been called to Iwanow's office one day. His door had been closed and he looked through the keyhole and voila! Iwanow and the lady doctor involved in very intimate matters.

He crept away quietly in his rubber boots and waited until he could see the doctor leave the office.

Apart from having a common interest in Dr Vera Rachmanova, Schneider and Iwanow have one other common interest. They do a roaring trade in medical supplies and drugs. There was another German doctor who however was hampered by having a conscience, so all that trading was strictly for the above three to the detriment of the plennies, who had to do without medication. A conscience is a luxury which Dr Schneider can't afford, if he wants to maintain his present living standards.

I am glad to say Sepp Pszybilla had no further news for me – I had enough for one evening! However there was one more thing. Black Katja, the translator for all the MWD, has 'shares' in Iwanow and hates Rachmanova with a passion. All useful information.

Sepp leaves the laundry and I follow suit ten minutes later. What a swamp I have landed in! My feelings tell me that I can trust Sepp. It's one for the book for me to be friends with an activist – they usually are the worst kind of men in a plennie's existence, but he must feel he can trust me too. Why else would he have told me all this?

The next few days are full of secretive activity in the camp. Two groups of one hundred remain in the camp, mainly the Hungarians. They spend the day clearing away all the scrap metal and later paint all the accommodation white, both inside and out.

Even the top and bottom pieces of our bunks are painted in bright colours. A lot of strange Russian officers are running about, the local officers look deeply worried. One day lorry loads of good earth arrive which is unloaded in front of the barracks.

Iwanow and Sepp run around with plans and give directions to the workers. Next day a group of plennies take off to the woods and return in the evening with lots of little birch and fir trees, still with their roots in place and plant them in fresh soil. What on earth is happening? I haven't spoken to Sepp for several days now, he is up to his eyes in preparations, for what? The usually bleak looking camp is almost unrecognizable.

The doctor too seems to be infected by this new desire for bright colours, her lipstick is startling red, almost luminous. We have to have a monthly health check, she pinches my bottom – not a show of affection – but a way to assess our general well-being. She has a way of sizing us up, like a farmer looks at cattle in a market. Today she even addresses me.

"Where you work?"

"In the laundry," is my reply.

"Perwiklass." (1. Group) she tells the Infirmary scribe. "What's your name?"

"Schmitt, Max Wilhelm."

She quietly talks to Dr Schneider as my name must have struck a chord. She inspects me carefully once more and puts a cross behind my name. Whatever that means it is bound to be bad. With her regrouping she had automatically taken me out of the laundry rooms, but she looks at me and says "You still in the laundry."

I suppose she must know about Schneider's task, and if I am in the laundry I am within easy reach.

Our camp looks like a miniature Eden, in plennie terms. Young, fresh, green trees line the paths. On the meeting place a pavilion has been erected and we even have a canteen where the plennies can spend their wages. It is hard on the men who do not earn any money. However, the number of men who previously were unfit to work has shrunk dramatically. The temptation of extra rations is too great, as many a man genuinely unfit still gets written off the sick list by Dr Schneider who doesn't even bother to check their recovery, just a tick on the list and they are fit! It is still a mystery all these preparations and changes, what is it all in aid of?

3

October 1947

On 1st October I have to report to the MWD. Only Black Katja the secretary and interpreter is present. The MWD counts out forty roubles, officer back pay dated to July. The ministry only now send the instructions. Russians paying back-dated money, an unheard of event! I can hardly contain my excitement and I am off to the canteen to buy rolls and some lard, but alas the rolls are finished so I buy tea and sugar.

Once back in my barracks I ask Captain Kovacs to invite the other officers for a cup of tea and until late at night we sit and talk. Conversation hits the old snag. We use Russian and French and it gets quite noisy at times. None of the other men complain and I feel they are pleased that their officers are having a bit of a treat – a rare event in their lives. Before long all the Hungarians greet me and gradually my own countrymen do as well.

Sunday we all have to attend a camp meeting. The Camp Commandant makes a speech to his people. He has three translators – a German, a Hungarian and an Austrian. He has decided that Austria is an independent state with its own language. That it's German too is quite irrelevant, but we seem to be close to finding out what caused all these improvements.

A delegation of East German women is to arrive on Wednesday to inspect our camp. We are to have Tuesday and Wednesday off work, but having to make up for that on the next two Sundays goes without saying.

On Monday four lorries arrive with new underwear, rubber shoes and blue work outfits. Everyone has to stay up through the night and Tuesday to collect their new clothing. It's like a funfair. The canteen is closed Monday and Tuesday to keep their stocks and to make sure the plennies have some money.

At long last Wednesday morning arrives. We line up for the morning count. Everything looks bright and cheerful and sparkling clean. All the Russians wear their best uniforms, even Dr Rachmanova is in uniform. She looks even more attractive than usual, a plain navy skirt and well-tailored jacket with a dark beret on her blonde hair. Black Katja too was turned out in her Sunday best. Iwanow surveys his two lady loves with a bright grin. Katja sticks to him like glue, but she has to keep smiling when Dr Rachmanova joins them. So, there we have it. Iwanow was now flanked by his two ladies and he puts me in mind of a peacock.

The Major takes up his position in front of the lined-up men.

"Sdrasdurtje, offizeri I Soldati," (Good morning officers and men).

"Sdrasdurtje Major," echoes back from the assembled men.

The Major smiles – what a sensation of ultimate power. He once more starts a speech and my limited Russian just picks up the repeated 'netsia', (forbidden). Severe punishment will be meted out to anyone who breaks these 'netsia,' rules. No individual chats with any member of the delegation. We are just about permitted to breathe when the German women are present.

We are dismissed until 10am when we are told to line up again. A lorry full of goods arrives in front of the canteen. Long queues form in the shop, all these unheard of delicacies. They have to open another counter to cope with the crowd. Around 9.45, ten dark Russian cars drive through the camp gates and what a picture they see.

Well-dressed plennies eating white bread and sausages! What thoughts must cross their minds, coming from the starving East Germany and here they see all these smiling PoWs munching their way through these peacetime provisions. You have to give it to the Russians, they can organize events, it's a perfect performance.

Were we to tell them how very hungry we are most of the time, no one would believe us.

The gong calls us to the meeting place, with our recent purchases under our arms. The women can see how well Papa Stalin looks after his PoWs. The delegation is carefully screened off from the prisoners. The leaders of the one hundred men groups report to the camp senior and he in turn reports to the Major.

"Camp present and correct!"

The major passes this onto the General who greets us as comrade officers and men. That's a new one on us.

I recall an officer of the Wehrmacht (German Army) trying to cadge Brownie points with a Russian Lieutenant by addressing him in Russian with 'comrade' to which the Russian replied in perfect German: "Your comrade I am not and never shall be." Suddenly we have been promoted.

The German women look careworn and needy. The clothes are very simple and look as if they have seen better days. Dr Rachmanova makes a snide comment to Katja and only an annoyed glance by the General stops their laughter.

The women's elected leader stands on a podium in front of us. We can see what an effort it is, not to break into tears. It must be the first German men she had seen behind barbed wire. So far she has only seen the trains with their load of misery arriving in Frankfurt on the Oder. Maybe her husband or son is still behind barbed-wire.

"I bring you greetings from your wives and children. You are at the forefront of Germany's attempt to recompense Russia for the evil done to it by Nazi Germany."

That sounded familiar, but I don't suppose she had much option. She was bound to be given a prepared speech. Katja translates every word for the General.

Now it gets interesting. "You will be coming home soon. We need each of you to rebuild Germany and for the democratic re-creation of a free country. Please study the example of free Russia whilst you are still here...etc"

We could have done without that. Just a quick conversation with Sepp could have given her a clear picture of life in free Russia for the average citizen. He could have told her about the appalling poverty, the corruption and ignorance that are rife. We know that tomorrow morning we will definitely receive our bowl of watery soup and 600 grammes of bread, but not every Russian has that certainty. It's a shame she played this old record we know it so well.

The plennies begin to lose interest long before she has finished her speech. They are now led to the Infirmary for an inspection, followed by the tailors' shops and the laundry, when they all disappear into the staff building.

The whole performance took half an hour. Nobody got the opportunity to speak to the women. We watch as they climb back into their cars.

We are dismissed and everyone runs to get a last glimpse of the women who are all crying and waving to us from behind closed-up car windows. We hope they understand what a game had been played here. Much ado about nothing.

From 11am we line up to exchange our new clobber for our old garb and by 5pm the old picture is restored: nothing but ragged plennies. Potemkin's villages revived, all an imaginary state for a short time.

Recently I met the German staff doctor. I had a minor cold and used that as a pretext for a sick call when I knew he was on duty, not Schneider. I found out that he used to practice medicine in Halle at a surgery. His wife was there after the war and after being raped repeatedly by Russian soldiers had committed suicide. His two daughters 15 and 16 years of age have vanished. How he can co-exist with that creepy Schneider is a mystery to me. He examines me carefully, but says little. I can't get him into conversation, he remains withdrawn. On top of his family's fate he has to put up with working under Schneider!

He covers the afternoon surgery while Schneider covers the morning duties. The latter refuses to put anyone on the sick list who isn't exactly dying on his feet and even then he takes his time. With people like him the Russians don't have to be cruel – the good German doctor does all their dirty work. Since he received a good beating from an irate plennie he always has a Russian with him as bodyguard.

The staff surgeon occasionally gets called in for a consultation, but it is usually too late and Schneider only does it to cover his back.

The doctors have to share a room which must be a punishment in itself. The staff surgeon once moved to an ordinary barrack, but the Russians insisted he return to shared accommodation. Dr Schneider has, as yet, not made my acquaintance. I salute him as he is part of the camp bourgeoisie, but he seldom or only casually returns my salute.

However, all this is to change. One afternoon when the laundry Starski and I are the only two working, Schneider enters and without even acknowledging my presence he tears Franz Ehrental (the Starski foreman) off a strip about the state of the laundry.

When the foreman asks what is amiss he tells him a button is missing from one of his shirts. Big deal!

Before long the two of them are shouting at each other and calling each other names in a language that strictly belongs to the gutter, no way is it part of an academic's (university graduate's) vocabulary.

I am just about to make a quick exit when he points to me.

"He can do my personal laundry as from now". When Franz Ehrental explained to Schneider that he has to ask me first, as I was an officer and wasn't likely to take a job away from one of the other men (it brought in extra pay) as he was a decent chap. Schneider did not like that at all and left the laundry in a huff!

He would sort it out with the Russians, he shouted as he slammed the door. Stupid man to brag about his Russian connections on top of everything else.

"You can kiss my arse!" was the Starski's reply.

He knew that Schneider would get what he wanted and it would be best for me to comply with Schneider's wishes. Paul who had done his personal laundry until now could help me and keep his extra roubles and cigarettes. I received ten roubles for being an officer and fifteen cigarettes anyway.

We arranged that Paul would do the washing, I would collect and deliver the stuff. So it was sorted to everyone's satisfaction and the peaceful balance in the laundry was maintained.

The next morning one of the medics came to us wanting to know who I was and the MO wanted to see me. However, Franz said I could only go once I had finished my quota.

The medic took off with a grin on his face. I completed my work and then took off to the Infirmary.

The medic pointed to the surgery and still grinning said "You have upset my lord and master, good for you!"

The room was large with ten beds, all occupied. The treatment room is in the annex where I find Dr Vera Rachmanova and Schneider. He shouts at me wanting to know why I hadn't come earlier. How grateful I am to Sepp who gave me an unofficial introduction to this man. I know he needs me, so he has to be careful how he treats me.

"Hope you are not speaking to me. Can I introduce myself? I am Captain Schmitt."

Schneider seems to be fighting for air. The lady doctor turns round and picks up a papyros (cigarette) oblivious of Schneider's discomfort. I light her cigarette and for my trouble she blows smoke straight into my face.

"Schmitt. The doctor is busy and overworked. His intentions are good and he wants to help you."

I notice that she uses the polite form of address, so she is giving Schneider a hint. When I pointed out that I, a fellow academic, expected to be addressed in the German fashion.

"Ah well," she continues. "You have to forgive him, he has spent so many years in such rough company you will have to re-educate him in the finer ways of communication."

That was the cue for Schneider to get back into the conversation. He apologises for his uncouth speech, but he once more requests politely that I should take care of his laundry and I concur.

We agreed on the usual payment and parted company. He had put his foot in it again, for just as I was leaving he addressed me as 'comrade.'

"My name is Schmitt, I am no one's comrade here, the ones I had are all dead." Which once more robs him of the power of speech.

"A right charmer you are," is the doctor's comment. I am again surprised at her excellent command of the German language. Maybe she comes from the Baltic.

I could take my leave, what had to be said was said. I make a polite bow in the doctor's direction and pretend not to see the proffered hand, but as I leave I hear her say to him

"Wottschelowek." (What a man!)

That's all I need, to be an object of her interest is not what I want to be. She is like a brightly burning flame which burns anything that comes too close, but gives no warmth. Things are difficult to keep secret in a camp.

Being a plennie brings the loss of being an individual, one gets sucked into the community.

Sepp Pszybilla knows that I had a visit to Dr Schneider – the medic passed on our conversation word for word. He also knows that I like smoking Machorka rolled in a piece of Pravda.

When we meet up one evening when I am on the late shift he explains it would not be a good idea if I was seen in his quarters. It would look like preferred treatment to the PoWs. He knows that his own position appears very enviable, he receives more roubles, is better dressed and gets better rations. He also is allowed the odd trip into Moscow as an escort. He is well aware that there are many who talk about him and are prepared to do anything to topple him, as they see his as an easy life. Little do they know of his wheeling and dealing with the Russians to prevent them being aware of some of the things going on in the camp.

I realize he is a very lonely man and the only thing I can do to support him is by listening. In the past he has seen so much wretchedness and bloody-mindedness, it sometimes seems to overpower him. His vision of our joint compatriots is a common bond between us. Many of the German PoWs seem to have developed brown nosing into an art form!

He has no real friends as he decided to keep the worst characters close to him, so that he could keep them under control. He would much prefer to be a normal plennie doing the usual manual labour. But who would do his job? He does his work in such a way that he can clear it with his own conscience. That's a luxury that very few others would allow themselves. He is surrounded by people who are forever claiming to be long standing Communists – whilst in reality most were big shots in the Nazi party, but he also knows PoWs with families in the western zone of Germany hope to be repatriated quicker, to theoretically fill the ranks of the Communist Party in the west. It is understandable, but he is under no illusion that these men will take off their "red mantle" the minute they cross the border. I would very much like to be of more practical help to him, but I know that he would only close up again were I to ask him direct questions. I have to exercise patience until I know that he is ready to open up.

It's once more Saturday evening. It's October and feeling quite cold. The Hungarian brigades drag in all manner of wood, even from the building site to feed the hungry stoves just to get some warmth into the quarters.

Once the nightly trading is over, the gypsies tune their violins. The first violinist asks for requests and I enjoy floating away on the waves of music.

The Primas (leading violinist) is of tall, slim build. Black hair frames his face. His fingers are delicate and seem to have a life of their own. He stands tall when he picks up his instrument and his eyes gaze into far distant places. His fellow musicians follow his lead and they drift off to the Pussta (Hungarian steppe) their homeland. The music paints a vivid picture of the vast meadows and fields, the rich corn fields moving in the gentle wind. I can feel the evening drawing in and the young people gather for the evening's entertainment. After a deliberate moment of musical discord all set off together to play the stirring notes of Czardas (dance) which culminates in a rousing whirl and comes to a sudden end when instruments halt abruptly.

All the Hungarians are up dancing their familiar dances – it is not hard to see and feel the burning longing for their homes, families and their country.

This is one of the few moments when being a mere plennie is a positive experience – such an inner feeling of brotherhood in its purest sense becomes reality. It is no illusion, this ecstasy builds a community of men who are joined together in this state of imprisonment, in their sorry fate of imposed loss of freedom.

Next Monday the medic from the Infirmary comes to me to collect Dr Schneider's laundry. No order, a request! My visit must have borne fruit. I suggested I might disturb the good doctor's siesta, but the medic reassures me that the lady doctor visits Iwanow at that time as the translator spends this time providing lunch for her sick mother and the field is clear.

Talk about a complicated love life for all involved players.

The medic is totally familiar with the rules of play and suggests I should join him for a quick drink of vodka after I have collected the laundry, to drink to the most beautiful woman.

She seems to be very generous with her vodka and her favours! He suggests abducting Rachmanova and theorizes about opening a brothel, with her as the main attraction!

I threaten him with a wet shirt and he takes off with a wide grin on his face, but not without slipping me a few cigarettes. No doubt, part of the doctor's supply. He seems to have a share in all the doctor's things, may even be part of Rachmanova's male harem!

4

About 1pm the brigades have all left for work and I make my way to the Infirmary. Konny the medic tells me I am expected and enter Dr Schneider's consulting room.

He is lying on his examination couch with his boots on. He stretches out his hand and today I cannot avoid shaking it. He appears to be pleased to see me and invites me to take a seat and keep him company for a while.

I sit down and to my surprise he calls for Konny and asks him to pour us drinks! Konny pours three tots, drinks his and then disappears. The atmosphere between the doctor and Konny in peculiar, to say the least. Not at all the senior/junior relationship which would be the norm. I wonder what Konny has on Dr Schneider?

Dr S notices my puzzlement and tells me how much he appreciates my being an academic and cultured person.

"One forgets how to relate to civilized humans after a while. Having to deal with this common lot all the time, it's easy to forget how to relate to a more intelligent person."

He pours us a second drink, no doubt hoping to get me to relax and lose my inhibitions. If only he knew how anxious I am about him he would be less generous with his alcohol.

The opinion of the majority of the plennies is very poor. Very few have much faith in his medical know-how and it's common knowledge there are quite a few men who have fallen victim to his ignorance. Only the presence of the other German doctor has prevented too many casualties from becoming mortuary cases. Schneider is fully aware of his junior colleague's low opinion of him, so he manages to provoke him to make an anti-communist statement which will cost him about eight days in solitary.

Through Sepp I managed to get a look into Schneider's personal details. He was born in 1923 in Saxonia. He claims to be a surgeon which is impossible as he was a mere 22 years old when captured and it was a physical impossibility for him to have acquired his medical degree, plus the necessary experience to qualify as a surgeon.

I am more inclined, judging by his demeanour, language and so called medical treatment to look on him as a butcher. Just looking at his hands: short, fat ugly fingers tells me these are not the sensitive hands of a doctor or a surgeon. What the Russian lady doctor sees in him is a mystery to me.

Dr Schneider produces a packet of cigarettes, a really posh make with a gold filter, something I have not seen for years. It seems quite an effort for him to offer me one of his hoard, but I am relaxing and enjoying my smoke. If he only knew how well informed I am about him! He is trying very hard to start a conversation without any help from me. In an effort to start things off he yells: "Tea for two!"

I point out to him that I should leave to get his laundry done, but he says there is no urgency as long as he has it in time for his Banja (bath day).

Konny arrives carrying a tray containing two cups and saucers – even two teaspoons! Konny is a clean living and looking young man and helps out frequently in his position as medic. A much more professional person than this so called doctor. He has of course, also got the German and the Russian doctors' number, but he wants to keep his position and he plays along with them.

As the conversation is still flowing I just sit back and enjoy the luxuries. I can sense Schneider's feeling of antipathy, but he has to be patient if he wants to be successful in his job as a traitor and spy!

I am enjoying my two cups of tea with lots of sugar in absolute silence. I notice that he is beginning to sweat, no doubt he had imagined it would be an easy job to get me to talk and to open up. I know it will cost him many a cup of tea plus cigarettes to get me to talk and tell him things the Russians already know with a few minor additions!

At long last he comments on how hot the tea is and I respond by telling him how he is sweating! He changes colour rapidly in absolute rage, murder lights up in his eyes, but there is a job to do.

I help myself to another cigarette and he removes the pack and the remaining cigarettes. I take pity on him and compliment him on the quality of his tea, but tell him how it would be even better if we could drink it at home in Germany. Quite, quite, but before that we have to be politically re-educated. He should leave the thinking to horses, they have bigger heads!

In my days I have done a lot of reading, both Stalin's manifestos as well as Lenin's writings which young Schneider has not even seen. As a potential converter he is very ignorant and on very thin ice with me. He feels that my theoretical knowledge may be excellent but could I turn theory into practice? His own intentions are to widen his experience to be able to offer his services to the homeland, once he is repatriated. Poor Germany, poor patients!

He is not a fluent speaker and makes quite a hash of it trying to be politically correct and speaking high German! He states one stupidity after another, playing right into my hands, should I ever want to use it against him.

I have had enough of his pointless ranting, so I try a quick change of conversation. He falls for it hook, line and sinker, grateful for any co-operation.

I presume from his accent that he is from somewhere near Dresden (in Saxony). He seems thrilled to bits that I am willing to chat; I compliment him on his youthful looks and tell him how amazed I am at his medical titles at his young age and his healthy appearance. He points out that as a medical man he is well aware of the human body dietary requirements and apart from that he does regular exercises in his room. The fact that I know what shape his room exercises take, makes it hard for me not to burst out laughing.

He is obviously trying hard to appear older than he is, so I guess his age is about 31, which pleases him greatly. He congratulates me on my correct guess. 32 years is his assumed age.

When asked about his university time he claims to have studied first in Dresden and then in Yena. Unfortunately I did four semesters in Yena and remembered it well. Now the real fun could start! He falls for every trick I play.

I am really pushing my luck, mentioning non-existent pubs: 'The Pigeon Coot' which he proudly claims as his regular. I really should put a stop to my wicked game, but it is so tempting to go on and on. It is just like giving sweeties to a child.

Temptation to push him even further is hard to resist. The name of Professor Dr Ibrahim of Dresden (he did lecture in paediatrics in Fence University) once more a figment of my imagination, and Schneider automatically claims to be one of his students. He seems to be caught up in a roller coaster of lies, unable to stop himself becoming part of a fantasy story.

He daydreams about midnight walks along the River Pleisse. Unfortunately Dresden lies on the River Elbe, a fact known to anyone with the most basic knowledge of Saxonys geography. Leipzig is close to River Pleisse and the place of his moonlight walks is also familiar to me, not as a romantic hideaway, but it was a place where I fought my first fencing party.

Time to stop the wicked game and Schneider and I will meet again. I thanked him for his hospitality and told him how much I had enjoyed our intellectual discussion! For me it was highly fruitful and educational. What ammunition for future use. But, as I am about to leave Dr Rachmanova appears. She sits down and when I try to beat a hasty retreat she invites me to stay and sends Schneider off to make more tea.

He does not appreciate being treated like a waiter and wants to pass the request onto Konny but Dr Rachmanova repeats her request, now really an order and he complies obviously with rage. Rather like a dog who knows his masters voice.

Dr Vera Rachmanova brings both a breath of fresh air and a hint of perfume. How long is it since I had the sensual pleasure? My wife always loved "Uralt Lavendel" but this was quite a different scent which becomes more potent as she is moving closer and with her eyes checks me over, like goods on display! I have no idea what she is up to and for once would be quite pleased to see the 'teaboy' return. She covers my hand with hers and asks me:

"What are you thinking Schmitt?"

Her eyes burn with fire and suddenly a tear rolls down her cheek. What hidden life history is behind her brash and often offensive demeanour? Maybe her inner self is tucked away behind this cold outer façade. Her seductive exterior seems to be looking for someone to listen to her other persona, not the woman we plennies see.

She asks me about my wife and I tell her how much I miss Charlotte and our children and with that I have constructed a sort of protective barrier around myself. I know she is looking for a man, not a lackey who jumps when she whistles. The heavy atmosphere lightens with the mentioning of my family and we fall into casual conversation. She can behave like a lady, not just like a huntress on the prowl. Maybe I could help her as she is quite obviously a very troubled, tortured soul contrary to her public face. At this point Schneider re-appears, I have yet another cup of tea and then beat a hasty retreat. I shake hands with the lady doctor after cleaning my hand surreptitiously on my trousers following Schneider's damp handshake.

Konny waits for me outside and says that he is expecting me to be the Russian lady's next victim. But as I pointed out to him it takes two to tango, and I am not in the market.

He grins and admits to a one night stand with the temptress and ever since he hangs about and is tortured by jealousy every time he knows she is having her wicked way with Schneider.

What a confusing set-up. We drink yet another vodka, but we refuse to drink or toast to the lady in question. I still think there is more to her than a willing conquest. Konny can't get over my obvious refusal to become yet another sexual partner of the Russian doctor. He thinks I am playing hard to get and using a novel approach, to get her through her soul, if she has one!

In the meantime a heated exchange takes place in Schneider's room. Words like "swine" and "bastard" can be heard followed by a volley of oaths and swear words. I take off at great speed; it's never a good idea to witness arguments and fights of so-called superiors.

When I return, "Well, what was she like?" the Starski asks me with an ironic twinkle in his eye. Unknown to me Schneider's 'laundry boy' was always picked by Dr R.

As he points out, quite a succession of plennies have had the lady's pleasure. Paul apparently lasting longer than most. Apparently she has a large appetite and she has a never ending supply of more than willing partners.

How am I going to avoid being caught up in this game? I have never had to hide from a woman in my life, but she bared her soul to me, not her body, for just a second and much appealed to the healer of souls in me. Just like any other human being in trouble.

5

Once back in the laundry I put Schneider's laundry to work. 3 linen shirts, 3 pairs of underpants, 3 vests and 4 pairs of socks. I wondered where he acquired such good quality clothing.

Franz E has left to visit his pal, the kitchen Starski for a dish of fried potatoes, lucky man. And thinking of 'extras' everyone knows that Sepp Pszybilla quite unlike the majority of activists never uses his position to obtain more rations or supplies. Just as I think about him he joins me.

After our usual cigarette he presents me with a typewritten piece of paper, my conversation with Schneider, word for word. He may not be a doctor, but his memory is perfect or maybe Konny's. The original of the copy in my hand is already on Iwanow's desk to stop Schneider adding incriminating items at a later stage.

Sepp advises me to add some of my own personal details at my next meeting with Schneider, preferably in a more public place such as a hospital ward.

He knows that I have found the doctor's secret, but advises me to file this away for future use, and he also warns me at all costs not to incur his jealousy. One or two plennies have suddenly died after a routine vaccination. What a weird position for a plennie to be in.

I have to admit that I am fascinated by the woman's face and I have to confess that I am not blind to her feminine appeal. What makes an obviously intelligent woman into a wanton, who bestows her favours on many a Tom, Dick or Harry without being too selective about it?

Sepp P changes the subject and sits next to my laundry tub. Obviously he has other pressing problems. He finds it very hard to be at the end of his dreams, having reached the Soviet Union and finding that the reality of communism is no way lives up to his ideal and it was no satisfaction for me to tell him that realized dreams very rarely live up to expectations. He had spent his growing up years getting more and more involved with the communist movement. I suppose it is really difficult to be a convinced, fully functioning communist without giving up being a German.

Sepp tells me there were many genuine communists, but most lost their lives under the Nazi regime according to Professor Jansen in Lloxio. As a young man Sepp being on the register of communists had the stark choice of staying in the concentration camp or being conscripted into the penal company. He opted for the latter, knowing that a dead communist is of no use to anyone. But even that reasoning misfired. Looked at from a Bolshevik angle, he was still not trustworthy. He deserted first chance he got whilst stationed on the Eastern Front. He owed his life to the political commissar, as the regular soldiers were about to shoot him. He was sent to a Russian propaganda company from where he did broadcasts to German troops. Even then he began to have second thoughts in spite of his totally genuine idealism. I could still not see what his problem was, his political opponents were conquered, he was still in the cradle of communism able to enjoy it at its purest.

My political ignorance needs updating. Communism had only reached its first development stage: Socialism. There is still a long way to go before Utopia is reached and a lot of bodies will fall by the wayside. He seemed to be in full flow and I could hear the influence of his time in Lloxio where he underwent intensive re-education.

Marx and Engels both Germans, brought the original ideas to Russia, but only when they were transformed into Russian theory and practice which once more is being brought back to Germany. Sepp is getting really cross when I ask him why he now objects to this. Don't you understand, Germans as a rule do not accept meekly ideas (unless they are afraid) without thinking and questioning them. Germans are prepared to work until they collapse, but they have to see something at the end of it.

He tells me nothing new, I have discussed this subject ad infinitum, with other safe and trustworthy plennies. The Russians have moved a long way from the original ideals, what remains is a powerful force intent on conquering the world at any price, under cover of a world revolution they are involved in a gigantic colonial political movement unmatched by previous dictatorships.

It would be easy to convert a load of German PoWs but they had been allowed inadvertently to look behind the aptly called Iron Curtain, the Russians degraded the plennies to work animals. Had they kept us interned for a few weeks, treated us in accordance with the Geneva Convention and sent us home, we would almost to a man all have been living and propagandists for Communism. (Still being fully aware of how Germany treated Russian PoWs), but instead hundreds of thousands died – for what?

Still Sepp feels Germany could still evolve into a communist state which could eventually provide a way of life suitable for Germans, which is not covered by feelings of revenge.

That ideal was far from the political plans for Germany. Ulbricht stated in his lectures that there was only one type of communism – the Marxist-Lenin style. He also said that one of his major aims was to destroy the German workman's allotment garden mentality.

Sepp regretted never having had the chance of ever speaking to General Mueller or Lenski or any of the others. "They might have made a lot of profit out of my ideas and thoughts." Still the eternal optimist is Sepp! Had his wish become reality he would have been one of the many who disappeared in the depths of Russia.

Sepp had news from his wife. The family had to leave Oppeln and after a tortuous journey had reached Halle with her sister Livech. One has to be able to read between the lines – how very hard life is for them and oppressive. Not surprisingly the more dominant and oppressive are not the Russian administrators, but their German deputies. An unfortunate character trait of Germans is to be more *pious than the Pope*. It's a trend frequently noted even in the camp. It's enough just to read the camp newspaper where General von Lenski writes that it was historically correct that the Russians took East Prussia.

As for General Vincent Mueller, I saw a Corporal giving him a right smack across his rear end and asking him how he was doing. Why did the good General put up with and join forces with creatures like the corporal? They thought their grovelling would get them home quicker. Everything will be the same in the new East Germany, it may appear less crude, but basically no change.

I personally remember a real conniving evil chap called Baecker who earned himself a fearsome reputation as Inspector of Works in

Nazi Germany. Like many like him, he did a successful backward salto and once more ended in the butter! He had amassed a fortune under Hitler and now earned his keep by spying on his fellow Germans for the Russians. He had big plans for his future in the new Germany and no doubt he will make it too. Unless he disappears suddenly in the camp – these things have been known. Basically the Russians don't care, they like and use treason, but despise the traitor. People like this Baecker are like mushrooms, when one disappears another one pops up.

It is a great sadness to Sepp that he knows this type of people will once more be at the helm of the new government. At first I suspected him of having similar aspirations. But no, not Sepp. He just wants to live in peace with his family and work. He knows his limits and is not in it to gain favours for the future as a camp elder.

We both agree that in the East it is 100% communist. Russia and the west are trying to pick up where they left off in 1933. We know our compatriots only too well. All in all we will end up with governments with feet of clay on both sides.

6

Dr Schneider does not seem to like my company either. I collect his laundry from Konny and so far there have been no complaints. According to Konny the good Doctor walks about like an injured lion, but it's none of my business, anything for a quiet life.

The Hungarian officers remain as polite and friendly as ever in spite of the language difference. I collect our daily food ration, this way I can save them a job when they return from their exhausting work. I have also discovered that the hospital cook is a fellow Silesian which makes him a bit more generous when he measures out our soup and sometimes there is even a minute extra helping for everyone. I can do without any extra helpings because my additional helping is kept warm for me at the laundry.

At first work in the laundry was difficult as I was a total stranger to the work and the workers, but once they realized that I spoke their language (didn't act as if this kind of labour was beneath me) and was willing to learn from them, I was accepted in their community.

The most interesting character is Hans from Berlin. He was a tiler and must have made a small fortune when all the new barracks were being built in Berlin. He used to buy the little used clothes of a well-known film star. He used to do the Doctor's laundry for me.

There is news of the Hungarian repatriation. We all hope it does not all go down the pan like so many of the Russian plans do. They are all being fitted out in new padded clothing, still not a dead cert but close. A supply of cooking pots and kettles as well as the metal tubing which is installed in the train wagons will be arriving soon. The catering department too is on high alert and new supplies are rolling in. All appears well.

It's like living with a swarm of bees at night. Everyone is excited and making plans. I am not able to follow their conversations but the hope and joy is almost palpable.

Captain Kovacs confirms the rumour. He is usually so calm and collected but he too is absolutely bubbling with excitement. One of the officers presents me with a small packet of tobacco, which he has been saving from his meagre ration so that I too can share in their joy. I am reluctant to accept this precious gift as I am sure it would be useful for bartering on the train and in Budapest, but he calls the Captain over to translate his feelings of disappointment before I accept his gift, so I accept gratefully.

Doctor Schneider has no time for me at present, all the Hungarians must have a thorough medical examination. There still has been no general official announcement.

The Russians may have quite different alternative plans, they might not all go home, maybe just a select few. It seems doubtful for the Russians to send off some of their best workers.

In the meantime the general office produced a thank you letter from the Hungarians to Papa Stalin!

Captain Kovacs translated it and it was signed by every Hungarian often unread, but they really had no option. I read the German translation and wasn't the least bit surprised. It just oozed eternal gratitude and goodwill to the liberating forces.

My contribution to this piece of doubtful literature was a quick iron-over as it had got badly scrunched up.

The tension is almost unbearable, until at long last there is an official proclamation. All the Hungarians are celebrating, the Gypsies are playing their wonderful music which troubles my heart and makes me more homesick than ever. The primas (lead musician) tells me he will play something just for me to make me feel less sad. The music he plays is almost indescribable; it's sad, it's happy it just fills your soul with longing and conjures up a different and better time. The men dance and as suddenly as it started the music stops, the primas takes a bow and I shake his hand and an overwhelming storm of applause surrounds us. It is very late when everything finally settles.

I am left with a desperate longing for home and my family. When will my time come? This is the first time for many of us to actually witness a major transport going away from captivity. It's like a millstone round my neck to see it all and to know we are staying behind. I do know that the Hungarians are returning to a very uncertain future in their homeland, but anything has to be better than here.

Next day they receive their new clothing, a German work brigade prepares the trains. Every wagon is fitted with a stove and sufficient coal and wood to prevent any untimely deaths. That would not look good would it?

At long last they are ready for the off. What little luggage they have is strapped to their backs, but before they are allowed to leave they have to undergo a very thorough luggage and body search. Not one bit of paper is allowed not even papyrossi (Russian cigarettes) are allowed in case the paper covering the cigarettes contains messages. Once the Hungarians leave their barracks they are separated from us by a heavy line of guards to prevent any possible contact. At last they are ready to finally leave this awful place. They march off in strict formation singing their hearts out. After passing through yet another control where each name is carefully checked, the last few wave to us, and then they are out of sight.

Many of us had thoughts of somehow mixing in with the departing prisoners, but the repeated controls made it impossible; a mouse had little chance of getting away with it much less a grown man.

The biggest deterrent would be our own compatriots – if I'm not getting out neither is anyone else!

7

The big factory hall is now empty. It will not be used to house people in the future and I am once more on the move. Sadly I lose my good mattress, and only reluctantly a spare is allocated to me in barracks but it does not bother me greatly as I spend the day in the laundry.

Hans is one of my co-workers in the laundry. When I tell him about the adverse conditions where I now live, they ask me to move into their barracks. The short time I spent in the previous barracks was difficult, as most of the workers had well paid jobs in a furniture factory. This allowed them to buy extra rations, they could not understand that I could control my envy and it was better to be away from that barracks.

After the Hungarians departed I was called to see Black Katja, (a Russian) the interpreter, in her office. She informed me that there was mail from my wife and family which was wonderful.

I felt she was in a good mood so I asked if she could help me. I said, I have been restricted to the camp for some time and was not sure why. She informed me that all my papers have not arrived, they only have my discharge papers from my stay in prison.

So now I can concentrate on my post from home, the card had been on a long journey, first to my old abode. What luck somebody did not rip it up and chuck it in the nearest bin!

This was a very special card, my wife tells me that Michael my eldest has been confirmed, he has been presented with a Hymn Book containing the following verse:

"God created the way and the wind, but sail and helm to reach a safe harbour are yours."

It stirs me and starts off a new train of thought, what can I do to speed up my repatriation? I am no hero or daredevil to plan an escape. I am also aware how many others would have to pay for my escape attempt, successful or not.

If I was any sort of specialist I could work like hell to establish some sort of record, but chances are my fellow inmates would do away with me, as they would be forced to achieve the same sort of workload!

The Russians would not want to part with me either as I am such a wonderful worker.

I am gifted with two left hands, I have learned the basic tasks to keep me safe in the laundry, but that's it. I am the usual plennie, underfed and lacking in any extra strength. Sadly my son's confirmation verse does not apply to PoWs, our sails and helms have been removed when we become prisoners.

In some ways I might differ from the rest of the plennies by the very fact of my privileged upbringing, education and social status, but there is nothing that would speed up my repatriation.

Should I suddenly turn into a convinced activist standing up for all that I mistrust and detest, it would do little for me. The Russians would use me and my intelligence and squeeze me like a lemon, but it would not move me an inch closer to home. It is easier to remain my own man. The idea of becoming a 'Soup Communist' is quite repellant to me.

The Revolution celebrations for the Russians are over. Major searches throughout the camp for knives and other weapons are completed; two days of rest passed peacefully, an axe was found in the laundry behind the stove. It was given to the Starski with a message from Black Katja – hide it better next time!

Fireworks in all the larger squares in town had been seen from the camp and were quite magnificent. The Russians love it, there is so little colour in their lives apart from fireworks. A lot of Russians get well and truly drunk on cheap vodka.

In the meantime I got used to my co-workers in the laundry and they to me. Most are younger than me but they are a thoroughly decent bunch, it makes me think there is a glimmer of hope for Germany in the future. All they need is a firm hand and a decent leitmotif for their way of life, once released from captivity. But just how much has been ruined for them to really think of that?

To me it often feels as if in the future the huge continent of Asia wants to just annex that little bit of Europe and swallow it up. There were great men once who were prepared to stand up and fight for their ideals, especially the nobility, but their time is in the past.

During the time in the Republic people lost their convictions and ethics and basically were up for hire. A whole people allowed themselves to be used by a select few, whose aims and goals were alien to any decent human being. The German people's enthusiasm and readiness was channeled to enrich and improve only a select few.

It is quite disgusting to think what was done to people; when I was a troop officer I lived with my men. I shared their fears often being more scared than them, as I felt it was my duty to be the first out of the dugout. I also had to watch how these brave men lost their idealism and not only in the PoW camp.

It was tragic to watch how the communist activists persuaded them that everything in their former life had been wrong and evil. They ended up feeling guilty and worthless everything was our fault and we had to pay for everything.

Of course these activists left the paying to others, they just enjoyed the privileges of being an activist.

How will it ever be possible to integrate these beaten people into a whole healthy unity? No one is saying that German misdeeds which were beyond the pale should be ignored, but there has to be a rebirth sometime where Germany is part of a new Europe.

As in the past shameless leaders persuaded normal people to do things which they would never contemplate under a good moral leadership. There's evil sides to all of us, but in most they remain hidden and never surface throughout our lives.

The influence of evil is not a German phenomenon, it is international

It was impossible for Joe Bloggs to realize what was going on with the Brown shirts and by the time they did the cancer was already too advanced.

Our children will have to bear the guilt and the task to prove that there is hope and decency within a true Germany. The present generation will find it difficult to ever trust anyone again.

The church too has to once more take an active part in rebuilding the new country.

Initially the Nazis adopted a lot of the churches ways, but once the clergy realized what had been done often in their name, it was too late.

People just stopped attending church services and joined the new religion. World domination by National Socialism. Such discussions fill many an empty hour in the plennie's life, it makes you forget who and where you are.

My enthusiasm in the laundry is becoming a worry. I have to find something else to take my mind off my longing for home and wanting to be an active participant of the rebuilding of Germany. Even the Starski tells me to put the brakes on my work efforts. Do I want to do it all on my own and put them all out of work? So my discussions with Hans come to an abrupt end. We both agree that the renewal of Germany must start with each and every one of us starting from scratch.

This is all very well, but as Hans put it, we would have to be angels. There's little chance of that.

Dr Rachmanova has been absent for quite some time, she seems to have no interest in me, and I no longer have to worry about her intentions. Even Dr Schneider hardly notices me these days, but I still drink my vodka with Konny, care of Schneider.

Konny tells me the atmosphere between the two doctors is less than amicable. He even heard the sound of a resounding slap and we both know who was on the receiving end.

Konny is busy adding on a small cupboard to the already existing drug cupboard. Apparently new medical supplies are in the offing. Will Dr Schneider misuse his status and use the extra medication for barter?

I arrange with Konny that I will personally collect Dr Schneider's laundry in order to get to the bottom of things. Before I get round to that, we have to overcome a more difficult problem.

8

Winter is fully with us and the minute we hang up washing it freezes solid. The cold tears our skin and once back in the laundry the hot water in the tubs make it very painful. As usual German ingenuity won through; a couple of blacksmiths devised a special iron with a very large main part which retains the heat longer. We can dry iron the wet clothes, it takes longer, but time is something we have.

In the evenings I offer to stay behind by choice to boil the laundry. I like standing there in the comfortable warmth of the stove with the light turned off. The wind and the snow are howling outside and I lose myself in the flickering flames which conjure up pictures of home. Loudly I sing one of the plennies' favourite songs about the linden tree in front of my father's house. It is a bit sentimental but it suits the moment.

Suddenly I feel a hand touching my shoulder. In sudden fright I turn round to find Dr Rachmanova standing behind me. I had been so immersed in thoughts of home that I had been deaf and blind to my surroundings. She had crept up on me in her padded felt boots.

She offers me a tin of hand cream to soothe my broken skin. I feel like a silly schoolboy found daydreaming by the teacher. I thank her for the ointment, she looks at me as if to say – well, is that all you can manage?

Before I realize what's happening we are talking away like old friends.

Apparently Sepp had told her that I was doing the night shift, she seems to have changed into a real person, gone is the superior Dr R who could barely be bothered to look at a plennie properly never mind talk to him like a human being.

Apparently she had been wanting to talk to me for some time without the whole camp using it as the latest bit of gossip. She is actually concerned about my good name and my reputation!

I thank her for that, but she suspects a hidden bit of sarcasm. However, as she puts it, she just needs to speak to a person from time to time who is not looking for special privileges or has more personal designs on her.

To ease the tension a little, she tells me a bit about herself. She comes from the Baltic region where she learned to speak German as a child. Her father was a well-known surgeon and established a clinic in Moscow during the First World War. He survived the Revolution but her mother did not due to her father's useful connections to several high powered Bolsheviks she was admitted to university in spite of belonging to the despised intelligentsia.

She subsequently spent many months in prison. Whilst in prison she had a baby which was taken away from her. She never found out what happened to it, despite searching for years. The memory of these awful times shakes her visibly and big tears roll down her cheeks.

When she was discharged from prison she couldn't find her father or husband anywhere, they disappeared like so many during that time in the bottomless pit that is Russia.

She spent some time working in a factory and then became involved with a man who helped her finish her studies, but she had to revert to her maiden name. She managed to pass all her exams and just threw herself into her work in order to forget her short spell of happiness with her husband and the loss of her baby.

By then the war had broken out and she was working in a field hospital. The horrendous conditions and the ever presence of death filled her with an untameable desire for life and to find love. She had no problems finding willing lovers, one following another, but her way of life was beginning to tell.

She was secretly relieved when she was transferred to a PoW camp. I pointed out to her that sharing her life story with me was punishable under Russian law and she put a lot of trust in me, am I worthy of this trust?

She tells me more about her situation. How she was in a position to get her hands on drugs and was able to sell them on the black market.

The plennies' chief surgeon would not countersign her drug sheet, but Schneider had been a willing partner as had been the political officer – all getting their cut.

She had reached a point where her way of life revolted her and it had to stop. She had to talk to someone who would listen to her without using it against her at a later date. She picked on me.

Now I had to be very careful to find the right tone. I used Vera, her first name, without giving it any thought. I put it to her as a fact, not an empty compliment that she was a very beautiful woman. Finding a good husband should be one option, someone who would love her for who she was, not what she could provide him with.

She had been round the block too often and so far had nothing but disappointments. If marriage was not the answer she could lose herself in her profession, be a real doctor to the many sick prisoners whose previous treatment had been less than cursory at best.

Many changes were already taking place in the camp but I was still concerned about her connection with Dr Schneider. Why does she not replace him with someone more able such as a genuine doctor? Now I find out that the good Schneider has found out as much as he can about her, which is not that difficult in a place where the walls have ears. What could happen to him should he betray her? He was already in prison, memories of her time in prison are still very much alive in her mind and she could expect very little help from Iwanow. He was a trué Russian and Black Katja was waiting in the background to take her place in his bed.

Schneider was the big stumbling block, he had to be effectively silenced without causing too much of a stir, but how? I assured her that I am honoured by her trust in me. I would remain her friend and would do everything within my power to find a solution. It was like a gift to me that she found me worthy of so much trust and treated me like an equal.

A plennie loses any feeling of self-worth after years of being treated like a piece of useless flotsam.

As quietly as she came, she vanishes. I take her to the door and soon she is swallowed up by the driving snow. I feel glad that I can once more help a troubled soul. If I can achieve a solution for her problems my time as a plennie shall not be wasted.

When I move Vera's stool I find a small lady's hankie. This will remind me of this hour when it will seem like a dream in the drab life of a plennie.

I resume my laundry duties, as that only takes up a minimum of concentration. I go over the recent conversations with Dr R. Will she remain steadfast and not revert to her old ways? Posmotrim (we shall see). Of course I could use all this knowledge as a lever for my own ends. Repatriation looms much closer but as quick as the thought popped up I repress it again. I haven't sunk that low yet.

After completion of my daily norm (my allocated work) I leave the wash house. The snowfall is reduced to just a few odd flakes. In the light of the arc lights the snow glitters like a collection of diamonds. How often did we curse the snow on our retreat when it hid obstacles or when we used the cover of snow for one of our dead comrades as a last resting place? Or, when as a group of plennies already half-starved in the forests of Kama, sank into piles of snow often too exhausted to fight our way free.

When I passed the watchtower, I called up.

"What time is it Ivan!"

Poor bugger. He was fast asleep; automatically he grabs his shotgun but its okay I am not in the dead zone and he lowers his gun.

"What are you doing here?"

I tell him I am a laundryman nightshift worker. He checks the time on his watch which looks as big as an alarm clock. It's 5am and he asks me for a cigarette and when I agree to give him one of my precious hoard he leaves his tower and climbs down to the other side of the fence. I take careful aim and throw the cigarette across to him.

He thanks me politely which is unusual, so I take a gamble and ask him for matches. With a laugh he throws me his and climbs back up to his post.

Suddenly the world seems a better place. I feel at peace with myself and all that is around me. It's stopped snowing and a wonderful silence rules. Before I enter my barrack room I turn round and look at the huge town – a million different fates exist within her. A number of large towers throw their dark silhouettes. What a magic picture!

To think that within these walls the fate of our world today is being decided. A world where according to the powerful there is no room for God in spite of the many churches and spires, where he is still praised and prayed to. So much effort has been put into removing his name out of the heart of the people. Did he not choose me last night as his tool to listen to and lighten a woman's lot?

A clear dark winter sky lets the stars sparkle in unending glory. I think about His words. What is man to you, oh Lord that you think of him and the Sons of Man and take pity on him? A last look and I am off to catch a few moments of sleep before the usual plennies' day starts again.

The idea of a bedroom for two is a long way from my present accommodation – wide open windows to face a panorama of the Riesengebirge (Tatra Mountains) were just a dream these days. Its man next to man, and the air thick with the unfortunate side effects of the food we are given.

9

December 1947

The days pass quickly and Christmas is just around the corner. Sepp asked the Political Officer for permission to hold a Christmas service but he was turned down.
What he has arranged is a communal celebration with a Christmas tree, a political address and presents handed out by Father Christmas. The gifts have been made by the prisoners.
The men in the laundry have decided to have their own 'do'. I want to present Sepp with a new pipe. Maybe Dr R will buy it for me in town? I have seen Dr Schneider on several occasions but we just greeted each other politely. He has lost weight and his usual self-satisfied demeanour is less certain in appearance. No more hanky panky with Dr R!
Through Sepp I know that he is not reporting to Iwanow about me. Konny watches him carefully.

One day after lunch I go to the hospital to collect Dr Schneider's dirty laundry. Konny is in on the act and he just points to the treatment room, a very abrupt "Come in," is the response to my knock.
As usual he is stretched out on his examination table and he stares up at the ceiling. I wonder what thoughts are going through his mind. He gets up and points to the seat, please sit down.
Apparently he is bored to tears and wants a chat. He complains that in this clear winter weather hardly anyone reports sick. I suggest he should accompany the work brigades – he would find plenty of patients there. He thinks I am joking with him, joining the ugly smelly working plennies? Not likely!
With a perfect straight face I ask him about his relationship with Dr R. Surely that would brighten up his boring life?

All I get is a filthy look and a comment about "a Russian whore" – so definitely not a gentleman.

This time he doesn't offer me a drink, even his supply of cigarettes has dwindled. All that is on offer is a bit of Pravda. He really is on his uppers, his self-assurance seems to totally have left him.

He yells for Konny to bring teas, but even the tea supplies are down to zero. Only Konny's kind offer to lend him some provides us with a cup of tea, without sugar. That too has run out.

He has had a total change of heart about the wonderful Russia of his talks. He wants to go home to be able to do some proper surgery. God have mercy on his future patients, providing they are not cattle, which we think is his real profession.

His language again gives him away and betrays his real origin. How quickly our Romeo went back to being a rough street urchin!

My private visit seems to cheer him up, but unfortunately Dr Rachmanova has curtailed his supply of extras. I make him an offer he can't refuse. I do his laundry for nothing and he treats me as a private patient. He can't wait to accept being old comrades, it is now a gentleman's agreement. I want him not to be too quick with his 'old comrades', it could be his downfall.

I find out he no longer has access to the drug cupboard. Dr R has taken the key off him. As far as he is concerned Dr R suffered an early menopause and takes her rage out on him.

My commiserations must sound quite genuine. He doesn't seem to hear the hidden irony. He even went as far as visiting Iwanow who throws him out without even listening to his complaints. Well now, I must make use of my status as a private patient. I have pains where I presume my appendix is. Dr Schneider calls for Konny to bring a spatula and I get a bit concerned – from which end is he going to check the state of my appendix. Relax, it's my mouth he is looking at and he assures me all is well, just a slight reddening which a good gargle will clear. I am trying very hard not to laugh, we have all heard of people who have bits in the wrong place, but to inspect an appendix through the throat is a bit, well unusual to say the least. Even Konny has to leave the room to conceal grinning.

This confirms once and for all Dr Schneider is not a qualified medical man he is a simple fraudster – probably worked as a trolley pusher in a German field hospital, and there watched doctors' behaviour.

I ask him would he be kind enough to check over my tonsils as the cold weather occasionally caused me problems in that department. Ever obliging he asks me to remove my work shirt and jacket, but after listening to my chest with his stethoscope he assures me all is well.

Just a minor jump from tonsils to bronchi but in the day of the good Dr Schneider it seems perfect. I put my clothes back on and offer my doctor a cigarette which he gratefully accepts.

He decides now is the time to do a little prodding – probably needs something for his report to Iwanow.

How did I spend the war? I tell him all the facts which are already carefully documented. Had I been to Russia before coming as a PoW? No, I had been an officer in charge of a company until 1943, then following a serious wound I had been transferred to military intelligence in Berlin after a short spell in Paris.

That was enough for today as laundry work called. I made my excuses with the promise to return for lots more interesting chats, to provide more fodder for his reports to Iwanow.

In the evening I attended sick call to get a chance to speak to Dr Rachmanova. It's a fairly quiet evening, just the usual crowd who need their regular supply of tablets.

There are a few minor abcesses to drain, a few plennies are quietly talking when Dr Schneider appears. He decides to give us a major dressing down: time wasters, malingerers etc are some of the words he throws at us. One of the prisoners, a tall strong man says if he is on my train for home there will be one less by the time we get to Warsaw.

We hear Dr R ask Dr Schneider to administer a whiff of Ether to one of her patients who has to have a toenail removed.

"What the hell. Can't he take it like a man!" but Dr R does not lose her temper.

"Just follow my instructions," she says and that's the end of that.

The plennies all smile and say our lovely doctor is okay, which is good praise from the prisoners.

I can see that the jobs Dr Schneider is allowed to do are strictly those of a medical orderly, like putting on bandages etc. Dr R looks at me a bit uncertain and asks me what my complaint is, but before I can answer Dr Schneider butts in and tells her that he has already examined me re: pains in my appendix.

I keep my fingers crossed that she will join my game. I was only there to collect my tablets for gargling. Quite right says Dr Schneider, just a little reddening, nothing dramatic.

Her face flushes with fury, but I manage to wink at her and thank goodness she understands and quickly turns to the drug cupboard and hides a touch of the giggles with a cough. She hands me a roll of pills and tells me to come back if there is no improvement.

Dr Schneider assures his colleague that he has listened to my tonsils…that's too much for Dr R and in a mad dash she leaves. I take my pills and do the same.

When I later see Konny he wants to know the cause of Dr Rachmanova's hilarity he has not seen her laugh so much for ages. I could tell him but I decide not to.

Only four more days to Christmas. The 10 laundry workers have decided to buy extra food supplies like bread, butter, sausages. Instead of individual presents we are to have a major Bolschoi Prasnik (big feast).

Very much to my surprise I notice Dr Schneider taking part in an expedition to the forest to collect Christmas trees. They had hardly left when Konny turns up and informs me that Dr R wishes to see me.

When I hurry across to her hospital I find Konny chopping wood, not one of his favourite jobs. There are storm clouds on the horizon so I am forewarned.

The hospital ward is nearly empty, only the beds close to the stove are occupied. Contrary to my expectations Dr R looks cheerful enough, she managed to send Dr Schneider and Konny on their errands, so she could speak to me without an audience.

Vera wants to warn me again to curb my efforts with the so-called doctor Schneider. She is fully aware that he is not a doctor, but she is also aware of how much he knows about her and what harm he can do to her. She is convinced that one day he will hopefully trip himself up without my help.

He could do me a lot of damage with Iwanow by just making up stories. I have no control over his written reports to the Camp Commandant. Through her connection with Iwanow she can find out what he has reported, true or false.

She is quite happy to obtain the pipe for me (Sepp's Christmas gift) and she won't accept my roubles. Before I leave she gives me a box of metro, a mediocre brand of cigarettes. Anything else would cause a stir. Konny watches me as I come out of the Hospital.

I tell him the doctor gave me a telling off about the quality of the clean laundry, this way he is not suspicious.

In the evening the commandos arrive with the fresh Christmas trees, every barracks has its own tree. Originally there was to have been a joint party but this had been called off. Sepp has been trying to persuade Iwanow that a big do would have been big propaganda value. But "Niet," was all he got from him.

Sepp and I sit in front of the stove watching the fire, each one of us following our own dreams and thoughts. He comments on the many positive changes in the last few weeks especially in the hospital, the infirmary and the kitchen, all due to Dr R, but as he says - women, what makes them do the things they do?

"I could never figure out my old lady at home either, we had many an argument and I always thought I knew her, but she always managed to surprise me."

The same applied to Dr Rachmanova, she used to be such a vindictive uncaring person, and virtually overnight she has turned into a human being.

She even avoided the early morning roll call, but apparently that's not all she is doing without. Dr Schneider no longer enjoys her favours. In fact quite the opposite, she gave him a few resounding slaps. From a cold almost brutal non-caring woman, she has changed to a caring professional doctor. Every plennie will put his hand in the fire for her.

The only one who does not appreciate this change is the good Dr Schneider. Sepp hands me a copy of his latest report re my activities to Iwanow. Between Sepp and Konny they have organized a foolproof system, using blotting paper and copy-paper with Schneider's heavy hand it is easy to read. Konny has passed on the contents of mine and Schneider's conversation, it's just as well he is on my side.

Dr R joins us, she is looking like a picture for sore eyes and cheers us both up. Sepp is initially a bit self-conscious but she soon puts him at ease, a packet of cigarettes gets handed round when she joins us near the fire. She enjoys her smoke and admires our Christmas tree. She likes the way Christmas is celebrated in Germany. It reminds her of her own sheltered childhood.

Sepp then tells us about his Silesian Christmas. His wife used to start by baking about four weeks before 24th December. When he came home from work he had to help her kneading dough. The dough was then left to rise near the stove and the next morning the Stollen would be rolled onto oven trays, and the children would take them on the handcart to the bakery for baking.

Then Sepp remembers all the different Christmas cookies his wife used to make. His children were all for eating them before they were even cooked; his wife used to carry the key for the cooking cupboard around her neck, and it wasn't just the children she wanted to keep out.

Sepp's wife and children now live in East Germany and they are finding it very hard going.

My family live in the American Zone and there too are severe hardships. My wife earns a few extra marks as a seamstress and occasionally does some typing for a factory.

Dr Rachmanova looks at us both and with a sad expression tells us not to envy her freedom, her restrictions are equally hard, and we one day will be able to go home.

As to what her future will bring, who knows?

When she leaves, she accidentally forgets her cigarettes and hands me two small packages, after taking her to the door I return and I am afraid in case Sepp makes a comment which will destroy the peace of the hour.

But all he says is because it's Christmas he is prepared to believe in miracles. He confesses that he originally was scared of Dr R as were many others. She had the power of life and death – her decisions used to be fairly arbitrary, more an expression of her mood, than a diagnosis of the plennies health or ill health.

It would be easy for Sepp to draw the wrong conclusions out of this evening's visit by Dr R. the opposite is true, I am trying to give her back the faith in herself, make her realize that the past is the past and to be able to face her future. She has to regain her own self-worth. Sepp is surprised I have never taken on the role of an activist, but I still have effected more positive changes in the camp than he has despite all his effort.

I tell him that it was a question of saying no to the easy option rather than go for the other option of trying to listen and to understand. How could I say no is a mystery to both of us, but something gave me the strength and it was not the thought of my wife which held me back. It was more.

My version is that God meant me to help Dr R in a different more permanent and less transitory way. Sepp and I shook hands, and I wonder if he knows how much I value his friendship. I am very curious to find out the contents of the two packages.

One will be the pipe for Sepp, but the other one? It is flat and soft. I feel like a child at Christmas looking through the key hole into the Christmas room. The temptation is strong, but no, I have to wait for Christmas Eve and I put both packages in my rucksack.

10

By now it is Holy Night. We have stopped working in the laundry, we did the extra quota yesterday. Our Starski – Franz Ehrental decided to decorate the tree for us. All the laundry staff are walking about the campsite all a bit lost, but full of anticipation for the things to come.

The laundry is shrouded in mystery. The windows are covered with blankets from the inside. We meet up in our work room, a lot of grown men excited like children full of anticipation for the evening. Franz even blocked the key hole – he knows us so well.

Even Iwanow laughs at our carry-on. Outside the laundry our Christmas spirit must have touched him too. The guards are joining into our snowball fight. The canteen is open all day today and business is brisk. New supplies arrived yesterday, the working commandos gave long lists to the people remaining in camp to do their shopping for them.

The people left in the camp are either permanent invalids or plennies on temporary sick leave. When shopping for their comrades these plennies get a few extras for their efforts, a bit of bread and dripping or butter. Their financial remuneration has been severely cut as they are not able to work.

This way they get a few extra Christmas treats. Nobody will be without extra rations tonight – Christmas Eve.

Just for once everyone will not go to sleep hungry. Even Dr Schneider seems to be full of Christmas spirit, he will no doubt celebrate in the club for all the communist activists. I doubt if anyone else will want his company. Even there he is persona non grata, but I doubt he will have noticed anything amiss, he is so thick skinned.

I also run into Iwanow and Katja as well as Dr Rachmanova. All seem to be infected by the prevailing festive spirit and Iwanow's response to my greeting is almost genuine – a novelty coming from the political officer.

Vera and Katja appear to be the best of friends – wonders will never cease. Vera gives me a secret wink as she passes. Around lunchtime we see our Starski heavily laden returning from his trip to the canteen and he turns down offers of help but asks Hans to get him two boards.

We continue to offer help so he won't be worn out by nightfall, but no luck. After all offers of help have been turned down I take off to visit my Silesian countryman in the kitchen.

Even the kitchen is surrounded by an atmosphere of tension. The doctor is expected to test the food, and the first plennies arrive to queue up for their lunch; when Vera arrives, the Chef takes a spoonful out of each container and ladles it onto a metal plate, after a good stirring of the contents, otherwise it is only water with very little substance in it. A wonderful aroma of roasted meat comes from the Russian kitchen. The only professional German Chef cooks for the Russians. On today's menu are fried meatballs accompanied by fried potatoes. He presents his selection on a beautiful plate with proper cutlery on a black shiny tray for Dr R and takes it to her in the small room where she actually does her testing.

When the German Chef comes back and asks for Schmitt, I am most surprised. He takes me with him to Dr R and whilst any other plennies are receiving their usual helping of slop, I am assisting Vera, as she does not feel hungry!

It does not meet with the Chef's approval as usually he passes the leftovers onto his favourites. Dr R totally ignores him, but he has to assert his position, so he shouts at me and orders me to get my plate. Had Dr R not been present I would have thumped him, but the doctor recognizes the tension between us and calmly orders another set of cutlery, so off he goes and returns with a dirty bent set.

Vera throws the fork at him and calls him a son of a bitch and various other choice expletives. No doubt he thinks he is irreplaceable in the kitchen as he is the only trained Chef, and as he bends down to pick up the fork she kicks his sizeable behind.

I have to admit I enjoy every minute of this performance and feel I am getting my personal revenge for the many times I have been humiliated by one of my own countrymen. There is nothing quite like a German with a bit of power, real or imaginary.

He takes off at great speed and presents her with a perfect set of clean cutlery on a small china plate. Dr R dismisses him but he hesitates near one of the bubbling boilers and he once more gets another kick to finally get rid of him, very much to the quiet cheers and grins of the German kitchen staff.

After a few minutes there is a cautious knock at the door and the Chef appears with a glass of tea so that I can digest the unaccustomed rich food, No doubt he thinks I am the doctor's latest conquest, you can virtually read his thoughts. Skinny bloke, bald and wearing glasses, just a normal plennie, but why him?

I however enjoy every moment of his discomfort and suggest a cigarette would just about round off my lunch nicely, so the Chef has no option but to offer me one of his precious Metro cigarettes, and to add insult to injury I manage a mighty belch.

Once I return to the laundry word has spread about my special lunch, and the others have shared my camp lunch between them. It's not the end of the story, apparently Iwanow sacked the Chef from his job very much to the delight of all the staff. Ah well, no need for the Chef to go on a slimming diet, normal plennie work will soon reduce him to a plennie shape.

The afternoon hours pass very slowly, finally the working commandos return to camp. We receive our supper rations and at long last it is time.

The Starski calls us in and in good order we enter the laundry. A magic country just for tonight, all lit up by the Christmas tree decorated with home-made decorations and burning candles. He used the most basic materials to make intricate decorations and he hid them all in the boilers in a corner covered over with blankets. The laundry tables and the bed boards are covered by white sheets decorated with small twigs of fir here and there and burning tea lights brighten up the centre of the table.

Everyone has a piece of white and brown bread, a dollop of lard and margarine and a sausage. On the glowing stove a metal bucket is heating water for our tea. Franz really has done us proud. Before we partake of our sumptuous feast he asks me to tell the Christmas story and from memory I say the eternal and all so familiar words.

And it came to pass that an edict from the Emperor Augustus was proclaimed so that everyone should be counted...

Everyone listens quietly far away in their thoughts with their dear ones, and many a tear is shed.

After the Christmas story we sing one verse of Silent Night and wish each other all the best for Christmas. The Starski serves us all our tea which was bought together with all the other things with our carefully saved roubles. At long last we can eat our precious food.

I think of my wife and our five children who will all at this time be on their way home from Christmas service. No doubt she will think of me and worry about me. Little does she know how comfortable and pleasant our Christmas Eve is. Bit by bit it gets pleasantly warm in the room. We all take our jackets off and relax, but suddenly there is a knock at the door and Sepp the Camp Starski arrives accompanied by Iwanow, the Captain of the MWD, the interpreter Katja and Dr Rachmanova. We all stand to attention and through Katja the commander wishes us all a good festive season.

A German Christmas carol is requested and we sing one of the oldest German carols followed by *Silent Night*. I didn't realize we had such good singers in our group, we even managed to sing in harmony. The Russians are emotionally moved as I see their faces relax. I also see Dr R has left the room to hide her tears. Even Iwanow has shed his iron image a little, on his way out he quietly tells us to enjoy Christmas as soon, we will all go home.

In a loud voice he announces that tomorrow will be an extra free day. It almost seems too much to cope with. On his way out Sepp hands me a little package and when I open it I find it is a little pocket Bible - a few pages at the front are missing (no doubt used as cigarette paper) but otherwise it is complete. Rather an unusual present from an activist but very much treasured nonetheless.

In all the excitement I did not give Sepp his gift and I quickly return to my barrack and collect the package Dr R gave me. A beautiful gift of a pair of socks and a warm scarf. I hope to catch up with her later in the evening.

When I look for Sepp I find that Iwanow's parting words were not just an empty promise. There actually is a transport of 300 men planned to leave for Germany. I suggest it's just a plan to keep us all happy over the festive period but Sepp advises me not to spread the word and sadly neither he nor I are on the list.

As we walk towards the Activists' barracks it's obvious that they are celebrating with more than tea! Sepp dreads joining them, but has no option as it's his home for the duration. I hand over his present and he is thrilled to bits with the new pipe. We agree that we should keep quiet about the giver of his present, neither of us can be seen as favourites.

As I pass the Infirmary on my way back to barracks I decide to drop in to wish Konny a 'Happy Christmas'. The few remaining patients are in a cheerful mood and tell me Konny is with Dr R in her office. Dr R comes out of her office as she had heard my request for Konny and invites me in and asks me to join them for some tea. I wish both a happy festive season and thank Dr R especially...'no need to make a big fuss over a plate of food.'

No mention is made of my present of socks in Konny's presence as the walls have ears, even at Christmas.

There does not seem much to say and there is definitely something in the air. So I leave them and make my way to my barrack room. This is a clear cold night, the heavens are full of stars and everyone's thoughts will have turned towards home. We really are better off than the families at home, we only have to look after ourselves but our wives at home have to care and worry about the children and the old people. How have they been able to celebrate Christmas however modest it may have been?

We men have always thought of our wives as the weaker sex and now the women have to carry the whole responsibility of their families.

Not only have so many had to leave their homes and their friends, they now have to find a new way of living for their families. Will those others who lost very little be compassionate and helpful to their compatriots? Or, will those more fortunate block their ears and doors to the refugees' misery and needs.

It will be a time of growth for most of the women, they will discover hidden strength and abilities and before long they will manage perfectly well without us men. The same applies to the children – will they still need their fathers when they come back?

I wonder if the women have any inkling that a transport will be on its way soon. I pray that I will be on the next one. The words *'Your will be done,'* go through my mind, but it is harsh reality. What can I do to hasten my way home, the longing at times is unbearable. I want to scream 'I want to go too,' but that would not achieve anything.

I have to be an invalid as the Russians have no use for a sick man who cannot work, but what sickness could I have? All my internal bits and pieces are in reasonable order in spite of the poor food. When my thoughts wander towards having a hand or maybe a foot sacrificed towards going home, I recall a plennie who accidentally lost a finger whilst working with a circular saw. His hand became infected due to the lack of antibiotics and he had to have his hand removed. When he had fully recovered he got an extra 25 years added to his sentence for deliberate self-mutilation.

The news of the expected transport has done away with all thoughts of Christmas. Everyone wants to be on the list. There is sufficient food left over for us to have some extra rations for the 25th and we all feel for once that we have actually eaten enough. The next day passes quickly, the camp has turned into a mad house of wild and weird theories of who will go home.

Konny knows Dr R has made a note of all the genuine invalids, so that's what they were doing on Christmas Eve and both knew that I wasn't on the list and felt bad about it.

The plennies are driving each other mad with their theories. It occurs to me that some, once home, might actually miss their guaranteed 600gr of bread, two helpings of soup and one helping of gruel, just enough to survive. Compared to the uncertainty of home.

Among the laundrymen are five with a working ability of 'Three', so they stand a good chance of going home. My being an officer and working ability of 'One' makes me a definite no.

No doubt Dr R would like to put me on the list but it is just not possible. I will try to feel glad for the people who do succeed and leave this awful place. I can always hope to be on the next transport.

The third evening after Christmas the official list is published. There are 300 names, mainly the chronically sick, working Group 3, men unable to work and a few from Groups 1 and 2. A few activists are included and before long an unbearable atmosphere hangs over the camp. Why him and why not me, goes through many people's minds. Many take steps to get on the list.

Next morning a new list is printed, those poor fools do not realize that the Russians are playing their devilish games with the plennies' minds.

I for once keep my thoughts to myself and my mouth shut, even thinking aloud at present is dangerous. In the evening a third list appears. The camp spies are working overtime, trying to blacken each other's names in an effort to get their names on the next list. It never ceases to amaze me that Hitler could maintain an active kind of fighting force with such material.

However, it is totally beyond my understanding why Dr Schneider's name as well as that of the demoted Chef appear on every list. Rumour has it that neither of them will ever reach Germany in one piece.

Sepp shows his stony face these days, he never goes anywhere without his trusted cudgel as minor fights are likely to break out anywhere and his cudgel puts a quick end to them. His life is even in danger when the serious fights start. What few realize is that it is better to get a whack from Sepp than to get a Russian bullet in the head. Iwanow has threatened the use of guns should there be any revolt in the camp. Doors are guarded by two Russians instead of the usual one man. The men in the watch towers have been supplied with machine guns and they appear highly nervous and all set to let loose with a round or two.

As always there is a calculated plan in all this, to set one plennie against another. There is no unity; friendships which have lasted for ages, break. What the Russians have wanted to know about many a plennie's past comes to them without any effort. They seem to think…if I am not going home, then neither is he.

We are all working hard in the laundry, the Christmas spirit is very much a thing of the past. Five men's names are still on the list, but for how long? I feel very sorry for an old Home Guard man who is sixty. He has very bad Oedema which could easily be cured with proper medication, and give him a few more good years at home. So far his name hasn't been on any list. I try to console him with maybe tomorrow's list, but he seems to have given up.

Iwanow seems to love every minute of his performance. Orchestrated by his repeatedly changing lists. I know I shall not be on any list, so I stay clear of any arguments.

Katja and Vera look tired and exhausted. They are obviously not enjoying the political game. I meet Vera one day and try to put in a good word for the old Home Guard man. She promises to do what she can for him. When I mention the two doubtful much hated characters Schneider and the Chef, she just grins and says the last list is not up yet.

I reassure her that I know that I shall not be on the transport home.

The next day a commando unit follow an order to prepare the wagons. The plan is to add our convoy of released PoWs to a train coming from Moscow based camps, which will bring the food and supplies, with kitchen wagons.

When I meet Schneider he expresses his sorrow on missing out on further intellectual discussions with me. As the infamous Chef joins our discussion he offers to contact my family. Thanks but no thanks. I would hate my wife to be contacted by this rogue.

Anyway, in this instance I believe I know more than he does. Schneider has great plans regarding the medical care of the returning PoWs. Still I am prepared to wait and see.

When I meet Sepp he just takes one look at these two evil men and fears what will happen to the new Germany with people like them in power.

The last few days have taken their toll and Sepp is looking old. The mood continues to be highly charged – one wrong word can start another fracas. The majority lie on their bunks staring at the ceiling.

First thing in the morning Sepp arrives with the ultimate list. The lucky men have to report to the stores for their travel clothing. Anyone not on the list reports for work as usual. You could hear a pin drop it's so quiet. Sepp reads out the names and every name alters somebody's life and every name that is called is followed by a heartbreaking sigh by the named man.

All the 5 laundrymen are still going as well as the old Home Guard man. But neither Dr Schneider nor the Chef are called. Another man breaks down in tears. This last list is very much like the first. Iwanow just loves his satanic games.

I notice there are 302 names when originally there were only 300. All the new information Iwanow has received from the plennies eager to buy their trip home will now have to be sorted and added to the accused names. Now nobody trusts anyone. There are a lot of disappointed faces contrary to the happy ones who have won in life's lottery.

There is a lot of hustle and bustle near the stores. The men are called in alphabetical order to receive their clothing. The camp itself is a minefield. Everybody treads carefully to avoid any friction.

The poor old Home Guard fainted and had to be admitted to the Infirmary. He has had a severe stroke and is not expected to survive for long. Vera takes good care of him but you can almost feel the proximity of death.

All the other patients are lying on their beds fully dressed but very quiet.

About 4 o'clock everyone who is part of the transport gets called for roll call. The camp guard Major, Captain Iwanow and Katja the camp translator are there except Vera who is keeping death watch. The Major gives his usual and frequently repeated speech that the plennies should tell the truth (according to the Russians). A lot of talk about democracy and the usual gratitude Germany owes Stalin for their deliverance. It just washes over the men, they have heard it many times before.

Then everyone is lining up again in rows of five and marching towards the gate. As they march past the Infirmary Konny and Vera bring out the poor old Home Guard and everyone going past removes their caps as a sign of respect.

It looks like Dr Rachmanova arranged and timed the old man's final departure with that of the fortunate ones. Dr R walks towards the Budka (Guardroom) as she had to be present for the final formalities.

It takes ages. Everyone's name, age, birth date and home address get called. Their few pathetic belongings get searched for any written bits of paper, the Russians are a bit rattled by the old man's death.

Two Germans were not called. Why? Nobody knows, but they have to return to their barrack. It was one of those sick jokes the Russians love to play.

The two men return to the stores and hand over their travel clothes and then join the rest of those left behind. Both are weeping. Such pointless cruelty, but by now they should be used to it.

11

Then I have a wicked thought. This is the perfect time to visit Dr Schneider. I could console him and check if his removal off the list has shaken his newly acquired political convictions. I am not going to laugh at his misfortune (well, not much) but it will be an education to see how this activist reacts to the vagaries of plennie life.

I pick up his laundry to have an excuse for the visit. Konny of course is still there as well as two new patients who missed the transport by a few days, what unfortunate luck.

Schneider is as usual in his room stretched out on the examination table, his mood is at an all-time low, so I make an effort to be on my charming behaviour. I point out to him that the recent events were maybe a trial to find out how genuine this communist idealism was. He sees it quite rightly as game playing by Iwanow. As far as Dr R is concerned he thinks the two of them have joined forces against him, according to him the whole Russian caboodle can kiss his arse. In future he will refuse to practice medicine and only work as a helper.

Well, that's new. Not a bad job for a Vet's assistant or a trolley pusher as we suspect he spent his pre-camp days.

Any suggestion to use his spare time to increase his political awareness falls on stony ground. He feels he has proved his reliability in so many ways and many an unfortunate sick plennie can give witness to that. The ones that survived this arbitrary treatment that is. So very many are buried in the camp.

I put to him that a man of his firm conviction would be absolutely wasted at home and that his talents are put to much better use here in the camp.

There is a plan behind his political conversation. I would like him to abandon his medical reading and lend me his books.

The man has no idea that I am playing him like a finely tuned instrument; he says he plans to give up his medical work in favour of more political activism. As far as he was concerned patients who were politically unsound had no right to his services anyway.

Dr R gets really rough treatment (in her absence of course) by Dr Schneider but what angers him most is being put on the same level as that rogue Chef.

He is putty in my hands now and it is very tempting to send him off in some weird direction. He is aware that he is very low on the other plennies' popularity list so he does have some insight. I suggest to him that further education in the realms of politics should be his main aim in the future. No doubt the other activists will not appreciate this born again activist, but the patients will benefit from his non-intervention, and stay alive, after massaging his ego a bit more.

I once more suggest that he should lend me some of his medical books and without much fuss he lets me have some of his books.

He invites me to his living quarters which he shares with the genuine German doctor. Their living spaces are divided by blankets and I see on Schneider's side a pile of medical literature. I suppose it is an attempt to give him the intellectual look.

The walls are decorated with drawings from a book called 'The Perfect Marriage' a publication for mature adults, but in his room it's just a dirty drawing to titillate a dirty mind which also proves that he is better fed than the average plennie. With the rest of us, sexual thoughts have a very low rung in all the pervading thoughts of feeling hungry, scared and longing for home.

A bit more study would have shown him where the appendix is in the human body, but I suppose he concentrated on the reproductive system. As he hands over the books he worries whether I will have a problem with the Latin words. Silly fool. He should know that Theology students' knowledge of Latin and Greek are on a par to that of a medical student.

On my way out I see the surgeons' quarters. Spartan and clean, totally different and separate from Schneider's who has his accommodation done up like a whore's boudoir. It must be a daily trial for that good man to be in contact with that awful and often dangerous fool. Sadly, no doubt the former will put me on a par with Schneider (show me who your friends are etc) I would dearly like to speak to him but at the moment it suits my own purposes to cultivate

Schneider as I have a minute germ of an idea of how I could achieve my own repatriation.

Things go on as normal until one morning Sepp appears with a new list of names. Apparently Iwanow is putting up this list for a group of plennies to join a transport from another camp. 200 names get called, they are to be ready by 10am to be taken to the other camp. The selected men are reluctant to show any relief, they do not trust Iwanow and fear that they are just going to another camp. They are fit workers, some activists as well as the Chef.

The activists are easily recognised, they are better fed and all dressed in old Russian uniforms and they have good boots (a plennie's most wanted bit of clothing). But, the activists lose these special clothes when they have to wear the same outfits as the other men on the list. The spectators know that schadenfreude (delight at someone else's misfortune) is one of the lesser human traits, but it does cross our mind.

Especially when the activists have to hand over their wooden camp-made suitcases and their contents. The men, who for quite a while enjoyed the special privileges of an activist's life, are now reduced to the status of an ordinary plennie. No more status symbols are in evidence. All of their communist notes and booklets, and all other special belongings stay in camp. Even the Russians are enjoying this little performance – the guards grin and put in a special effort in their searches.

Now its lunchtime but the 200 have to eat their soup standing outside in the freezing cold. We have worked out that the 200 men are the people who have been denounced by their fellow plennies and are to be shipped to a stricter camp.

Nobody waves or wishes the departing men good luck. Outside the camp a heavily guarded convoy with dogs awaits them. Anyone who still has any delusions of their fate must live in cloud cuckoo land. In this way Iwanow has washed his hands of them and saves himself a lot of paperwork.

In the meantime our laundry complement has shrunk to 5 but as the camp population has 500 less plennies we manage well in spite of the pervading bad humour throughout the camp. We have managed to maintain an area of calm, we all took out our anger and disappointment on the innocent laundry. It never looked so clean.

The night boiling at the laundry has become my chosen responsibility, it gives me a chance of solitude and frequently I can take a bath. I like going back to my bunk when all is quiet. I do not want to talk to anyone I just want to drift off to sleep.

Like everyone else my main thought is of going home. I simply have to do something to be on the next genuine transport. With the reduced numbers in the camp it should not be that far off in the future.

The Russians could of course transfer prisoners from another camp, but I hope that the first will become a reality.

I only have two options. Either I am included in the transport which is doubtful as I am an officer, or I increase the odds in my favour by becoming an invalid. But how?

I hope an in depth study of Schneider's medical books will help.

Next day I try to see Iwanow but he is hard to track down and I just get to see Katja. She presumes I am here to complain about not being included in the transport home. I assure her I am trying to find out why I am still confined to the camp area. When she offers me a selection of other posts, including that of Head Chef, as I am so keen on fried potatoes, I tell her I prefer to stay where I am in the laundry.

She explains to me that my papers have still not arrived and until they do I have to remain in the camp area. I want to go home, but not just for myself. I am a married man with 5 children. The war is over and I need to do what fathers do: look after and provide for my wife and children. From what I hear life at home is not a picnic. Only very much later did I find out that life in the west was bearable.

The eastern part of Germany however has barely sufficient food to feed the Party big-shots. The average 'liberated' citizen however suffered greatly and everything was in short supply.

I know I am not able to trust anyone with my as yet unformed plan. It would just endanger their lives as well as my own. What a way to get a free ride home for someone, it would just be too much temptation. I could not even tell Vera however much her help would be invaluable. She too has much to lose.

It's a totally mad idea which I want to put into place, but as far as the Russians go I am too guilty to ever go home. My posting to the counter espionage centre in the Eastern front had been passed on to them by one of my compatriots and cost me several teeth in a very hands-on interview.

First I tried to drink liquidised tobacco. It tasted awful and I was violently sick and then fit as before, by the following day. My second attempt of mixing sugar with petrol has the same result. Hunger strike is a waste of time. The Russian way of artificial feeding is barbaric but effective. It was Konny who had unbeknown to him sown the first seed, when he told me the old Home Guard had suffered a fatal stroke. How about me having a not so fatal stroke?

I know nothing about the symptoms but this is where I will use my newly acquired reading material. Surely no one else has gone down this route before and my chance of success is better. I firmly believe the more outlandish the idea is the more likely it is to succeed. I read my medical books at night so as not to cause suspicion. I can concentrate my reading to the chapters dealing with Apoplexy.

Neither Vera or Sepp must catch me, I am always surrounded by laundry under which I would hide my book and the windows are covered by frost so no one could observe me through them. When I do see Sepp he looks beaten, tired and hopeless. He is still far too useful to be allowed home. He is heartily disillusioned by the behaviour of many of the activists. He feels the camp is heading for closure and dreads the thought of being sent to another camp, where he does not know the spies and the peculiar workings of another communist camp leader like Iwanow.

The guards differ little and it all very much depends on the officer in charge. Our Major has very little contact with us, it's all firmly in Iwanow's hands and mind. As far as I am concerned it's all a question of Nitschewo (who cares…what the hell?) and he heartily agrees.

This word covers a multitude of emotions within the Russian dialogue and communications; this word describes well the mentality and feeling of helplessness which follows the Russian daily life and frequent misfortunes.

We both leave the laundry together and I go back under the pretence of having forgotten to put more wood under the laundry cauldrons for tomorrow's washing.

Sepp goes on without me, but invites me to go in for a minute. Now I am stuck with the book which I put inside my trousers. It is well hidden by my padded jacket but I don't intend to pay a long visit to Sepp so I should be ok.

He is very concerned about Schneider's newly awakened zeal. Apparently he suggested raising the workload and the other activists had no option but to agree. However the proviso was his signature to be under the new work plan and his personal participation in an ordinary working detail. Of course he tried to get out of this and nearly ended up getting a good hiding. I think I will keep my distance from Schneider. He is really getting to be a very dangerous man to be associated with.

On closer night time study I find that only three pages are dedicated to the diagnosis of a stroke. Upon reading it again and again I decide that a stroke which would effectively cause paralysis on one side of my body would be the area to concentrate on. I find that it depends on the size of the ruptured blood vessel and its position inside the brain.

It takes a lot of thought to decide which side of my body should be paralysed, in simulation. It never occurred to me that I might not be able to go through with it. I am not the most physically able man at the best of times, so I decide I can do for the time being without my left side. If I am successful I can always have a spontaneous recovery, once on the transport on my way into West Germany.

Which means my right side of the brain has to be the origin of the stroke. I start practicing on the quiet with the left side of my mouth hanging down a bit. In fact I have to be careful so much so the Starski makes a comment one day regarding my odd shaped face. So it's strictly when I am alone I can start practicing my symptoms; sometimes I think I am planning to take on too much. How am I going to be able to control all the automatic reflexes on the left side of my body when I am being examined by a doctor? There are many other symptoms I have to produce to appear genuine – high blood pressure, flushed face, speech impediment and drooling are just some of the points. Plus a marked loss of sensitivity to stimuli like pain, heat and cold. I have time on my side so I can practice.

I find the control over my reflexes the most difficult. I wish I was an Indian mystic, they can control their bodily responses to perfection. But how to raise my facial colour? I run to work and check on my precious bit of broken mirror that it worked, the veins stand out and my heart beats much faster.

Then I try another experiment. I hold my breath as long as I can and again I notice my face getting redder and redder, but I know the heavy breathing would trip me up. Even an idiot like Dr Schneider would smell a rat, so I have to practice to breathe very slowly and evenly outwards. My feet are my biggest worry. I am very ticklish so I have to manage to reduce sensitivity. I also slowly get quite skilful at rolling my cigarettes with one hand which is an essential function to any plennie.

Dr Schneider is the most likely person to examine me, which should not be a problem. Dr Rachmanova is a different proposition. I am hoping she will mainly use her eyes and not suspect any fake symptoms. Dr Schneider still owes me several roubles for my laundry work so he will try to avoid me which suits me.

12

January 1948

It is getting towards the end of January, the days are getting longer but the biting cold persists; it is cosy at night in the laundry. I turn the lights off and watch the play of the fire. All I need is the smell of baked apples, but I don't have time for daydreams. I must persevere in my efforts to master the art of suppressing my body's instinctive reaction to external stimuli. I feel I am progressing well and feel fairly comfortable about the path I have chosen to get my hands on a free ticket home. No one else will suffer because of it should I fail.

Whilst I am planning my day of falling ill, I hear footsteps towards the laundry. Vera enters the laundry, she looks very much better since she has recovered from all the stress connected with the transport and death of the old Home Guard. We have become friends which suits us both, a fleeting relationship of a different kind would have been of no use to either of us. We address each other by the much gentler Du (instead of Sie) which comes natural to both of us when we are in each other's company.

She wants to know if I feel very sad as I wasn't included in the transport. She was horrified at the behaviour of some of the plennies, how they tried to outdo each other and betray their fellow sufferers in an attempt to get on the transport.

The first list was the correct one, the other lists were just part of Iwanow's game to see how he could set one man against his neighbour. There was a fourth list but Katja refused to co-operate. I asked her if Katja knew about my illicit Christmas lunch with her.

"Oh yes, I told her, by far the quickest way of quelling a rumour!"

Vera takes out a packet of good cigarettes and a small bottle from her pocket. After she takes the first drink I take my turn. It is lovely, sweet and strong – something similar to cherry liqueur. She gives me a cigarette and lights it for me. She gives me a very thoughtful look and tells me how much she looks forward to our occasional get-togethers. She knows I will go home one day to family and freedom. She knows my priorities but she is still glad our ships passed. I managed to give her back her self-respect, her pride in her profession, and a bit of hope for the future.

Here in Russia it's rarely possible to totally trust anyone, even married couples have learned to be careful. We know that only Sepp and Konny know of our meetings, the same guard is on duty on the nights of her visits and she is keeping him sweet with a supply of medication he could not normally obtain.

Carefully I try to find out when the next transport is scheduled as we are all aware that the camp population is now severely shrunk after the departure of the last two transports. Surely something else is on the cards. As Iwanow is in charge of such decisions she has no real news, but just knows that the camp Major has hinted at another transport. My curiosity is raised about Schneider's fate. I am astonished he hasn't been on a transport.

Sometime ago Schneider caught Iwanow in a weak moment which he can never forget or forgive, especially as it was with a plennie. Schneider made a bad enemy which will very much affect his future.

Vera suddenly leaves me and I realize she is having a hard time to keep our friendship on a continued platonic level. This is the reason to put my plan into action sooner than later.

I am glad my wife does not know of my plans, the fear and uncertainty would just about kill her. When I think of home I know that it will be different now. The Poles now live there, will they now feel like we once did? That our home was our castle where we lived safe and secure. I do not envy them the ownership of our goods and chattels. I could weep when I think of all my precious books. No use to anyone now, it's a foreign and hated language to them.

13

February 1948

As the year turns to February the sun's rays are beginning to show a bit of warmth. The plennies get together in a sheltered corner and make the most of the sun.

When I meet Katja she jokingly reminds me of my meal of fried potatoes! I also come across Konny. Apparently Schneider is nowhere to be seen; he keeps his head down, a wise move for someone rarely given to bouts of insight.

He also tells me the senior doctor is not allowed to practice medicine due to instructions from the Works Minister. He does however frequently visit the working parties and assists with advice and suggestions to anyone who needs his help. Schneider couldn't afford to do that, it wouldn't be long before he had a fatal accident while visiting the plennies. He is universally hated by all Germans and Russians alike, his only remaining safe place is in his quarters.

Schneider has visited Iwanow on several occasions first to thank him for being on the first two lists and then to query his removal off the final list.

Iwanow said very much the same as I. He needed him in the camp to keep up morale and uphold the communist ideals. He also asked for protection from his fellow plennies, according to him they hated him for his zeal and work towards the communist goal. He forgot to mention he helped to reduce their numbers through his medical skills or lack of them.

I return the medical books to Schneider when I know him to be on one of his rest periods in the Infirmary, but when I do run into him he is in a foul mood. He is surprised that I am there again in search of laundry. I assure him that I only wish to return his medical books. He cheers up no end when I tell him that it was all far above my understanding and, as he suspected I had difficulty with the Latin words. Just to push my luck I asked him what Cystoscopy means.

He jumps off his table and disappears quickly. Has to go to his meeting!

I visit Konny, we enjoy a glass of Schnapps together. This latest brew tastes just a bit like medical alcohol, but it's the only way he can make a bottle of Schnapps last a whole month!

I ask him would he be my go-between with Schneider with his laundry. This way I could avoid my chats with him and keep a little more out of his way. I know he is now desperately looking for material to get him back in Iwanow's good books. I depart quickly in order to avoid Schneider when he returns from his imaginary meeting.

Tonight is a dress rehearsal for me at the laundry. I shall have a very thorough bath, then I want to check how far I have progressed in my control over my instinctive reactions, a packet of metro cigarettes will make the night more bearable.

On my way to the laundry I pass the kitchen and exchange two cigarettes for an armful of resinous wood and some bark which makes it easier to light the fire.

The Starski has already put the laundry in the cauldrons, so I start straight away to light the fire. I chop some wood into smaller pieces to use for kindling which makes it easier to light the fire. There is plenty of wood stored for drying so I shall have enough for my bathwater as well as the laundry.

I clean out the bath as it's been used for soaking the dirty laundry and then I have time to just sit down and watch the fire, just a quick stir of the washing now and then. Otherwise all is peaceful and quiet. I am used to the smell of the bubbling laundry and for once I hope neither Vera nor Sepp will choose this night to visit.

In my mind I reconstruct the three pages from Schneider's medical book. I hope my body will be as obedient as my spirit when I am admitted to the Infirmary. I am convinced I can maintain the deception for two or four weeks or until I have bought my freedom.

After separating the laundry for tomorrow I clean out the cauldrons and add clean water for my bath. I pull the tables normally used for ironing close to the stove and cut a piece of wood down to a fine point. I shall have use for it later. The bath is as usual a physical pleasure, it's great to have a really good scrub whilst I am on my own. The time spent in the laundry has served me well. I am a much healthier looking skeleton now, no extra weight but no starvation figure either.

One of the pre-warmed sheets serves as a towel. I just have to explain to the Starski tomorrow what I used it for and why it needed re-washing and ironing. After that I have thoroughly scrubbed the outer man I lie on the prepared table and try to totally relax. It takes me a whole cigarette to achieve this aim. I feel totally calm, I pull up my knees to get my stomach muscles to relax as if a set of small waves wash over my abdomen which is the correct result – according to Dr Schneider's books.

After that I check on my left arm and leg and they respond correctly. The most difficult bit is my left foot, but there too the reaction is minimal. I have to make sure there is a marked difference between the reactions of my right and left side of my body.

Both Dr Schneider and Dr Rachmanova have to have convincing evidence to enter into my notes. So far so good, but back to my nightly chores. I get dressed in clean clothes and put everything back to its normal place, the light is back on, I have unlocked the doors and I am ready for the last part of my rehearsal.

My breathing exercises. I hold my breath for as long as possible. I can feel my veins sticking out of my head, my lips turn blue and I am close to suffocating when I gradually release my breath. It has to be done very gradually so no one would notice an increase in the rate of respiration.

I am now ready to face the public. Any time will do now, there is nothing more I can do. When I check in my piece of mirror, I see that a red line has formed across my chest.

I do not feel too comfortable with the fact that I will have to deceive my few real friends and the other plennies. The latter group I owe nothing to. I have seen how they behave during Iwanow's lists, one against the other.

Weighing against my guilty conscience is evidence of not involving anyone else. How often have I seen that? One plennie's rash and thoughtless attempt to make a break-out has made the rest of the plennies already unbearable lot even worse.

Rations were reduced, workloads increased and what little free time there was would be even more limited. An evil practice on recapture was to make the escapee run through a gauntlet of his fellow plennies who would have to beat him with whatever was to hand. That was, after the guards had finished with him.

They too had to pay dearly for allowing him to escape on their watch. Many a recaptured man had to spend many weeks in the hospital, some never recovered.

It was totally inhuman to do that, but only a man who is really starving and at the end of his tether can know what a wild anger and fury builds up against the cause of his increased deprivation.

I do not intend to put the burden of knowledge of my personal plan on anyone's shoulders, if anyone is to suffer it has to be just me. That is if my plan fails.

As I leave the laundry I meet up with Sepp. He asks me to follow him to his quarters. Here he informs me that everyone is going home. The camp will be closed down and Russian workers will take over the production line. A group of Russian foremen will arrive soon to familiarise themselves with the inner working of the various works. He has this information from the Major not Captain Iwanow, so it does sound possible.

March 1948

Today is Sunday 7th March 1948. I had planned my day of action for the 15th. I shall continue with my plans as it will guarantee me a place on the transport and they can always attribute my stroke to the sudden onrush of excitement of going home.

No news of the forthcoming closure is heard. Monday 15th arrives and I plan to proceed according to schedule. I have had a hard time in the last few days concentrating on the routine of daily ironing and work. I have to make a real effort to be my normal self. I even started to sing at work, the Starski reckons its spring fever.

I can barely sleep the night before that fateful day, I know I shall remember it for the rest of my life.

I go through it in fine detail and consider the morality in deceiving my friends, but here I am a plennie, a person without any rights totally subject to the Russians' goodwill or lack of it.

This war has been over for three years, according to the law I should be home by now.

I know I want to go home and be with my family but I also want to live a little. I cannot spend the rest of my life contemplating the rights and wrongs of two World Wars and paying penance for the German nation's part in them.

That evening I found out that it is the German Staff Surgeon's turn to be on call the next day, so I am quite relieved to see him leave the camp with the work force.

I force myself to act normal. I cannot eat, it seems impossible to swallow my soup.

Now the moment is here.

I bend over to tie my shoelaces and deliberately fall against the table leg. The laundryman working at the table shouts and swears at me to get up, but the Starski notices the commotion.

He comes over to get others to help him to pull me out from under the table. He opens my shirt and feels my heartbeat, it's thundering rapidly, but he can detect no breathing.

He gets four men to carry me over to the first aid post. Konny happens to meet my group and tells them to take me straight to the Infirmary and he will call Dr Rachmanova. I have my eyes shut through all of this.

Vera will be here in a few minutes she must not suspect a thing.

"Quick, get a move on his lips are turning blue," shouts the Starski.

Once we are in the Infirmary I can hear Dr Schneider yelling.

"What piece of shit have you brought today?"

The Starski tells him that this particular piece of shit is Max Schmitt and if he does not pull out all the stops he will be for the high jump.

I did not think our usually quiet Starski could shout so loud and be so emphatic.

The other laundrymen also maintain a threatening stance against Schneider. He quickly changes his tune and complains that the bearers have lost their sense of humour.

They gently place me on the examination table and remove my clothing. I would never have credited these hard men with so much gentle handling. Schneider politely asks the men what happened and the Starski briefly explains my collapse under the table.

I slowly open my eyes to avoid Schneider opening them for me and he asked what happened, but I just look straight through him and stare into the distance.

I resume near normal breathing and allow the left corner of my mouth to droop. My heart still beats very fast. After trailing up and down my arm Schneider finally detects my still racing pulse. He is about to administer some drug by injection when Dr Rachmanova arrives.

My laundry bearers leave the room sure in the knowledge that I will be in safe hands; with a look of horror she sees the injection in Schneider's hand and takes it off him and yells at him in language that would make a sailor blush. Schneider gets the message and leaves the room. She then proceeds to listen to my heart as I control my breathing again and stop for a few seconds, then restart breathing.

My arms get checked over next, first my right arm which is fine then my left one which just flops back on the bed. The hands react the same way, she asks Konny to hand her a sharp pointed object and as expected checks my abdomen. First it's fine on the right side but on the left side only a faint reaction is present.

To my distress I see tears running down Vera's cheek. It is difficult for me to remain an impartial observer – from the inside looking out, as if it all concerns someone else.

She once more becomes the consummate doctor she is and continues with her examination. She checks my eyes, as hoped the result is as expected. The right is fine, the left reacts very little to the torchlight.

Once more I shut my eyes so I don't have to see her distress. The red mark on my chest seems to be another point of worry. She asks me several questions but I opt not to answer, just pretend to move my lips as if I were trying to answer.

Konny arrives with the Starski and they cover me with blankets and move me very gently on to a trolley before transferring me to the camp hospital.

It must be years since I lay in a proper bed covered in clean crisp white linen sheets – which I had probably washed!

Konny brings an icebag and places it on my head according to instructions from Vera Rachmanova. It's very hard not to shiver but then I hear the doctor whispering to Konny that I have had a stroke.

I have succeeded so far, now I can make the most of my beautiful bed. I turn to my left side in an attempt to further deaden my arm and leg.

Vera gently touches my face and tells me not to worry, she will put me right. For the time being I need lots of rest, so she will give me an injection to effect that. Gradually I feel myself drifting off into a feeling of pleasant weightlessness.

Konny tries to turn me back but Vera tells him to leave me in my chosen position, the objects in the room become fuzzy and with a big sigh I feel myself fall asleep.

I sleep soundly and when I finally wake up it is evening as the light is on. I feel as if my head aches just above my eyes, possibly the effect of the icebag.

I find myself in the same position on my left side and have to force myself to open my eyes as things begin to steady and I feel less woozy and I can recognise Vera, Iwanow and a tall slim Army Captain. All three are watching my attempts at trying to re-orientate myself, but I know the side effects of my sleeping drug can only positively confirm my stroke symptoms. The Captain is also a medical man.

Vera turns over the covers and Konny helps her to remove my hospital gown. I realize I have genuinely lost all strength and feeling on my left side. While the Captain talks to Vera I stop breathing as I had previously practiced to raise my blood pressure. When the two doctors came back to the bed the Captain notices the reddening around my neck and he carefully listens to my chest with his stethoscope; my respiratory rate has returned to normal and he measures my blood pressure with the result 170/90. He is not happy with that and he then proceeds to undertake a very thorough neurological examination.

I am secretly grateful for my weeks' of preparation, even my feet react correctly.

I suddenly have a dreadful thought I might have done too well – am I now too ill to go on the transport?

The Captain suggests treatment, Vera points out the cyanosis around my lips which contradicts the use of that particular drug. Iwanow who has been watching with interest throughout the examination seems to have got bored. He quietly whispers to me that he hopes I will get better soon and to return home.

I hear Vera and the Captain discussing my illness again and again I hear the word stroke. I had not counted on an examination by a neurologist, but it seemed to have gone all right. The visiting specialist comes to my bed before departing with Vera and assures me that everything possible will be done to clear up my condition.

I am glad for Vera's sake that she managed to get a second opinion should things go belly-up, her back will be covered. The confirmed diagnosis will be a ticket home for me and no problems for her.

Vera returns and sits next to me and strokes my right hand and I can feel hot tears on my hand. I have to shut my eyes tightly, I can't bear to see her cry but as the professional that she is she soon regains control. Unfortunately there is very little one can do in the treatment of strokes.

I am to be moved into a separate room to ensure perfect peace and quiet. No visitors are allowed for the time being and I should keep as still as possible and be safe in the knowledge that she is taking care of me.

Konny with the help of the Starski and two laundry workers will carry me into my new room. I hardly feel them moving me they are so careful. They quietly depart wishing me all the best. Sepp turns up the light, he strokes my head gently with his heavy hand and he too wishes me a quick recovery. The sympathy of my friends is a blessing as well as a feeling of guilt, to deceive them is the worst part of my so far successful plan to get home.

Not being able to speak has aided the confirmation of Vera's diagnosis. She returns after her visit to other patients. Konny once more applies the icebag to my head, I suppose I just have to get used to it. When Vera returns she tells me that the visiting neurologist signed a form that I, in spite of being ill, was fit enough to go on the next transport.

It's really hard not to grab her hand and thank her. Konny sits with me when Vera isn't there but does not say a word following her instructions. Later I get another injection and as before I drift off into a dreamless sleep.

When I come to in the morning I notice that Konny removes the foldaway bed where Vera had spent the night keeping watch over me. I also note rather to my shame that I have been incontinent during the night. Embarrassing as it is, it's another plus point in my diagnosis as I have not eaten. Control over my bowels is not a problem as yet. Vera notices my accident but assures me it will pass.

Konny with the very helpful Starski changes my bed and night clothes with the ever faithful Starski giving me a wash and once again I am safely tucked up in bed and he opens the window to get some fresh air in the sick room.

Konny quite rightly presumes I can hear him and he passes on the increasing rumours re another transport home, but as yet nothing definite.

Konny is a bit concerned about my lack of intake. I haven't had anything to eat or drink for 24 hours. He waves a piece of bread in front of my eyes, but I show no interest. Vera enters at that moment and decides not to worry me with food and promises me a special breakfast later.

Konny has to tell her about my lack of bladder control but she confirms that it is part of the stroke symptoms. I feel embarrassed at having to put my friends in a position where they had to see to these very basic needs, but it is unavoidable. I once more get another injection with the awful icebag back on my head and I am soon off to sleep again.

I vaguely realize that Konny is dishing out the morning soup and a piece of bread. The issue of the bread is allocated strictly by rotation as it is elsewhere. It is the only substantial bit of food there is to use one's teeth on.

When I wake it feels as if I am on the outside looking in. I know it's the heavy tranquillizers that submerge me in such deep sleep but added to that is the nervous exhaustion due to all the effort in the previous weeks.

I watch myself gradually rising to the surface of this drug induced hypnotic trance. I need all my strength to just open my eyes, it's still a grey fog only broken by the rays of light from the lamps.

Vera sits next to my bed reading *War and Peace*. As soon as she realizes that I am awake she puts down her book. She tells me what a good patient I am and that I will sleep myself to good health. She tells Konny to sort out my bed and make me more comfortable. I cannot talk to her so I shut my eyes and daydream of home. Everything is vague, I know my children are all four years older since I last saw them during my last Army leave.

Time passes and in the early hours of my third day in hospital I suddenly wake, something is crystal clear. I see Konny sleeping on the fold-up bed, as soon as he hears the slight sound of my right hand moving he tells me that Vera has slept over in the Admin block and is on call should I need her.

I manage to convey to him that I am fine, my bladder has let me down again in spite of not drinking anything. Suddenly I feel a raging thirst and Konny reads my mind and feeds me a few sips of water.

When he has left I once more check my left side and find that all sensation has gone. I once more fall asleep and when I awake I see a very excited Vera standing next to my bed.

"Good morning Max. You are going home! There is a transport in seven days but you must try to stay as calm as possible."

I close my eyes tightly to hide my inner turmoil. She must guess the wild emotions racing through my body and soul. Apparently everyone has had the good news the night before, but Vera decided I needed my undisturbed sleep. Vera decided I need to start taking in some nourishment to get my strength back for the long journey home.

She takes four eggs out of her handbag and a small packet of sugar. Some milk gets warmed up and mixed with the lightly beaten eggs and sugar. First she feeds me by spoon, then she uses the feeding cup.

I have decided now is the time when I gradually regain my speech. To my surprise I find it quite difficult and it's not put on. My stuttering is quite genuine. Non-use of my vocal chords have made them rough and tender.

Once Vera had made her morning rounds it's my turn. I once more find myself stripped in the gentlest possible way. Everything gets a real going over. I find that I have really lost almost all sensation on my left side, even my left foot is almost without feeling.

I no longer get the injections but as my general circulation has improved I receive phenobarbitone morning, noon and night. The awful icebag still gets used.

Sepp Pszybilla and Franz Ehrental visit in the evening and bring my rucksack - all my few worldly goods are carefully packed and stored in it.

Like many other plennies I had always said, if we had to, we would go home in the nude just to leave Russia. Now it seems to be a reality. I am surprised how attached I am to all my bits and pieces; I am most attached to my halfway decent pair of shoes. We all make an attempt to look as respectable as possible. Who knows what life will be like at home? I intend not to give up anything without a fight.

What will await us at home? I remember many of my earlier conversations with other plennies. Some think they will just return to 1939, especially the ones who hoped for the 1000 year Reich. They think the years between 33 and 45 will just disappear like a bad memory. Many a man admitted that he really had not changed at all, which in itself is the key to the German problem.

Konny arrives with the phenobarbitone. Its effects are not as dramatic as the injections but it still guarantees me a good night's sleep. I have got used to the urine bottle between my thighs, it saves me the morning embarrassment of a wet bed.

When Vera turns up in the morning to give me my breakfast of raw eggs and milk she tells me how pleased she is with my progress. She knows that I will have access to all the specialised equipment for treating and diagnosis of strokes, not yet available in Russia.

Just another three days in camp and three days travel until the transport arrives on German soil; and no doubt up to five days debriefing and lectures on the evil of western capitalism in East Germany. That's where I intend to stage my recovery scene.

It will not be that easy to separate myself from my illness, it will probably be a lot harder to get well than it was to have a stroke. The moral load weighs heavy on my shoulders, it is not an easy thing to betray and deceive real friends. I am in a vicious circle and I am damned if I do and damned if I don't. The only comfort I get is knowing that I have not hurt anyone else by my actions. Would my friends' ignorance really stand up to a typical Russian court of law?

"Konspiratia" will be the doctor's offence and Konny and Sepp as well as the Starski would disappear in the endless maze of the Russian prison system.

No one would believe me was I to tell them I had no help. It would cause an avalanche of terror to a lot of innocent people. I am however unable to do a single thing to stop it. I must be consistent to protect them all and last but not least, myself.

Vera wants to find out if my bowels are beginning to function normally again after six days of inactivity, and as if her question has started a reaction I make urgent signs to Konny who produces a bedpan.

My inhibitions to use the bedpan in spite of my best efforts with an audience came to nothing. To my horror Vera orders Konny to bring an enema. I must have looked absolutely stunned.

"You are my patient now, too much exertion could cause another stroke," Vera says and after the procedure is over I feel greatly relieved all round. The open window airs the room quickly

As I am now talking a little I can converse with Konny, he wants to know what to do with my accumulated rations of bread and cigarettes. I suggest he should share the bread out amongst the other patients and divide the cigarettes out to the Starski, himself and me.

I wanted a cigarette right now, he is very reluctant but gives in and I enjoy my first one, but after a few puffs I have had enough.

It was about time I found out what had happened to Schneider since the incident with the injection he was about to give me when Dr R entered the room.

He had been forbidden to enter the Infirmary. Dr R had in fact thrown the ampoule in the bin, but later retrieved it to use it when necessary against Schneider. Things could not get any worse for him.

The lists are ready for the transport. Every name is on it. The Infirmary has their own list with the Staff Surgeon in charge of the care of all patients.

Schneider has invented a new job, he is writing new guidelines in the communist style to be stuck to each wagon. Even the Russians are sick of him – his services are no longer required.

Another funny thing happened, the store manager turned up in Schneider's quarters and removed an extra blanket he had. One blanket for each plennie that's it. The phenobarbitone continues to give regular periods of sleep. When I awake from my afternoon nap Vera is busy writing my case notes, the little notebook getting bigger by the day.

Having nearly regained control of my speech I look forward to a long talk with her tonight. Suddenly Konny calls out.

"Attention!" Iwanow stands in the door, he wishes me good health and a continued recovery. Then he turns to Vera – my Russian is not good enough to be privy to their conversation. I am surprised at this visit. Plennies usually do not rate a get-well visit from the politico.

Vera tells me that so often matters in Russia turn out to be totally unexpected; the Captain has apparently requested that special food should be supplied so that I would survive the transport.

Vera looks sad, she knows one more day and another evening and I should be on my way home towards family and freedom. Soon I will have forgotten all about Russia, the bad as well as the good moments.

Her situation is so different from that of ours, she will never be really free. She too has made plans - in a few months she will leave the camp, she has offered her services to a new Komsomol on the River Jenissai where a new town is being created. In Russia when you say "goodbye" it's forever. I can feel what an inner battle is taking place within her soul, she is making an all-out effort to make the parting easy for both of us. Any careless word could ruin what we had. We are like two people on a railway station waiting for the train to depart.

She leaves quickly, only to return later to give me my sleeping tablet. She leaves a message with Konny that he can reach her anytime in the Admin building.

The next morning 300 plennies leave the camp, they are going to prepare the wagons for the long journey. Stoves in each wagon, a kitchen in one and another wagon is being adapted for the patients and medical supplies. Wood and coal are being allocated to each wagon. The usual German love of order and organisation is running at full swing. A wagon foreman is chosen and everyone is allocated to a particular wagon.

Schneider wanted to carry on with his slogan writing but his equipment is confiscated and he had to return to the camp. He has not learned to let sleeping dogs lie, raging mad he went to see Katja who told him to just be patient. Things would be made clear to him soon.

In the camp each wagon is called by number for the men to be kitted out in new clothes. I for my part make a real effort to finish my soup and gruel. Vera arrives with a surprise. A jar of stewed apples. It's very refreshing and I eat quite a bit of it, keeping some for Konny.

I am amazed at myself, how well I manage just using the right side of my body.

Konny went to the store to get all the supplies and equipment for the Infirmary inmates. Everybody is busy trying on their new gear. I am not allowed to exert myself so Konny and Vera choose for me.

For a change I get a fur hat, but also my icebag is back in place before long. All my attempts to try on my new gear apart from the hat are thwarted by Vera.

"Wait till tomorrow," is her advice.

Schneider has at long last met his fate, He has been sent to prison. We hope he will not try his activist activity in prison – not a good idea.

Sepp pays a visit. He is planning to travel in the Infirmary wagon, it's amazing how nebulous everything already seems, the only reality is the next day and home.

I do know how very fortunate I am. Schneider's fate could have been mine.

I think about all the people involved in my scam and would they forgive me should it all come to light?

It's a pity we have to go via East Germany, but it cannot be helped.

"Nitschewo," as the locals say.

The sleeping tablet is as usual very effective. I wake up early and refreshed. Konny told me Vera visited twice during the night, as she too is an early riser she comes and checks my vital responses. She removes the icebag. If I remain nice and peaceful she says the danger of another haemorrhage is virtually non-existent.

"Your good doctors in Germany will soon have you fit and well."

The other patients are all wearing their travel gear, if they didn't all look so ill, one just couldn't believe how excited they all are. Konny decides to give me an enema so I don't have any problems with my bowels during the journey.

We were just about to get me kitted up when there is an urgent call for Dr R she tells us to keep things on hold until she returns.

In a very short time she is back. She is chalk white, her body movements are robotic and she virtually collapses into the chair next to my bed. Tears are streaming down her face.

"These criminals, these inhumane criminals!"

A decision has been made high up to transfer me to a plennie hospital. When she argued with Iwanow that the shock might kill me he just blandly told her that we all have to die. Whether I die in Russia or elsewhere, what's the difference?

She was forced to sign a chit that I was unfit to travel. The real reason however is on my recently arrived papers carrying a 'Not To Be Released' stamp in red.

Iwanow did tell her that he was quite ready to let me go without papers, but as these had arrived an hour earlier his hands were tied.

The only thing Dr R can still do for me is accompany me to the plennie hospital. Apparently everyone is upset. Katja is crying, Iwanow in spite of his usual communist bravado shows a softer side, but all in vain.

I am to be collected by an ambulance in one hour, a special privilege granted by Iwanow. Konny is crying, but being my usual realistic self I have to quickly consider new plans. No paper is allowed to travel with the plennies so I ask Konny to memorise my German address.

The message to my wife is that my state of health is the same as it was in August 1939. I tell him I had a similar incident then, in reality I couldn't have been healthier.

He promises to do his very best and I put special emphasis on the last part of the message as it will counteract all negative news about my present state of health.

In August 1939 my wife and I had been on holiday near Sagan where I was stationed as a newly recruited soldier. Three days were all we had but they had been magic days. I ask him to write to my wife and forget all about my present sickness just concentrate on the fact that I am receiving good care. I trust Konny implicitly and know he will do the right thing. He proves his honesty by bringing my rucksack. He thought I would prefer my treasured possession – my shoes, to the wooden clogs the other plennies are wearing.

The storeman arrives to collect my going home outfit. Dressed once again in my old plennie clothes I lie on my bed. It's amazing what a man can stand. The disappointment is only now becoming a reality, but my motto is 'Nitschewo' so I will just have to bear it and cope with whatever fate decides to throw at me.

I must continue in my present state, a sudden recovery would possibly mean that my house of cards will collapse. At worst I might join the good Dr Schneider in his present abode.

Vera did me a good service by informing me about the red stamp on my file. Nobody is going to put a hopelessly ill plennie on trial, so hopelessly sick I have to stay.

My symptoms have become so real that I no longer have any control over my left arm or leg.

Vera appears in full uniform which will give her a bit of status when we arrive at the new camp. She too has become all common sense and any emotion is well hidden.

Both Sepp and the Starski come to wish me well and to say goodbye. The Starski returns with Konny and they place me on a stretcher, all supervised by a very tall Russian Sergeant who carries his machine-pistol Russian fashion, across his back.

Vera gives me another sleeping tablet to ease the problems of the journey. Our ambulance is surrounded by a group of plennies.

"Don't let the bastards get you down, keep your spirits up," and many more shouts of advice follow me and Vera into the ambulance.

The Sergeant sits up front with the driver after making sure that all is well in the ambulance.

I am slowly drifting into a deep valley of sleep and sorrow. I have no idea how long the journey took, but gradually surface to the sound of the wheels crunching through the snow and slowing down.

The searchlights shine into the ambulance.

We have arrived.

PART THREE

1

**A Camp Hospital
1948**

We enter the new camp. What will it bring, how long will I be here? German words reach me: 'Na mate what's up with you then?' Vera Rachmanova watches as the two men carefully carry me down some steps. This new Infirmary is built into the ground rather like a deep cellar to protect the inmates from the cold.

The room consists of a row of two-tier bunks filled with sick plennies; all eyes follow my arrival. I feel fairly lethargic but still take careful note of my new surroundings. The doctor hands over my fairly extensive case notes to the German. He asks my bearers to deposit me in a single bunk at the end of the double bunks.

One of my orderlies takes my clothes off and is about to give me a good wash when he is stopped by Vera. I am once more dressed after just a lick and a promise, into clean hospital clothes. A young Russian nurse enters the ward, and the way she and Vera greet each other makes me think they have met before. Before I realize it Vera has gone, she just turns at the door and gives me a wave. One of the orderlies shakes his head.

"Shame she is not stopping with us."

I have just enough strength to roll over on my left side and as far as I am concerned the rest of the world can kiss my arse!

I quickly fall asleep until I wake quite early in the morning. The tall German orderly sleeps on the bunk closest to me, the room is filled with the noise of sleeping men. Everyone is in their own valley of dreams, good or bad.

When it gets a bit lighter the German Starski arrives and wakes everyone. The walking sick see to themselves, the others are washed by the orderly and I am last in the queue. By his accent I can tell he is a Berliner, he introduces himself as Paule from the river Spree, his mother was Miss Schmidt.

He proceeds to give me a good wash down, he seems to be a decent chap with a good sense of humour except his non-stop chattering may get a bit too much at times. Before he gets a chance to relax and cheer me up with more of his stories, the Starski mobilizes him to get everything spick and span before Maria the Russian nurse comes on duty. The Starski's name is Gustav who also offers his assistance. Gustav is wearing a beautiful pair of officers' boots, maybe he is the activist.

Two heated trolleys arrive and together with a piece of bread all patients receive their morning soup. Paule (or Paul in high German) arrives full of his usual chatter and proceeds to feed me my breakfast, he is very deft and gentle in his movements. He puts me in mind of a St Bernard dog with his big body, gentle face and big brown eyes. He tells me the Starski had tried to impress Vera but had got very short shrift. The Starski arrives with my allowance of sugar and cigarettes and he suddenly addresses me with the more formal 'Sie' after the nurse pointed out to him I was an officer.

Paul too apologizes in his usual humorous way and he tells me that his one wish had been to be a batman to an officer, and eureka, the prison camp had fulfilled his dream. His other wish was to have his own bed and in Russia that too became a reality.

This man is the salt of the earth, a true Berliner, very rough round the edges but with a heart of gold. I tell him I am perfectly happy with the informal 'Du' as we more or less share the same surname, anything else would have been silly. Paul tells me he had a vast number of fathers to choose from, so he decided to stick to his mother's very Arian name; disappearing up a chimney was not a way he wanted to end his life.

Suddenly someone shouts "Attention!" and a little round person wearing a fur hat, quilted jacket and trousers with boots rolls through the room. She goes into the clinical room, but not before Paul advises me not to judge a book by its cover.'

A few minutes later a slender little person with a delicate face and beautiful eyes with an abundance of blonde curls not very successfully hidden under her nurses' cap, comes back into the room. She tells me Vera has commended me into her care. The doctor will visit later but for the time being I will have my usual tranquilizer to keep me calm. To my logical mind it seems a bit odd to give me medication before the doctor's visit, but never mind. Nitschewo.

But now the Russian lady doctor arrives, I use the term loosely as she looks more like a cleaner with her scruffy white coat, a dew-drop is hanging from her nose, her hair is uncombed and her eyes are little black slits in a very Asiatic face. She smells of tobacco and unwashed body. It's instant dislike on both sides.

"How are you?" the doctor shouts at me.

I reply in very broken Russian that I don't understand much Russian. The nurse is called to translate, it's a bit like day and night between the two women. Maria the head nurse gives a fairly sharp but accurate report of Vera's diagnosis so far, and the treatment.

The doctor suddenly becomes very professional and checks out every sign and symptom presented by Maria. I get the full benefit of a close up of her face, a slight beard, a big hairy wart all accompanied by a whiff of garlic. Poor woman she really was at the back of the queue when good looks were handed out. Maria gives me a quick wink, so Vera's recommendations have had some effect.

The doctor makes some attempt at a neurological examination but just drops my left arm with a wallop on the metal side of the bunk. Maria shouts at her and before you know it the two women are up to their necks in a verbal catfight. Russians really have developed swearing and maligning into an art form. The rest of the ward is obviously quite used to it and everyone listens. It's part of the daily entertainment.

The doctor is generally referred to as Dr 'Kakdjiela' (How are you?) as that seems to be the only thing she says to the patients.

Paul gives me three boxes so I can store my supplies, a board above my bed will keep my boxes as well as my drinking mug. He explains the relationship between the two women. The older doctor envies the nurse Maria not only her youth but also her very useful relationship with the political officer. He does say he feels sorry for the 'old girl' from time to time but she just can't win the very uneven battle.

When Paul talks I notice from time to time bits of a Breslau dialect mixed up with his Berliner twang, that's probably where his mother came from before she discovered sex and the men of Berlin.

Phenobarbitone has been my medication for so long that I think I can overcome some of its effect by sheer willpower. The effort makes me grey and withdrawn which can only be good. Another doctor arrives, he is Dr Metzener. He proposes to do a thorough neurological examination. When asked about my ability to speak I informed him that I had lost the power of speech totally at the beginning, but that appeared to be improving. He comments on the quality and thoroughness of my case history. With Maria's help he removes my clothes and as he is about to take my blood pressure he realizes that a part of the apparatus is missing. He apologises and I use his absence to hold my breath until I nearly suffocate, but it achieves the desired effect when Dr Metzener returns he finds me grey and exhausted with very raised blood pressure.

Nurse Maria writes down his findings and comments, the only positive thing is my general appearance and the state of my physical health. Apart from the obvious signs, my time in the laundry has improved my previously almost skeletel appearance, as we were never exposed to the horrendous winter temperatures.

The doctor talks Russian to Maria, to me he just says my blood pressure is still too high. My eyes are next and the result doesn't seem to please him either. God bless phenobarbitone! Then he checks out my reactions. Maria has to put the brakes on for she can't keep up with his speed of dictation. Once he has completed his examination he asks me where I come from in Germany. I tell him that my family lived in the Waldenburg area, but that we lived in the Silesian Riesengebirge, the Tatra mountains. I notice that Maria raises her eyebrows at the mention of Riesengebirge, and it appears to be familiar to her.

When the doctor has had all his findings documented I know that they bear out Vera's diagnosis. When I try to push him for the diagnosis he states that it looks like a stroke, but I am too young so he will do more tests. As from tomorrow I will have to manage on a salt free diet – horror of horrors and a specialist for internal medicine will be asked to give his opinion.

Paul is allocated as my personal carer, he is, as the doctor puts it, totally reliable. I realize that the reliability of Paul also refers to his political views. As we speak another elegant man enters the room and introduces himself as Dr Kilian. He intends to check my innards in case anything is in need of repair. He orders a blood and urine test first thing in the morning, he gets me to breathe in. He doesn't realize he is talking to an expert here.

I get a second blanket for my bed as I feel the cold more than the others due to the lack of movement.

As both doctors were leaving I just managed to stay awake to be dressed again by Paul and Maria.

I give in to my medication and once more fall into a deep sleep. When I wake up Paul is with me and I offer him one of my cigarettes. I know I shall have to rely on him in so many ways, and he does not have to do much else as he is my special carer. He just asks me not to sleep too much as he likes to chat and wants a bit more than just carrying and fetching my bedpan.

Apparently he has been shot through the lung during a battle, and a 'conquering hero' had whacked him over the head with a spade to make sure he was dead, without success. But he did suffer infrequent attacks of shaking, shouting and general mental disturbances, possibly some brain damage.

Paul soon brings me my boring salt free lunch of potato soup and soya-gruel. I lie on my left side, I can manage to feed myself quite well, but Paul is horrified he has just got himself a cushy job, and here am I trying to do him out of it. He tells me to behave myself or else. I give up after a few spoonfuls. I hadn't counted on Paul's persistence. He is taking his job seriously, I get him to taste my food and he agrees as to the taste and he offers me some salt. Just then nurse Maria walks past and threatens me with a feeding tube if I don't stick to my diet; so Paul to the rescue. He tips my food into a bowl and eats the lot. For his height he should get extra rations, he is always hungry. After lunch I sleep for a few hours.

Gustav the Starski and activist gives me a numbered store tag for my personal belongings. Once I leave the hospital everything will be there for me. As I plan to stay here for a while I want to get on

Gustav's good side and I offer him a few cigarettes which he accepts; he promises me that once ambulant I can join him in the clinical room as smoking is not allowed on the ward.

Only now am I properly settled in and fully awake. I get a chance to survey my surroundings. On the other side is a bloated looking man who is also on a salt free diet, no soup poor man, only gruel and he is constantly thirsty. The patient on my left says very little, he just seems to be there with his eyes taking in everything that's going on.

I am beginning to feel reasonably secure. Dr Metzener's findings more or less confirm Dr R's. It is also quite likely that he wouldn't question the diagnosis of a Russian doctor. As far as Dr Kilian is concerned I have no worries. He is only interested in the state of my internal organs and those seem to be fine.

It is highly unlikely that they have any advanced medical technology in this hospital, so it looks as if I am safe for the time being anyway. But, I am still full of hope to reach my ultimate goal through this unorthodox method. I still cannot quite fathom the meaning of the dreaded red stamp (not to be released) on my papers. Is it because I was an officer and only other ranks are to be released? But there may be a totally different reason. I am amazed how quickly I have recovered from my disappointment of not being repatriated.

'Nitschewo' Tomorrow is another day.

My present situation has to remain static for a while, I can't afford a sudden recovery. I must sleep on my left hand side to maintain the existing paralysis. One attempt to lift my left leg got me nowhere, my arm is the same. I can't lift a single finger. To carry on with my daily existence I have to develop a fairly thick skin. I do worry at times if I can carry it through. Time is in plenty of supply – this is Russia. The worst part of the plan is not being able to talk to anyone about it. I can't trust anyone as I would put their lives in danger. There seem to be a lot of German specialists here, they have all had a prod and poke around.

Dr Kakdjiela does her usual morning round, but that's all we see of her. She could make the healthiest man ill! Nurse Maria obviously is in charge here, she is efficient, obsessed with cleanliness, but otherwise a good and popular human being.

She keeps the Starski Gustav and one of the other orderlies permanently on the go with dusters in one hand and a broom in the other, the patients too keep as tidy as possible. All to maintain the atmosphere of cleanliness. She does not seem to have any favourites among the patients. Gustav tries very hard to get into her good books. Through other activists he has contact to many of the workshops and can have items produced which are not available on the open Russian market.

Maria accepts the gifts as if she is bestowing an honour on him by accepting them, but he will never reach his ultimate goal. Maria is just too far out of reach for him. She still shouts at him if she discovers any dust or suchlike anywhere. If it wasn't for smelly Dr Kakdjiela this would be an almost perfect life measured by plennie standards. When Maria does night shifts we all look forward to her singing. She doesn't have an outstanding voice but her slightly rough voice gives her songs from the homeland an unusual poignancy. Her face reflects her inner feelings of homesickness and despair to pleasure, love and joy. She sings a special song of the wives and mothers of fishermen waiting at the shore for their returning men.

What I wonder is her own private story, another of the many souls lost in the endless country that is Russia. But she is so young compared to us old timers. Russia is the land where orient meets occident within its people of many hues and origins.

Paul too is deeply touched by Maria's singing, his intentions are totally honourable – he dreams of leading Maria down the aisle, the whole works: parson, registry office and music. In Berlin he worked as a casual labourer usually tied up with clubs and general nightlife. He always worked and earned his crust, he never was a scrounger.

Dr Metzener has not shown his face for a while, just our regular morning visits by Dr Kakdjiela. Paul has increased her German vocabulary by a few additions. "Bowels how?" and "Appetite open," and most patients reply with a straight face if possible. Very good and regular in that order.

Maria nearly collapsed with mirth when she first heard this exchange. None would ever offend Maria this way, quite the opposite everyone adores and respects her.

When I see Dr Metzener on his next visit he is no longer wearing his padded suit under his white coat, just a tracksuit and lighter shoes, so it must be spring.

Spring is a magic time in Russia, the sky is clear blue with little bits of fluffy clouds sailing across it in a variety of shapes and forms. Spring is a time when plennies get restless and with the bursting signs of life around the wide open country their hearts are ready to burst with the longing for home.

We see little of spring in our ward, with our little cellar windows we just see a little bit of blue sky.

Oh, I would like to throw away my self-imposed shackles and get out into the spring air, but now I am not only a plennie but also in a prison of my own making.

Even Paul gets affected by the general air of melancholy, he asks me to say a poem that I recited to Maria one night. It was one of Moerike's poems, he is a poet of the people, using simple words which go straight to the heart. Paul is in the midst of carving a little wooden box for Maria, and I can see his eyes shining with emotion. He is very dexterous in spite of his size and can produce some very delicate work.

A book regarding the dreadful fate of the Titanic is doing the rounds just now, and we all read it in a sort of relay, chapter by chapter. It passes the time and takes our minds back to another place and time.

On Dr Metzener's most recent visit he notices the rigidity of my limbs has worsened. He plans more tests before massage treatment can begin. When I listen to him I almost feel that I actually have had a stroke. My vast history seems to get bigger every time I see a medical person. When Dr Kakdjiela adds her comments it looks as if a drunk chicken ran over the paper.

Paul is requested to ensure I no longer sleep on my left side, which is quite a relief in a way. I still sleep on my left side when Paul is asleep.

When Dr Metzener examines me next he asks somewhat hesitantly whether I have had VD. I can answer, no never.

But now I think of it, I recall a man in Breslau who had a peculiar kind of limp due to the effects of VD. He still has to do a Wasserman test in spite of my negative reply.

The two beds next to me are now occupied, but the bunk below Paul is empty. One of the new occupants has a severe case of meningitis and he is unconscious, totally oblivious to his surroundings. The other man is Karl from East Prussia with a severe chest infection. The two German doctors examine both new patients within minutes of their arrival. How lucky they are not to be examined by the likes of Dr Schneider.

Sadly, all medical help is too late for the meningitis sufferer, the poor man's agony lasted for two hours. It seemed an eternity. All I can do is pray for him as all talk stops. A sudden silence tells us that he has found his release. Maria gently covers the dead man and Dr Metzener signs the death certificate.

Paul and another orderly transfer him to the mortuary and all necessary details are entered into a register.

Dr Kilian returns in the evening to administer a medication to the other newcomer, then he comes across and sits next to me.

"Penicillin would, if available, cure many ills, but as yet is not available."

Dr Kilian from Koenigsberg wants to know about his homeland – the hell where I became a PoW. He was married in 1941 and is full of worry about his young wife. His mother had been able to flee to the west but she had no contact with her daughter-in-law. I feel as if I am once more back in that hellish scenario. I could tell him all the gory details about what took place in his once beautiful homeland.

The Nazi big shot in charge of the town had prevented an early evacuation of the local populace and when the Russians overran the town there had been no time to warn them. Koenigsberg was retaken briefly by the Germans. The Russians had been encouraged to do their worst and they had! I had to take a statement from surviving women.

The words of the writer Ilya Ehrenburg a communist Jewish extremist. 'Kill, kill! There is nothing within the German nation that is innocent, even the unborn child., Follow the orders of comrade Stalin and forever kick to death the fascist animal in his lair, break down the racist women, they are yours for the taking.'

I have seen the results of the statement, and I will never forget those images, they will be with me for the rest of my life.

I do not think Dr Kilian would benefit from this knowledge, and I could not put that heavy load onto him.

I tell him of the death of his beautiful town, I recall the pointless death of many German soldiers who had the opportunity of saving themselves but were prevented by their senior officers. The SDC (security service) actually opened fire on their own troops as they were going into Russian captivity.

I try in vain to find a single anecdote to make the listening easier for him. There were the deaths of the two women I witnessed. One was the mistress of the Nazi in charge of Koenigsberg who of course had managed to flee to safety. The other woman was the secretary of another party big shot. The three of us are in a hiding place and I try to give them courage, they know what will happen to them once the Russians reach our dugout. I get called away for a few moments and on my return I hear the sound of two shots. Both the women are dead, whilst I know all the moral arguments of the sanctity of life I fully understand the path they have taken.

This is the last time I talk to Dr Kilian about Koenigsberg, it is now a closed chapter.

Maria starts her shift early next morning and totally confuses Gustav. He has not done his usual round of dusting, airing and cleaning. He hates being told off by Maria. If he gets sacked from his precious post as head orderly not even his membership of the activists group would save him. But Maria doesn't seem to notice the existing untidyness. She urgently demands to see Dr Kilian.

Paul rushes off to find him and when Dr Kilian arrives, Maria presents him with a box of penicillin. She has been to Moscow during the night and through connections had obtained the precious drug. This will help Karl E very quickly. Dr Kilian bestows a heap of praise on Maria, who glows like a proud little girl. As Maria is about to give the injection Dr Kakdjiela enters the ward in an absolute rage. How dare you administer a new medication without discussing it with her? Had Dr Kilian not intervened the precious drug would have been wasted. Dr Kakdjiela leaves the ward under a puff of smoke. Dr Metzener has also arrived on the scene, he intends to do a lumbar puncture to check CSF (Cerebro Spinal Fluid) and I have to lie absolutely still.

Maria holds my head and the process passes quickly and I am secretly relieved that it was not his Russian colleague.

Maria instructs Paul to ensure I lie still, I am not to eat anything, not even my treasured piece of bread.

Dr Kilian returns in the night to repeat the penicillin injection, his patient already breathes easier.

I have a favour to ask of Maria. My cigarette supply is growing daily although I do share them out from time to time, but I really long for a smoke. The walking sick all have the opportunity to smoke elsewhere. Maria consults with Dr Kilian who gives his consent for me to smoke in bed, providing I wait until Karl Ebener has improved a little.

Gustav gets informed and he passes the information on to the rest of the ward.

2

After I have had my night time medication I try in vain to sleep. Maria is on night shift and when she realizes I am neither in pain nor uncomfortable she suggests we should exchange our personal stories; talking and listening might send me off to sleep.

I tell her about my homeland, the beauty of the Riesengerbirge where I lived with my family and where my children were born. The longing for home puts words in my mouth which is like painting a mental picture.

Maria listens to me deep in her own thoughts. She says she can almost see the landscape. When I ask her quite suddenly whether that part of the world is familiar to her she surprisingly looks scared.

She gives me a long searching look, apparently Vera had told her that I could be trusted. She knows quite a bit about me in my previous camps as told to her by Vera Rachmonova. The women used to share a house in Moscow and occasionally went to the cinema. Maria is still in contact with Vera and promises to pass on any news.

But, then I ask about her perfect knowledge of German. She says it would be easy to say 'I was a good pupil' and learned to master the difficult language well, which is partly true, but she still hesitates to give away the hidden part of her life history. Through Vera she knows she can trust me.

She originally came from Odessa. She volunteered to work for the Germans when they occupied Odessa and she was taken to Hirschberg where she worked as a housekeeper for a butcher's family. That's how she got to know the Tatra mountains.

The family had been very keen walkers and took her with them on their trips, but when her own forces took Silesia she was accused of being 'konspiratia' and taken into custody to face a long term in prison. But before her case came to trial a Major in the MWD fell in love with her; his secretary had been killed in action, and in keeping with the topsy-turvy times it was not very difficult to take on the dead girl's personal papers and history. When I asked her was she still part of the MWD she confirms she is. She also tells me that she had fallen in love with a young German whilst living in Silesia, she would return there in her bare feet were there the slightest chance of meeting her young German again.

But I know her chances of this ever happening were very slim, my chances of going home were definitely better.

But unlike her, I cannot open my heart and tell her my most recent story; I know confession is good for the soul but not when it endangers another human being.

Poor little Maria had quite enough on her plate already.

Dr Metzener visits in the morning and he is glad there have been no ill effects from the lumbar puncture, both blood and CSF specimens have been sent to Moscow, but the results will take some time. However, time is what I have plenty of.

The days pass quickly and the only hope of an eventual trip home keeps me going. Karl Ebener has made a remarkable recovery, after his treatment with the antibiotics, he asks for a transfer next to me and seems to have developed a new condition: verbal diarrhoea. He talks non-stop about his precious homeland East Prussia and his hobby – bees.

Occasionally his stories are fascinating and Paul stops and listens to him, but I wish he could take the occasional break. But only meals and night time put a stop to it. Otherwise nothing new on the horizon.

My left limbs are rigid, so far all tests and examinations for a reaction to the paralysis have ended in a dead end. Dr Metzener would like to begin a regular regime of gentle massage, but fear of another stroke deters him. Today it is an in-depth examination of my eyes. Apparently the back of the eye and its consistency is an indication of some sort, a few drops are instilled and I quickly see everything in a haze and eventually objects disappear altogether. I ask Maria for a mirror and I can just about see my pupils being abnormally large.

But this examination is just another waste of good Dr Metzener's time, it leads to nothing except to another entry in my case history.

I get the distinct feeling that all avenues within the camp hospital have been explored to no avail. Dr Metzener sadly notes that whilst certain appliances are known in Russia, none are available for use in the treatment of plennies.

In the meantime Karl Ebener has developed (in his mind only) another hobby. The creation of a mink farm. Mistakenly I ask about mink and he proceeds to tell me in the smallest detail. He knows we all have to find alternative employment once we are repatriated, but does he have to go on in such detail with his latest hobbyhorse?

His wife now lives with relations near the River Neckar which would be perfect for his latest plan.

He pursues his plan right down to the fact that the mink once skinned would be edible, and the bones could be ground down for fertilizer. Surely there has to be an end to his fantasies. I begin to dream of roast mink, I wish he would get well and move and leave me to comparatively sane and realistic thoughts.

My wish is answered on Saturday. Dr Kakdjiela takes a whole lot of names off the sick list. Ebener is among them. The following Sunday they will be sent back to their respective camps to take up work again in the great Repayment To Mother Russia by the German PoWs.

My peace is short lived. An engineer plans to replace all metal tracks with glass tracks, is it something they get in their food or is it another case of going stir crazy?

Spring has well and truly arrived, the warm wind melts the last bit of frozen earth and the camp is turned into a quagmire of clay. Paul complains every time he has to go into the camp, his inadequate footwear cannot cope with the mud. Maria wears high leather boots.

She brings us news that the hospital may be moved to another barrack cleared for this purpose. Our ward has become quite empty, just a few chronically sick myself included, remain. The patient opposite my bed seems to get worse by the day, he is getting more bloated and is always thirsty. One morning he emptied a whole bowl of clean water which was intended for his morning wash. But to my amazement I see how a small opening is cut into his abdominal wall and a veritable fountain fills half a bucket. He seems to be relieved for a while but before long he is plagued by his thirst as before. One night I see him empty his urine bottle. I tell Gustav about this in the morning and he fetches Dr Kilian who takes a long look at the poor man and gives permission for him to drink as much water as he wants. He knows that this man's journey is nearly over, and that afternoon he dies. Another family who will wait in vain for a soldier to come home. We hardly knew his name, we never talked but I will always remember his whimpering requests for water.

Late in the afternoon there are some new admissions, amongst them is a mentally ill man. He is placed in a bunk under Paul and Maria assures me he is harmless, but I hide my pocket knife just in case.

The man looks drawn and grey, not a word passes his lips. He just laughs now and then.

Dr Metzener tries hard to make him talk but without success. In spite of Maria's assurances I feel a bit anxious as the man has spent some time in a Russian mental hospital and now I understand his awful appearance. What little we have heard of Russian institutions is enough to make one think of the middle ages. His name is Richard Brendel, he was a naval officer. They sent him to us as untreatable, ready for the next transport home. We all try to get him to talk and all personal questions meet with a blank wall, or an insane grin.

The only words we understand of his ramblings are "Food, food." He becomes livelier around meal times, he kneels on his bed and crawls to the end saying "Food, food."

His allocated rations including fat and sugar get eaten as fast as he can without choking. His bread ration gets torn to shreds and stuffed in his mouth in one go. Gustav had to remove the cigarettes as he was about to eat them as well.

Dr Metzener talks to him in a gentle paternal voice, he presumes that times of horrendous starvation and ill treatment have caused the rational part of his system to close down and he purely exists on a very basic animal level.

The doctor has little experience in this field of medicine. It is possible once repatriated he may recover, but too much damage may have occurred.

Paul takes Brendel under his special care, the giant looks after him like a baby.

But for me there is a special treat in store. In the actual camp there are 25 doctors with time on their hands. Dr Metzener intends to use me as a guinea pig in a demonstration and teaching lecture, but not only does he intend to teach but someone may have new ideas regarding my treatment.

I see no reason why I should object. Dr Metzener will give me plenty of warning, transport there and back will be arranged.

But Richard Brendel gets more and more distressed and his usual apathy is replaced by his continual demand for "Food, food!" Paul and Gustav try to quieten him down but Richard gets quite aggressive and bites Gustav's hand, who gives him a responding slap and before you know it the two of them are having a real set to.

Richard has got hold of one of Paul's wooden sandals and lays into them with amazing strength, eventually he has to be tied down by his hands and feet.

When Dr Metzener is called, he administers a tranquillizing injection which soon becomes effective. Richard visibly relaxes and falls asleep.

Paul checks his war wounds, he is severely battered and bruised, his wooden shoe was a very effective weapon. The surrounding area too has suffered in the fight. My store cupboard above my head had been broken and my goods are spread all over the floor.

Maria watches Richard full of pity. When Dr Kakdjiela turns up Maria gives her a detailed account of the incident, but Dr Kakdjiela obviously is not familiar with mental illness and she has a quick look at Richard from a safe distance.

Early afternoon Richard gradually wakes but is soon off again to dreamland after another injection. His restraints are removed, just a belt round his middle keeps him safely in bed.

Paul has strict orders to stay with him all day, another orderly will do the night shift, the patient is so deeply tranquillized that even breakfast passes by without him noticing it.

The following afternoon Dr Metzener intends to do his lecture.

Paul and I have a quick cigarette, I have official permission, he is just there for the company, but before we realize it we are caught in the act by Dr Kakdjiela. She gets herself worked up to such a degree I expect her to burst with fury any minute. Paul manages a quick getaway in spite of repeated shouts of "Nelsija" (forbidden). I try to look totally uninvolved. As my smoke is nearly finished I carefully put the butt in the provided dish and as the doctor spits like a cat when she is worked up, I pull my blanket up over my head.

I know that Dr Kakdjiela is really having a go at Maria, but as she cannot really touch her I have to stand in as a punchbag.

Maria saves the situation and she arrives just as Dr Kakdjiela pulled my blanket off my face and then spits right in my face and is about to hit me when her hand is pulled back behind her back, her knees give way and she lands with a bang on my metal bed.

I know that Maria saves me from a severe beating. Dr Kakdjiela would have taken all her built up anger and frustration out on me. The smoking offence was merely the excuse she needed, but as she was on her knees Maria whispered a few words in her ear and she went as white as chalk. The power of the MWD is far reaching and she stages a quick exit.

On her way out she collides with Dr Metzener who wanted to give her a list of the participating guinea pigs but he ends up with his list in front of him and she is none the wiser.

We do not give him any details just refer to the incident as a clash of opinions and leave it at that.

He knows that Maria is the wrong kind of person to be the doctor's assistant, her youth and obvious superior medical knowledge is like a red rag to a bull every time the two women meet.

Paul carefully checks out if it's safe to return and once more takes over his seat next to Richard.

Paul has changed his wooden clogs for a softer safer pair of footwear. Lunch passes without Richard taking any note of the passing mealtime. Maria arrives with a few blankets to get me ready. The quagmire in the camp persists, I am lucky I do not have to walk.

Paul wraps me up like an infant and transfers me to the stretcher with my pillow and bolster so that I can see something of the rest of the camp. Both orderlies are experienced at carrying patients, not a jolt or a stumble as we come into the bright daylight. The spring air does the body good and Maria promises to have me brought out more often once the temperature rises a bit more.

But once we hit the mud my two orderlies have a hard job to keep me straight. The man at the head of my stretcher slips and the inevitable happens, everyone ends up in the mud except me. Maria is furious, she looks like a pig that has been digging in the mud.

Other plennies rush over to my rescue, the orderly who has got the worst of it must have hurt his left leg as he has to be helped back to the Infirmary. Another man takes his place and without further incident we make it to the improvised lecture room.

This is the first time I get to see the camp. It consists of a collection of barrack buildings and bunkers similar to our ward. The bearers put me down for a few minutes rest and a smoke, but Maria, in a clean uniform, arrives before they can finish their cigarettes and tells them to get a move on before I catch cold. The other orderly broke his leg when he fell and now is another patient and as far as Maria is concerned that's a safe ticket home.

How did she find out about that? Well, now we know for certain that there is a transport home, there are always rumours but through Maria's careless comment we know for certain. Paul assures her that we promise to keep schtum.

There are twenty other patients waiting in the heated anteroom who are patients of Dr Kilian. Their history, diagnosis and treatment gets discussed in the main room, and then it's my turn. The orderlies carefully place me on a table and I am surrounded by twenty five, to me unknown, doctors.

I am totally relaxed and feel perfectly safe. Dr Metzener does the neurological examination pointing out the difference between my left side and right side. I hardly think there is anyone amongst this group in whose interest it would be to prove I was shamming.

The last test with varying degrees of water temperature are known to me for different reasons. Our soup is always very hot so my left hand is used to support my hot bowl so that's not a problem, but my right hand is much more sensitive, as long as they do not use electrical impulses those would be beyond my control.

But once everyone has had their say Dr Metzener requests my return to my ward. I feel exhausted not only by the unfamiliar fresh air, but also a bit of stress and fear make me long for my familiar bed.

I am still bothered by my guilty conscience, what I am doing is not right, all my efforts are geared to keeping my conscience quiet.

Dr Metzener had ordered a course of gentle massage which would allow me to very gradually improve. And with all the excitement I doze off to sleep as does Paul who is sitting on the end of my bed.

I suddenly awake to be faced by Dr Kakdjiela. She kicks Paul awake, her face bodes nothing but evil. The air is suddenly full of tension, all the other patients have fallen silent and pretend not to watch.

She tells Paul in a very unladylike manner to leave. That he does at great speed and she rips open my shirt and jams a stethoscope on my chest quite deliberately trying to hurt me. But the smell of her breath is enough to make me feel ill, she is determined to get revenge for the events of the other day. She will get at Maria through me.

I keep my eyes open for Paul, so far no sign of him. By now the other patients quite openly watch what's going on, it's too good to miss, a bit of excitement in the daily boredom.

If she intends to give me an injection I shall hit her with my right hand, there is enough strength there to stop her; a few of the others have got out of bed ready to come to my assistance.

She puts a little tray next to me and takes my left hand and puts it flat on the bed. Out of her dirty white coat she produces a bottle and soaks a ball of cotton wool. This she places on my open hand as I shut my eyes to get more distant. She yells at me to open them so she can see my reaction, then she puts a match to the cotton wool.

I can smell the burning skin but instead of screaming with pain as expected I break out in a hellish laughter, this is too much for her, she once more gets her little bottle of petrol, but before she can do any more damage Maria comes running into the room. She grabs the bottle and throws it out of the open window. She slaps Dr Kakdjiela very hard on both sides of her face who then attempts to kick Maria, but the nurse is too quick for her and a ball of fury. The Doctor ends up on the floor with kicks raining down on her, but Paul manages to separate the two women as neither are a match for his strength and size.

By now Gustav and two other plennies have arrived to help Dr Kakdjiela off the floor and push her to the door.

Paul takes a bow in front of Maria.

"Clear victory knockout of our enemy!"

Maria realizes that Paul has saved her from committing a real stupidity by striking a senior person, not even being a member of the MWD would have saved her. She is gradually calming down and gets Paul to lift her down from his bunk where he had put her out of harm's way.

She now wants a detailed account of what had happened. She inspects the burnt area of my hand and covers it with powder and then puts on a protective gauze bandage.

We both know that Dr Kakdjiela's experiment was a direct go at Maria, she suspects that I am one of her favourites and hoped to get to her through me.

Maria assures me that Dr Kakdjiela does not have a leg to stand on. She used state property and put us all in danger. With the Russians, endangering state property is very high on their list of priorities – the bunk, the bedding and all the contents of the ward could have gone up in flames. The plennies fate is secondary.

When I asked Maria what would have happened had she actually killed the doctor, she looks at me as if I was a silly child; surely I must know ruining state property turns Dr Kakdjiela into an enemy of the people. If my thoughts are going along a different avenue, I obviously don't know Russia as well as I thought, but luckily she winks at me while she spouts her MWD propaganda.

I thank her regardless of her motivation for her action. Even Richard cheered from the bottom of his bed where he has been sitting in his usual position, he looks quite animated and involved.

At suppertime a new plennie arrives to get introduced to Gustav as he is now a fully fledged orderly. Paul warns him about Richard but I think nobody has much to fear from him as he seems to have turned a corner.

The whole camp knew that an incident had occurred but had got their wires crossed somewhere along the way, the returning workforce were under the impression that Richard our resident loony had made an attempt to escape, but everything was now calm and we could eat our supper in peace.

Richard is still sitting there smiling quietly to himself, what a nice face he has when he is not troubled by his fears and worries.

3

April 1948

Spring has come with a vengeance, the air is cool and gentle and birds sing in the trees and bits of green show in the fields. Paul has got a touch of spring sadness. We spoke quietly and I know something is bothering him, rather than talk he asks me to recite a few poems. I dig deep in my memory and start with Lenau's poem *'Lovely Was The Night In May'* that seems to be his favourite, but he listens to all the other poems of my school years. Little did I know where and when I would recite them and to such a captive audience as Paul and all the other plennies. They all clap when I have finished. Richard as well, not just to follow suit but with genuine appreciation. I can see how he tries his utmost to say something.

Maria sings her favourite song of the fishermen and when she has finished everyone cheers including Richard. Total silence follows until Paul comments on the quality of the entertainment: "as good as any Winter Garden."

Maria reverts back to being a nurse and gets us all settled down for the night. She stops at Richard's bed, and gently strokes his hair and wishes him "Goodnight." I may have made a mistake but I am sure I heard a very quiet "Goodnight, Maria" coming from Richard's bunk and his eyes followed her as she leaves the ward.

Nobody is in the mood for chatting, it would ruin a lovely evening, its time to dream.

The moon appears in the shape of a small crescent through the small window, a few wispy clouds sail past, a night straight from a picture book.

As always my thoughts travel homewards, I know now that another transport is being prepared but I am not hoping for a miracle.

Before I close my eyes I look across at Richard, he is on his side looking across at me.

This time I'm sure he says "It was very beautiful.". The man looking at me is transformed from the "Food, food" shouting disturbed human being. The man is as sane as I am, or however sane one can be after going through the mill of the Russian PoW system.

To confirm my thoughts, he once more says "It was very beautiful tonight."

All my tiredness has left me and I repeat, yes it was beautiful.

Everyone else is fast asleep when Richard moves a bit closer, so there is only a few centimetres distance between us. Richard tells me I have no need to fear him he is quite normal, he just now felt the overpowering urge to open his heart to another human being.

He has been simulating madness for two years and I decided not to say anything, just to allow him to speak and make no comment. As always my mistrust is deep seated as I do not trust anyone. I am surprised when someone trusts me. Trust for a plennie is a dubious gift, once given you cannot recall it and you are in the other's hands. I do realize that poor Richard has reached the end of his strength, he simply has to talk to someone.

I reassure him that he is safe with me, nothing is further from my mind than to betray him to MWD.

Now the gates are open it all bubbles to the surface. In a quiet whisper he tells me he came to us from a lunatic asylum in Moscow. He was locked up in a large room with Russian inmates and he would have spent the rest of his life there, had he not been discovered by a clerk in administration who was responding to a request from a punishment camp near the Kara Sea.

He had made two attempts to explain his situation but both had resulted in the famous Russian cold water treatment followed by isolation. This was worse than living in the communal ward.

When I asked him why he had chosen this particular path he felt that it had been his only option at that time. He had hoped to effect a transfer from the punishment camp to a normal PoW camp.

His story is long and involved. He was a Commander of a minesweeper in Norway and had tried to get into Swedish waters with his ship and crew just before the end of the war to avoid being taken prisoner by the English or Norwegian forces. Once interned by the Swedes his life was reasonably safe as the officer in charge of the internment camp had given his word that he would not hand them over to the Russians.

One morning the camp was surrounded by Swedish troops, and the Swedish officer had shot himself as he could not cope with the shame of broken promises. An indescribable bloodbath ensued. The German captives went to any extent to avoid being handed over to the Russians, some hanged themselves, others chose self-mutilation, but nothing made any difference. Apart from the dead men, they were all taken down to the harbour and handed over to the Russians.

The journey by ship was too gruesome to describe. They landed in Riga and from there they were split into smaller groups and sent to different PoW camps.

He managed to get away and fell into the hands of Latvian guerrillas who did away with anything which vaguely looked Russian.

But one day they were ambushed by a vastly superior group of Russians, four of their group were killed and the rest were taken to Riga to stand trial.

I stopped him briefly to make sure no one was listening, but they all seem to be asleep, the usual way prisoners sleep with their blankets over their heads to keep out the ever present light.

Richard's story is so moving that sleep is out of the question, everyone here has a story worth listening to.

Richard's tragic fate surpasses most others. He chose total isolation which culminated in his simulated madness which could lead to the real thing if the valve is not released, so he can open his soul to someone.

I can help him by listening. I do know by this simple act, we leave both our lives open to a lot of danger. One simple unobserved listener is all it needs to get the MWD started on one of their particular kind of interviews which make a stone speak.

It is not easy to practice what we preach. Many a time I have given a word of comfort and faith to a man on his way to an interview. But I know exactly what shape these interviews take. I have the gap in my teeth and days spent on my bunk unable to move.

I could only keep quiet because I could not answer their questions, had I known what they wanted to know I might have told them. With Richard I have already passed a stage where ignorance is bliss. I am into it as far as he is, so I might as well hear the whole story.

My faked illness is nothing compared to Richard's. I feel that as he tells me his story he can consign it to the past as it no longer is a pressing millstone. When he asks me whether I want him to continue I nod and he carries on.

At their trial five of the guerrillas were given the death penalty and shot. It took a lot of effort on his part to prove he was an escaped German PoW so he ended up getting sentenced to 25 years in the Kartoga (chain gang).

From Moscow he was taken to Kirov, the camp was close to the Kara Sea and the existence there was beyond what is humanly acceptable.

Escape was impossible, therefore the only way out for him was to simulate insanity.

His fellow prisoners, all Russian, made an all-out effort to beat him to death until the camp leader noted that there was something amiss.

First he was put in the camp hospital, then transferred to a local lunatic asylum. He spent all his time with Russians, never a German word, and he could not drop his guard as he would have been sent back to the camp near the Kara Sea.

After a lot of transfers to other mental hospitals he ended up in an institution near Moscow.

Again he made another effort, in vain, to tell them he was sane. The more he tried the more they thought he was genuinely insane.

Suddenly we hear a sound of one of the patients going to the toilet and we decide to continue our conversation another night, to stay safe when the other patient returns to his bed.

I see Richard has quickly fallen asleep, his face peaceful and relaxed and I hope he does not regret talking to me. I am not sure what his situation is. Is his sentence still valid, if so will he never leave Russia?

As he has been transferred to a normal plennie camp one could presume his status has altered and he might well be on the next transport home.

Nothing is definite. I always fall back on the old plennie saying: *'Nothing is impossible, everything is probable and if so, it's usually the least expected.'*

His transfer is due to someone's bureaucratic whim, who knows? A simple stamp underneath a signature makes it an order. The machinery is running and Richard ends up with us.

My neighbour's fate weighs heavily on me; it was good for him to speak to me. I shall not reciprocate in kind, he had enough to carry with his own load. It will be curious to observe his behaviour in the morning.

By morning I find the daily routine and continuing waiting from mealtime to wash time is beginning to be mind-numbing. I have to find some kind of occupation to fill my mind and time.

When Dr Metzener visits he is accompanied by Dr Licht the ENT specialist. He checks out my respective bits and pieces and tells me he will remove my tonsils as they do not look too healthy. I assure him that I have had no problems with them, he efficiently removes a few bits of pus with an orange stick. He also inspects my teeth, they too are in need of repair.

He wants to know whether I had a bad fall and I explain I had several hands-on interviews.

So, that's a change? Not what I had in mind but a change of scenery anyway. First the dentist, then my tonsils. Dr Licht the ENT doctor seems a nice chap but I would like him even better if he left my tonsils alone. I usually avoid the dentist as much as I can, the thought of the drill makes me come out in a cold sweat.

In about eight days I am to undergo this treatment to remove any possible cause for a further stroke, because of this they will remove any totally ruined teeth under general anaesthetic. More bits to add to my already extra-large case history. I might as well have it done here as I have time to spare, at home time will again be a valuable commodity.

Through the doctors' visits I have been prevented from checking on Richard, but it is as if last night never happened. His eyes are almost closed, his facial expressions are apathetic and distanced. No one would have believed the change. He is back to crawling to the bottom of the bed and calling "Food, food". When nobody is watching I look very carefully at him, but all the lights are on but nobody is at home. He does not even flinch.

This reassured me in a way. I shall continue to remain his patient listener, but nothing will persuade me to expect the same from him.

One of the medical technicians measures my arm to document the extent of muscle waste.

Dr Metzener will order the promised massage to begin in about two weeks, there is a very experienced masseur in the camp who will spend time with me. The delay in starting this treatment has been necessary to avoid any further strokes. He promises that everyone will handle me with care, its all in aid of increasing my mobility bit by bit.

When the young dentist comes to check over his new patient, he confirms that my teeth need a good tidy-up. He thinks a local anaesthetic will cover it and all I will feel is the initial injection. Easy for him to say!

I have had my fill of medical visits. Whatever other specialists there are in the camp can forget about me for the time being.

We do not have an x-ray machine which is just as well. I have heard some scary things about brain x-rays. It's been a busy day so I am quite relieved when I see Richard fast asleep.

Three nights later Richard wakes me by gently touching my face and within seconds I am wide awake. Before we start a conversation I check our surroundings for any possible listeners. He deliberately waited a few nights to allay any possible suspicion and he also wants to make quite sure that I still want to listen.

After I assure him of my continued interest and silence he went on with his moving story.

He told me he had been admitted to an insane asylum, which compared with existing in a punishment detail was a holiday. Before long he could no longer cope with life in the asylum and gradually felt all the insanity around him began to affect him.

In one instance when it all became too much for him he had lost all memory of what he had actually done and only came to his senses when the guards managed to release another inmate from his stranglehold. All he needed was a little push and Richard once more attacked another inmate. From then on he was confined to a single cell which was only lit from the outside.

How long he spent there he didn't know as he saw no change in day or night. When he was taken out of solitary he was placed in another communal cell, which differed little from the first one.

Playing the lunatic had become second nature to him and would hopefully take him home eventually.

But back in Moscow suddenly somebody understood his shouts of 'Woina Plennie' (German PoW). He had to change out of his hospital clothing into the usual padded cotton clothing and shortly after was transferred to this heaven of sanity, the German PoW hospital.

He realizes that he cannot suddenly regain his mental health, his sentence still hangs over him and he would automatically be sent back to the frozen north. He would have to maintain his status of harmless lunatic to even think of being sent home. As always there is nothing certain with Russians, their logic works on a different wavelength.

1st of May was a big holiday, closely followed by the celebration of the 10th May – the day the Germans capitulated. All we knew of it was the racket coming from the soldiers and guards accommodation. They had been given extra rations of vodka.

To celebrate the event the Russians undertook a very thorough search of their ward. Sharp tools and weapons were what they were after.

Maria comes with a Sergeant to supervise the search and to prevent any ill treatment of the patients; I make sure my pocket knife is carefully under my left side. Maria has been out of sorts for a while, she must be missing her young German man.

Her facial expression is in total contrast to the light spring clothes she wears. Richard too has ceased all communication, maybe he has sudden doubts about my reliability. Mistrust is the only way to remain safe in this country and what I have seen and heard during my time in Russia confirms this theory. Of course I am as guilty as he is, but then he doesn't know that. I know that a good German specialist who has access to modern tests and equipment would have been able to prove I was faking my condition, but by now I and a lot of specialists were up to our neck in this deceit.

On my last inspection by Dr Metzener he ordered regular alcohol rubs for my back as I was beginning to develop pressure sores.

When Maria gives me my daily treatment I try in vain to cheer her up, or at least find out the cause of her unhappiness.

May 1948

One May morning a Sergeant arrives with a pile of clothing and dumps it on my bed. I suddenly feel ice cold with fear, but it is Richard who is leaving us. He is being transferred to another hospital which is better equipped to deal with psychiatric patients.

When I look at him, he appears absolutely terrified, but before long the curtains are drawn as he puts up with being dressed by Paul and Maria who are being as kind and gentle as possible. All I can do is wish him well, I do not know his wife's address.

When Paul returns he is shaking with shock, outside the ward they had been met by a policeman, two soldiers armed with machine-pistols and Richard was being handcuffed, so we both know he is not going home. That dreaded punishment camp would once again take possession of this poor tortured man.

Maria came to see me that night, she had known for a few days but felt it better not to tell me. There was nothing anyone could have done, we both felt that Richard would have chosen death rather than return to that camp.

Quietly she said "Nitschewo"…a Russian answer to everything.

I realize my own situation was equally bad. I was now in a prison of my own making and if I did not want to share Richard's fate I have to be very careful. This awful burden is mine alone to carry, too many people are involved now.

I cannot afford to give in. I have to play my role until whatever fate has picked out for me.

Just after breakfast I am being collected for dental treatment. I am wrapped up in blankets and taken out into the beautiful spring day. I am dreading this and I am very scared, and when I am taken into a room full of doctors I feel even worse.

They put me in a dentist's chair, next to me a sterilizer bubbles away with my torture instruments.

But what is the explanation for the presence of all these doctors?

An ancient drill is pushed to one side, so that the dentist can get to work. He lifts several instruments out of the sterilizer and has them lined up on a glass plate. First he draws up an injection and I feel two cool hands holding my head and two more injections follow. I begin to lose feeling in my lower jaw. I don't feel a thing and just see the instruments being used. After the first extraction they proceed to pull out three teeth.

Next in line are my tonsils but that's for another day. For the time being I am on a liquid diet.

4

Big changes are afoot, a 1,000 man transport is being arranged. This rumour gains credibility when Dr Metzener informs six chronically ill patients, myself included, that we are to be seen by a Major from Moscow.

He will decide our fate. Does our continual illness cost the state too much? In the long run would it be our cheaper option to get rid of us on the next transport regardless of our plennie history?

Paul and I are two of his patients, the other four are Dr Kilian's. I am particularly worried, but Paul is full of excitement and plans, I do not want to dampen his spirits but I know from bitter experience how quickly one's hopes can be dashed.

First Dr Kilian's patients will be seen, then it's our turn, we have to wait for simply ages. We do not even have to be seen by the Russian Major, he signed our case histories after a detailed discussion with Dr Metzener.

Both carry a big stamp, I am almost beginning to hope that maybe this time? But I know Russia only too well by now and I have to be patient.

June 1948

By June we are moving into a well-lit airy barrack, above ground, the room we are allocated is smaller, it just contains four hospital beds, so far there are just Paul and I.

The first night in my new surroundings I cannot sleep, the ghosts from the past walk through my thoughts. I have only been in Moscow for over a year. Hans Schubert, Werner Berg, Vera Rachmanova, Konny and Sepp - all unforgettable characters who have touched my life. We walked together for a few miles on the long and winding road of life.

Paul is just about out of control, he is so bubbly and I find it impossible to warn him of the changes which will have taken place in the Berlin of his dreams. Here in Russia he is receiving his meagre rations regularly. Will he be assured of the same at home?

What will life be like for a war damaged man like him, will anyone be interested and support him? He is not qualified for life after the war, but he plans to work as an attendant in a petrol station. There will be very few cars owned by Germans, has he considered that? I try to bring him down to reality but he prefers to dream on. Anyway, who am I to wipe out his dreams?

Rumour has it the Doctors will come too, even the usually calm and collected are beginning to show signs of home fever.

But the downside of the expected transport is also once more in evidence. Shades of the previous camp show up, but otherwise a definite case of deja vu. Nobody trusts anyone and the atmosphere gets worse by the day.

One prisoner who could no longer stand the strain hanged himself. To put a stop to the Russian continued chicanery of repeatedly changing lists a general hunger strike breaks out in the camp, even in the hospital.

A very inexperienced man volunteers to see the Russian MWD to tell him the strike will be over the minute the final list appears.

Maria and her Russian helpers beg us to eat and she tries to persuade me to act as a strike breaker (a good example according to her) but I cannot do that. I have to support my fellow plennies. Even the fact that I am an officer gets an airing, but to no effect.

The suicide plennie is a heavy burden for the MWD, not in a humane way but because of all the ensuing paperwork.

Just one man who could be a pawn in their devilish game of having their last fun with the German plennies.

Next morning a bus load of officers and other Russian personnel arrive and the plennies are hauled in one by one to be interviewed. After two hours the camp strike is broken and we are eating again.

Individual plennies have been threatened with prison and trials of conspiracy which always result in transfers to punishment camps. Who wants to risk 35 years in the mines in Russia's almost permanently frozen north? Especially if you're not sure of the wholehearted support of all the plennies.

Dr Metzener leaves us to get our breakfast and Maria stays with us. She admits that she had lied and told the MWD that we were all eating, she wanted to avoid any of us being 'interviewed'. I also know that she and her Russian helpers would have had black marks in their personal reports.

The young speaker who had volunteered to speak for all had been speedily removed and was now on his way to a destiny unknown but easily guessed at.

Never again will he volunteer for anything.

By lunchtime normal life as we know it resumes.

Next day the preparations start for the transport. Everyone gets kitted out, myself included, but I hold on to my inner reserve. It's all happened before. Tomorrow night we are to be taken to the transport all dressed in our new outfits, blue engineer suits and red kepi.

I know I am just a grain of sand in the vast number of plennies and that I am of no importance to the Russians, so why should they pick on me again? I will slip through the net one day, why not now?

In spite of this I find myself thinking of home and all that it means to me. When I awake I try to hang on to the images. We have hopefully our last breakfast and we should have our lunch in the ward as well and by suppertime we should be in our wagon.

Paul has already left us, he is hardly functioning on his normal level. Maybe being hit on the head with a spade has affected his brain more than originally thought. Home will be hard for him. Who will be kind and patient with him in the hard struggle of daily life?

Paul takes off to check out what's happening in the general camp. He returns very distressed, as apparently the Russians have yet another list.

Once the plennies get to the Budka some of them get returned to their barracks. He is very scared that he will share their fate but I try to reassure him, but who am I to talk?

Reluctantly I let Paul help me into my new outfit, but before we are finished Maria appears. I know that look, is it Paul or me? The powers that be have decided that I have to stay, until I am able to walk again. She gives me two sleeping tablets and before long I hear the voices of Dr Metzener, Dr Kilian and other plennies from a long distance and their faces seem to be shrouded in fog. Paul who usually finds it hard to keep quiet is totally silent, he just gives me a hug whispering: "Soon, my friend soon."

They all promise to contact my family. Maria stays close and when I finally wake the next morning she is asleep in Paul's bed.

I decide never to get sucked on to this transport fever. I just cannot afford to put that burden into my soul. After years of war and imprisonment I am beginning to feel too fragile to cope with yet another disappointment.

Apparently I must have gone back to sleep, when I wake up my breakfast gets collected from the kitchen.

Maria decides that something has to be found to occupy me and fill my time in a positive way. I want to learn the Russian language properly with the help of Maria. Nothing like a living dictionary.

There are no German doctors, they all went on the transport, but a few days later a Hungarian arrives to take over our care. As he does not speak a word of German it means once more Maria will have to be the intermediary and Dr Laslo looks a trustworthy man. Maria gives him my case history, and luckily she avoids mention of the impending tonsillectomy.

Two new patients arrive both having Dystrophy and one plennie from our camp. A new activist announces himself, easily recognized by his good clothes, our new Starski treats him with caution and allows him to store his belongings in a sack under his bed. I wonder what Maria will have to say about that?

When I inspect this activist a bit closer I see that he is wearing my precious shoes. I am not prepared to let this character have them without a fight.

Maria hears my outraged shouts and comes to see what is happening. I tell her I have a receipt for all my belongings from the store room and show her the note about my shoes. She asks me to describe them which I can right down to the last detail, the newcomer calls me a traitor as I have involved the Russians, but that does not change the fact that he somehow managed to get my shoes.

Maria asks for my belongings to be brought to me and everything is there except my shoes. A pair of canvas shoes with wooden soles have been substituted for my shoes. The storeman and his assistant leave us quickly, no one wants to get into conflict with the MWD, just over a pair of shoes.

Maria turns to the activist and tells him to remove himself and his possessions, she will take him elsewhere.

I know I have made an enemy and to have an activist as an enemy was a dangerous thing. But no way was I going to give up my shoes!

The other two newcomers have watched the proceedings with interest, they both have read the situation correctly as has the new Starski. Do not mess with Schmitt or you'll have Maria to deal with.

As from tomorrow I will be able to spend a few hours in the fresh air. Both Dr Laslo and Maria think it is a good idea.

Amongst the plennies a few gardeners have got together and have managed to persuade the Russians to get some seeds that they have grown in their barracks over the winter period. Now these seeds have turned the camp into a sea of flowers. The short Russian summer brings the flowers to bloom. One of the orderlies made a very effective sunshade so I do not get burnt by the hot sun and I sleep so much better now.

The only cloud on my daily horizon is the regular masseur a veritable giant of a man. It is amazing what gentleness is in his huge hands. Initially he just massaged my left limbs, but now he is involving the joints and that is very painful.

He arrives every morning after breakfast. I put off the torture as much as I can by offering him a cigarette, but once it's over he carries me out to my place in the sun. Usually I fall asleep at once.

Today I get woken by a deep voice. I see a tall almost square man in the uniform of a captain. He is wearing a well tailored uniform finished off by a cap rather than the usual uniform hats of the MWD. He has a pleasant face full of character. Going by the grey in his hair I judge him to be about fifty.

After he asks how I am he tells me he is 'Sigi'. Sigi Kirschbaum. He is vastly different from the other MWD officers I have met. He has a reputation for fairness and justice, a rare combination within the MWD. He has been especially effective in the control of the over-officious activists. The activists in this camp have to watch their Ps and Qs. Sigi makes sure of that. He visits the stores and kitchen frequently and unexpectedly to avoid all insider dealings, he must have a very effective ring of spies throughout the camp because little happens that he does not know about – often before it happens.

Rarely have I met a man from whom such calmness and relaxed attitude eminate.

He squats down next to me. He had planned to see me before but Maria was against it as the journey to his office with untrained orderlies would be risky, the trained orderlies having left with the transport.

When I asked him why I had been taken off the last transport he shakes his head and told me what he had been told by Maria, but that really wasn't the whole story.

His German is perfect, just a slight Yiddish inflexion now and then, from whence did his destiny bring him to this camp I wonder? According to my plennie papers I belonged to the dreaded department of counter espionage. This is hated everywhere, whatever side of the war, the victors or vanquished.

He tells me I should be on the next transport if their investigations prove that I had not been actively involved in any action against Russia.

My personal agenda is not what is on the man's mind. He wants to ask my advice. His daughter, a bright 16 year-old has done well at school and is almost fluent in German. She now has to pick another language. What should she choose?

Without much thought I advise him to get her to opt for English. The future will show that there are only two camps in the world, one is ruled by Russia and the other will be under American influences and it is useful to be familiar with the language of the opposition.

Now he wants to know if it is the reason I wish to learn Russian. Maria now has permission to obtain the textbook by Professor Steinitz in Moscow.

He knew for whom she wanted the book when she applied for permission. As I said before, he is well informed.

He wants to return to his original conversation. What makes me think there will be a split between East and West whilst they are confederates just now. But as I point out to him, that was only a marriage of convenience and a temporary one at that.

He compliments me on my clear political thought process, he would like to send me on a course of 'political schooling'. I have to point out to him that the communist philosophy of life is totally opposed to my religious convictions.

Sigi was impressed. Usually this offer to attend a course is looked upon as a springboard to the next transport home, but many a man was transported to Siberia rather than home.

He is a plain speaker and tells me without any hesitation that should I be proved to be guilty of any crimes against the Russian people, I would be nursed back to health, but also I would die in Russia, or do I consider the soil of mother Russia too heavy for a German?

Should I be found innocent I would be sent home on the next transport.

He tells me we will meet again, it will be at his place next time. With that he shakes my hand, wishes me well and leaves. From our conversation I know that he is not only clever but also a well-educated man. I have nothing to hide from my military past. I was never active on the Russian front.

Dr Laslo is a frequent visitor as I am progressing well with my Russian studies with Maria. We are able to converse a little more. I can tell him about my previous contact with the Hungarians and how much I valued and respected them.

Summer is at its zenith, the hot sun burns down mercilessly on the camp. My masseur turns up daily, it's still painful but gradually I develop a degree of feeling and movement on my left limbs. I hope that my salt free diet will come to an end, but no such luck as yet. Next week I am to start my first attempt at walking.

5

The camp is always busy, people coming and going all the time. The same applies to the hospital. Most new patients are suffering from the effects of starvation, the others are unable to work due to their general state of health.

My Masseur Wilfried has just finished another session with me when a request comes for me to report to Sigi Kirschbaum. The Russian orderly keeps shouting "Dawai, dawai, Schmitt," until Wilfried pulls himself up to his full height and waves his huge hands in front of the Russian, a bit less of the 'dawai, dawai,' if you please.

Wilfried says he will take me there, and will collect me afterwards. He helps me with my coat and then casually lifts me up in his arms and carefully like a mother with her baby carries me to the MWD office.

All doors within the office are well upholstered and padded, nothing can be heard from the outside. He carefully deposits me on a chair opposite Sigi who arranges for the masseur to pick me up after our talk. The door shuts and we are on our own.

He thought it would be easier to talk if we had a cup of tea and a cigarette. He produces a teapot, two cups, brown sugar, spoons and half a glass of Morello Cherries.

Once, stationed in Poland I had enjoyed drinking tea in this manner when visiting a Jewish carpenter before the SS took over.

He seems to be able to read my mind. He knows that I am trying to work out where his roots are. I am allowed to serve myself, I am his guest today. And we are going to rewrite a curriculum vitae for me today. He is only interested in the life before I joined the army.

He hands me a picture of my wife taken in Amberg which she had to have taken to get her refugee pass. The local Bavarians had a different pass. She now lives in Amberg with my children.

"Nice looking boys and girls," he says, they are waiting for their father.

He lets me absorb these facts and I wonder how far the Russian Secret Service goes. Then out of the blue he shouts.

"What was your profession?"

I tell him that I was a parson of the protestant Lutheran Church, just as it states in my CV.

He replies with more sharpness in his voice, that he wants clear answers. Now if I had studied theology I should be able to read Hebrew and with that he hands me a Hebrew bible and asks me to read a paragraph. I tell him I can only oblige if I have a dictionary with the Bible. He intends to obtain one. Now I realize that there are doubts about my profession. On previous interviews the same subject had come up; why not officiate as an Army Padre. The vocational profession of a parson stands at odds with being an officer in counter espionage. That I really had no choice seemed irrelevant. He then asks for a biblical quote in Hebrew, all I can think of at the time is the 130th Psalm. I start off quite well, but when I get to the fifth verse I get a bit wobbly. Sigi carries on and it sounds like a prayer.

Next I have to write down the beginning of the Bible. I get as far as the first day of God's creation, when he puts a halt to my writing and promises me he will obtain a Bible for me. Then he changes tack and asks me about my Russian studies. I tell him I am now able to talk to Dr Laslo a little, and then he makes a surprising comment that it is not wise to be too clever and know too much.

When I ask him when the next transport home is, he laughs. He tells me to ask the other plennies as they always know first. Then I was dismissed. Just as I was beginning to relax he shoots a sudden question about my inability to walk at me. I tell him to look in my case history. He grins and says "Paper is patient."

When I am back in the safety of my bed I go through the whole event once more. This man is dangerous because of his intelligence, behind the mask of a nice man hides a very superior brain. He seems to be most unimpressed by my case history. In my life history before my imprisonment I have nothing to hide in my private life or as a soldier. That's how I see it, being merely a clerk in a counter espionage office seems to be my main crime. That I was only transferred there in the last few months of the war due to a war wound seems to be the extent of my crime.

Weeks pass and through Wilfried's good work my limbs are getting much more supple. Tomorrow is my big day, my first attempts to walk again. Maria, Dr Laslo and Wilfried are there. They lift me and try to stand me up, the first time in five months.

Wilfried holds my shoulders upright but the minute he lets go my legs buckle under me, even my right leg has lost its strength. I will have to start from scratch, like a baby.

On the following Saturday evening Maria is on night duty and turns up with the Starski and tells me the Captain wants to see me in the Starski's quarters. First they try to walk me between them but then the Starski lifts me and carries me to his room and puts me in a chair.

Sigi Kirschbaum presents me with the Hebrew Bible and the dictionary.

"There you are, read what you like."

I pick Isaiah, the story of the barren vineyard and afterwards translate it. Then he asks me for the 23rd Psalm, his favourite. I thought I had seen it all, a believer in the MWD but as before he almost reads my mind. It was his mother's favourite bit of scripture. She died in Auschwitz.

Like so many times before I feel ashamed to be German, the spectre of the common guilt lies heavy on my shoulders.

The Captain seems to believe my repeated statements that I am a Lutheran Pastor. But, the military part of my CV is harder to prove. Where can I get confirmation and witnesses to corroborate my statement? So far I have not come across anyone who was taken prisoner at the same time or place.

Once I am back in my bed Maria comes to see me, she bends down and tells me Vera sends her regards and good wishes. Before I can ask any more she has gone.

It has been a beautiful night and the meeting with Sigi K makes me very thoughtful. What horrendous events have formed this man, we all think our own experiences are the most important, but they often pale into insignificance in comparison to other people's lives.

When next I see Dr Laslo he prescribes treatment with ultraviolet light to improve my muscle tone.

On yet another evening I get called to the Captain's office where he gives me a piece of paper and a pencil. Again I am asked to write down my life history. He says many of the plennies insist on a very working class background and upbringing and try to put themselves into better light according to communist ideals.

My life history fills half a page. I know it all word for word, but in that short report there is enough to make the Russians suspicious. The fact I was not a conscript but a volunteer speaks very much against me. As expected Captain K wants to know why I volunteered and I tell him that my main reason was an attempt to escape the machinations of the Nazi party. As a religious man in the army I was very much left in peace by the political aspects of army life.

He thinks my motivation was totally different, I was keen to get my share of war booty. That's how he sees it, and it seems impossible to convince him of the truth of my personal history. When I deny ever being a member of the Nazi party organisation he shakes his head in disbelief, when he mentions the pogroms against the Jews especially.

"Kristallnacht." I tell him that in our little village far from the beaten track, agriculture was the main topic of interest. News from the big world only reached 24hrs later by radio and then it was an edited version.

Again he wonders how a country like Germany full of conscientious and industrious workers could fall into the hands of such political gangsters.

I try to recall the time prior to the ascent of the Nazis and describe to him what life was like for the average working man.

There was no work, our money was without value and the situation was getting worse rather than better; all the after effects of the 1st World War. There was nobody to give the worker work to earn enough to feed their starving families, all they got was speeches and soup kitchens.

That was fruitful soil in which the Nazi party successfully sowed its seed in the 'name of the people', that became the slogan of the day.

Why didn't I object to the deeds of the Nazi party? Because I was a coward like everyone else and I had too much to lose. My family was the most precious possession.

So, by volunteering for the army I guaranteed their safety, my children's education and a certain amount of protection, should the party ever turn against the Lutheran Church and those involved in it.

The Captain looks interested in my explanation and once more offers me a place in a school of political development. Again I tell him that I must refuse.

That seems to be it for the night and I am returned to my room.

August 1948

My walking exercises make good progress and I am able to walk after a fashion by putting all the pressure on my right leg and use my left as a prop. I cannot learn to walk too fast, that wouldn't fit in with the expected progress of a stroke victim according to Dr Schneider's book. I decide to stick to the status quo for as long as I can.

There are daily new arrivals, singly or in groups and they bring news from other camps. It looks very much as if our camp is a collection point for another transport. On a beautiful August evening the Camp Commander informs us that a transport of 900 men will be going home. Maria assures me that a separate list is being produced for the hospital, when I try to find out who selects the names she says it is Dr Laslo, but it still has to be approved by the MWD. Reluctantly she agrees.

"Everybody will go home sometime, if not now, then on the next transport."

It looks as if the Russians are not up to their usual trick of changing lists. The 900 men get kitted out in their travel clothes. But in the hospital no one is told or prepared for a journey, the tension is high and nerves are at breaking point. By lunchtime the next day all patients get their travel clothes including myself, in spite of that I find myself unable to participate in the general excitement.

At long last the time has come. The patients are to be transported to the wagons in a lorry, but when the men are called alphabetically it seems a lifetime until they come to the P, Q, R and S. Several names are called but no 'Schmitt'.

Once more I am left behind. I just about have time to wish them all a good journey and again many promise to contact my family, but now I am past caring.

From the room next door I hear the desperate weeping of a man. He is from Vienna and like me briefly worked in the office of counter espionage. I hear Maria's comforting words, she sounds like a mother bringing peace to her child. By the time she comes into my room I manage to show a smiling face.

Of course she looks right through me, she knows not to say anything, it would open the floodgates and all my carefully built up front would collapse. She just sits next to me and gently strokes my face and feels my sorrow, pain and disappointment.

Sigi Kirschbaum turns up like a spectre at the feast. He is surprised that I had unrealistic hopes of going home. That's the MWD man speaking, but there is still the other human side to him. He is trying to say a kind word but as always says 'I was only following orders,' exactly what I had to do, was my reply.

I was not in a position to pick and choose where I was transferred to once I was considered fit for active service after my time in hospital. He knew of course the same applies to soldiers the world over. However he promises to speed up my case, he just has to sort out a few grey areas before he can release me, with that he leaves me to my thoughts and misery.

Three of us are left in the hospital, even Wilfried the masseur, he is cool and collected which is my best medicine at the moment. He tells me that all active officers have been kept behind.

Poor Wilfried hopes that one day we too will leave. We cannot just rot and die here. 'Patience' is the slogan of the day, not always my strong point.

I continue with my daily walking exercises, except I cannot become too good at it, poor Richard's fate is still close and real to me.

6

Suddenly overnight its autumn, the asters are in full bloom. The wives of the MWD officers come to visit the German tailor who will make their winter outfits. Much cheaper and more tasteful than any of the Moscow dressmakers. The tailors are usually men from the Sudetenland and are in great demand, and everyone benefits. When the ladies return to Moscow they are laden down with big bunches of asters.

The clothes they are wearing are dull and off the peg, uniform in their utilitarian fashion. No wonder they all come to visit our tailors. Some of the choices created by the tailors often causes some hilarity. What women imagine will make them look elegant, sometimes makes them look quite ridiculous. Still, as my father-in-law used to say "If its fashionable to stick a feather up your backside," etc, etc.'

One woman sticks out amongst the visitors, she is delicate and slender with a slight Mongolian look to her face.

I have a new job. One of the Russian Sergeants asks me to hold watch over a tobacco field, ie: keep the plennies away. I am quite happy to sit here in the sunshine, nobody in their right mind would try to steal any leaves during the day, but it's nice to have a job of sorts, I am not totally useless.

It also means I get to check out all the lady visitors as they come past me on their way to the tailors, and I number them all from 1 to 10.

The 'Mongolian' seems to like me and one day she hands over a little bag of sweets but carefully checking beforehand that she is not seen. She waves away my thanks and quickly carries on to the tailors.

When she returns she is wearing her new suit. Very elegant I tell her, she does a twirl like a mannequin. I certainly unearthed the 'Eve' with my compliment.

Right at the bottom of the sweets is a small packet of Machorka and some Russian tea, now I can have a nice cup of tea tonight and think of my benefactor.

Big excitement in camp. There has been a delivery of mail. Wilfried shows me a card which came from Erlangen where an aid organization for PoWs had been founded. This card carries just a few words and many good wishes and is signed by Bishop Heckel. I try to remember why his name rings a bell.

He used to be the man in charge of the Lutheran Diaspora. When Wilfried comments that he has not been a churchgoer for a long time I suggest that he should enjoy his card even more – nothing like a lost sheep!

Lots of unknown plennies receive cards, strangely they are all former members of the SS.

Everyone is pleased that someone is thinking of them, and we are not all written off as a lost cause.

The first light frost kills all the flowers.

That night I get called to Sigi's office. He wants to know how I am enjoying my Russian tea. I think I actually blushed, I do not want to betray the kind giver of my tea and tobacco but he knows already; nothing is secret in this camp for long.

Once he has enjoyed my embarrassment he hands me a card across the table posted from my wife. It is the usual plennie card and my wife has attached a picture of Bernd my youngest son in his leather shorts standing in a meadow of flowers happy and full of life.

Then I tell him I saw Bernd for the first and last time on 12th December 1944 when I was able to perform his Christening. On top of this surprise he gives me a small package which was sent from the Lutheran aid agency for PoWs. My hands shake as I open the parcel and Sigi hands me his pocket-knife as my hands are shaking so much I cannot undo the knots. I keep as much as I can of the string, a plennie never throws anything away. I have to put the contents on the table so Sigi can compare them to a note attached to the parcel: one tin of butter, a sausage, a bit of chocolate, some sweets and a packet of cigarettes. I have to sign for the riches and then I can put them back in the carton.

Sigi decides I will be of no use to him tonight and I am released till tomorrow night. I can go off to my room and arrange a 'prasnik' (party) for my friends. The orderly goes to collect Wilfried and for his troubles I give him a sweet.

I have developed a certain skill in coping with just my right hand. My left I just use for passive support.

Again and again I consider my riches. I feel as if my Christmas and birthdays have all come on the same day. I too am not forgotten.

When Wilfried arrives I tell him we are going to have a party and I show him my gifts. Gently his hands touch the things from home. The orderly makes tea and I persuade him to accept a piece of bread with butter and sausage. In the middle of our get-together Maria arrives. She refuses the food but accepts a cigarette. A bar of chocolate is worth 30 roubles on the Russian black market and she has not seen or eaten chocolate for years. Still she refuses to accept even a little piece.

Thoughtfully she studies my little boy's picture.

I have to admit the German cigarettes taste a bit insipid compared with the much stronger Russian ones; oh, but the taste of the sausage sandwich!

When everyone has left I read my wife's card. The three older children have already started attending secondary school, they are all well and waiting for their dad to come home.

They only know me from a photograph taken many years ago. My wife writes nothing about the problems she must face daily on her own with five children.

How glad she must be to know that all our immediate family is alive and well Maria says, and I do persuade her to accept a small piece of chocolate and a sweet.

"Dream of home," she whispers as she leaves.

Next evening I once more return to see Captain Kirschbaum. I must still look pleased with myself but he soon brings me down to earth.

Once more I have to go over my military history. I start in the year 1935. He still cannot believe I joined up to avoid the politics at home. He says even so he almost believes me, he will have considerable problems to make it plausible to his superiors.

My military history only holds interest for him in as far as it takes place in Russia. I was in charge of a company of cyclists and we got as far as Smolensk. In a battle I was buried under a load of rubble and ended up in a field hospital. My second posting was 1942 to 1943 to the River Don and Sigi said I should have read the book: '*Quiet Flows the Don,*' instead I was wounded again on the retreat from the Don to Donez and ended up at home in a military hospital.

Now the usual questions. How did I get from the regular Army to the department of counter intelligence? Where was my Russian posting with the intelligence corps? Nowhere, as I was posted to Tilsit which was still German then, but now of course is Russian.

We could go on forever in this pointless discussion but I am not prepared to give an inch and when I was posted there a major retreat was already in progress and now Russians were employed to spy on their own countrymen.

Germany was falling to bits and most people were too busy trying to save their own skins than to think of espionage in the Russian field. What would have been the point?

The Captain is still trying to persuade me to join a political retraining school. He dreams of all the things I could achieve in the name of Marx, Lenin and Stalin once repatriated. The participants in those training schools have to give an oath of loyalty to Stalin and communism and a promise to devote their future life in the spreading of the Communist "truth."

Because I have already had my calling I could not break the promise to the church and God and still live with an easy conscience. Sigi assures me of his continued goodwill in spite of my questionable military career since the beginning of 1943. Many of my, in Russian eyes, unforgivable deeds could disappear and be forgiven should I put my name down for a political training course.

He warns me never to forget where I am at present and in whose power; he was giving me another chance before he sends off his report to Moscow. Again I have to tell him that there were certain things I could not do. I could not sell my soul for a possible ticket home. I also needed further hospital treatment; there was a hospital attached to the training school in Moscow, though that did away with that side of my argument!

Fighting windmills is the way the Captain describes my refusal and with that the night's interview was over.

October starts to bring us the first taste of the Russian winter. Heavy frost at night and much colder days.

One day Maria tells me I am to be prepared for a transfer to a specialist hospital for plennies. On the same transport will be the other two PoWs who had not been included in the last transport.

I am badly frightened by the news and all sorts of possibilities go through my mind.

Before I even have time to come to terms with yet another change of camp my Russian escort appears.

"Dawai, Dawai. Fritz."

Maria and the orderly help to get me dressed. Wilfried comes to say goodbye and off I go without a chance to say my farewells to Maria and before we know what's happening we are off to new horizons.

Ah well. Nitschewo!

A quick check at the last gate to make sure they have the right bodies and that's it for this camp.

Roll on the new place.

PART FOUR

1

**A Camp Hospital
Near Moscow
1948**

At this stage of my life a move of all my worldly goods is easily accomplished – everything fits into my backpack.

Our open truck drives at breakneck speed towards Moscow, no doubt the driver hopes to gain a couple of hours, time for a nice walk about in the metropolis.

My companion from Vienna is fast asleep through this hellish drive, he must have nerves of steel. Before long I get concerned it's not normal sleep. He must have taken something, as he looks totally out of it. He gets checked over by the doctor and we resume our speedy drive to whatever hospital we are aiming for. If he survives it will be a miracle.

After about three hours of lunatic driving we reach the outskirts of Moscow. The closer we get, the more excited the Russian escort gets. He changes out of his scruffy gear into a new clean uniform topped off by a pair of beautiful shiny boots.

We don't think he has seen soap or water for weeks – the stench from his feet is overpowering. As we are driving along busy roads one of our escort and one of the drivers leave us in order to check out the delights of the big city, while we park up for a rest.

Our man from Vienna remains the same. His laboured breathing continues and we make sure he is kept as warm as possible. We park near a street and before the other two men left us they bought a loaf of bread and a sausage and some beer. The remaining escort had some of the food and drink and then passed it to us plennies. When the semi-conscious man doesn't accept his offer he is most surprised – ah well, more for him!

People pass by and stare at us, they usually only see 'fritzes' from a distance.

One old lady in particular smiles at us as we are parked on the roadside. She returns after a quick discussion with our guard and hands over a pot of freshly boiled potatoes. Her son had been a prisoner in Germany and knew what conditions were like for a PoW.

The potatoes were turned into an upturned hat. Together with this she gave us some pickled gherkins. Luckily her son had been treated well whilst being a prisoner. On top of that a jug of well sweetened tea arrived to round off our meal.

The Russians are highly amused to see us eating the boiled potatoes without peeling them first.

"Nix cultura" they comment.

A small group of people has gathered round us and I see a Russian war wounded man push his way through to the truck. This could become nasty so we keep very quiet but he addresses us as comrades in passable German and tells us about his time as a PoW in a German field hospital. His medical treatment had been very good and the German doctors saved his life, and he was back home now.

When I ask him why he isn't fitted with an artificial leg he points out that without the artificial leg he is entitled to an Army pension, with it he would have to work.

I suppose that's one way of looking at life, anyway his wife goes out to work so everything is in order.

Everybody is getting quite chatty, cigarettes are handed round and we all have a good supply and we thank the old lady for our food and tea.

Before long we can hear singing and yelling coming towards us, the two city visitors quite obviously only got as far as the nearest inn and spent all their money there. They look the worse for wear especially the man with the nice shiny boots. He swears non-stop till he has removed them and we are once more exposed to his smelly dirty feet.

The remaining guard takes a dim view of the returning escorts behaviour but once they present him with a bottle of vodka he takes it in good spirits, after first savouring the smell of the alcohol, he takes a sizeable drink, then wipes the top and passes it on to me. I don't take such a big gulp but the stuff burns like fire.

We must get on our way which is easier said than done. All the guards, orderlies and the driver are drunk to a degree. The one remaining semi-sober guard hands me his pistol and pushes the drunk driver away from the wheel and starts the truck. Luckily the motor starts and we are off with our load of drunk guards, the semi-conscious plennie and the other bemused patients.

Before long I see the barbed wire enclosed building and barracks. We stop a few yards in front of the Budka. The Sergeant on duty shakes his head in amazement at the unusual delivery to his camp.

He allows us to pass, first having taken the necessary papers from the guard who was driving.

As it was dusk the artificial lights came on suddenly and bathed everything in the glaring light. Over the big gate flutters a Red Cross flag – this will be our home for a while now.

A group of about 50 plennies line up in front of the hospital, after a few clear commands we are welcomed by the song *'The Blue Dragoons'*.

They march past our lorry and wave to us. These are not ordinary plennies, their clothes are in good condition which tells us they are activists. Near the entrance to the hospital they stand easy then enter the brick building next to the hospital.

Suddenly I remember Sigi Kirschbaum. So, he has transferred me to the hospital cum training school after all. So far I mean to keep my own counsel and wait and see what happens.

A whole row of Russian women doctors and nurses are there to receive us. One tall blonde woman seems to be in charge. The look on her face when she saw the motley crew within the truck was priceless. A German plennie also well dressed, introduces himself as Herman Vogel, Starski of the hospital.

The doctor in charge climbs onto the truck to see her new patients. They expected us at lunchtime and were beginning to worry what had happened to us. The sleeping driver, orderly and guards told their own story. First the semi-conscious man gets carried into the hospital, then I get carried in after returning the pistol to the original owner.

The usual procedure follows. A warm bath and a set of new clothes are issued. All my possessions are checked over and taken away to be returned to me once I have been allocated a bed. I just managed to keep my pocket-knife, my ring, my purse and spoon.

I get transferred to the second floor, Room 5, which is under the care of Dr Weigert.

My room has four beds and two of them are occupied. My bed is close to the window and will give me a chance to see some of the camp tomorrow when it is light.

The Starski comments on the size of my case history, it will save a lot of time for the examining doctor to find it already documented.

The other two occupants are officers too. One is a Luftwaffe Captain a Von Lewandowsky, the other one is a neurologist Dr Schmolk. The Air Force man suffers from a colon infection, the doctor from a neurological condition.

The airman is the more lively of the two and before we know it, we discuss our favourite subject – food.

I am quite comfortable in my bed, I have two blankets and the mattress is still good and the central heating is situated right under the window so I shall not be cold either.

Soon I have the necessary information about the hospital. They don't have a German surgeon, so a Russian doctor covers this field and her assistant is Dr Weigert.

Just as I was about to doze off the Starski arrives with my number for my clothes. Realizing that I am an officer has changed his attitude a little, he has reverted to the more formal address of 'Sie' which suits me for the time being. I have to get to know him better before reverting to the more personal 'Du'.

We get soup made from beetroot and I like the taste, it is different, whether I will like it in four weeks time remains to be seen. I get my tablets and sign off for the day, tomorrow is another day.

The morning starts with a major clean-up. The doctor in charge must be doing her rounds and before long we hear the sound of many voices.

"Room five, three officers," the Starski announces and the lady doctor only spends a few minutes with the other two patients and then it's my turn. She introduces me to Dr Weigert who is carrying my case history. He flips through the pages and looks relieved when he reads Dr Kilian's name.

He explains that Dr Kilian is a renowned specialist in the field of neurology and apart from that he has found the stamp and signature of a Russian senior doctor, so the case history can be taken as read.

How to treat me now? Massage, infra-red therapy, strict bed rest, that's it for the time being. The usual checks are made and found to be corresponding to the same as on previous occasions. With that the whole medical swarm leaves.

The door has hardly closed when the two orderlies arrive to re-polish the floor.

The youngest doctor of the group, nicknamed 'the Pony' because of the sound of her high-heels comes and visits in the afternoon to make her own notes.

On my first evening a runner appears to inform me that I am required to visit Captain Semjonow on the third floor. I get carried up and arrive at a thickly padded door.

When I knock and enter I find a room typical for all MWD officers. A desk, two chairs and a table for paperwork. A bright light hits the visitor. In the shadow of the light I see a man of middle years and next to him a translator.

We go through the usual personal details and after that he turns the light sideways off my face.

When asked why I am here I tell him that I presume I am here to be made totally well again. He agrees with that, but also says as I had suspected that Capt Kirschbaum had put forward my name for the political school. There is plenty of time until the next course on December 2nd. I should be better by then and with that I am dismissed.

My two porters are surprised to see me return that quickly and helpfully take me back to my room-mates who welcome me back, but I can feel their suspicions. They are concerned that I am either an activist or worse, a spy and informer.

At their request I give them my history and tell them of the continued interest of Captain Kirschbaum and his idea of the political training.

Both retain their suspicions but gradually I notice a thawing in their attitude and eventually they seem to take my word as genuine;

they tell me that I will be put under a lot of pressure to attend the course. The mood in our room stays cool and introvert and in my thoughts I am with Sepp Pszybilla as well as Sigi Kirschbaum, both have been trying to persuade me to attend the dreaded course.

That it would simply be an impossibility for me to sign an act of total loyalty to a totally alien philosophy would be immoral as well as disloyal to my first responsibility, the Lutheran Church, my family and least but not last, to God.

I am damned if I do and damned if I don't.

I could quickly allay my room-mates mistrust, but I cannot tell them of my real reason for my present state. It would be too dangerous all round.

The next few days and weeks pass without any major incidents, my infra-red treatment is undertaken by a very chatty orderly from Upper Silesia.

Then my treatment gets taken over by an elderly Russian doctor who has seen better days. She finds all this very confusing, on top of her medical duties she has to attend a political training course and spends most of her time trying to learn communist tracts word for word. I am tempted to ask her if she understands it all. After the infra-red treatment I get taken back to my room.

From my window I can observe the rest of the camp. I see plennies leaving in the morning and returning at night, exhausted, tired and weary, but I also see the activists' busy going through the camp. They are better dressed, much better fed and very much disliked by the other plennies.

I cannot possibly sell my soul by becoming one of them and attend the political school.

Even if I did not sign anything (which is nigh impossible) as Sigi K suggested, it is just not going to happen.

Another patient gets allocated to our room. A Captain who has been in the Stalingrad division. As he is carried in we can see both his legs are missing. And his name is Horst Zimmerman a minesweeper Captain.

He too has been part of the intelligence corps and so a ready victim for the MWD. He was told his position would vastly improve if he agreed to attend the school. One day he was presented with a signed document which accused him of having trained Russians as agents, so he really has no option. He volunteered to attend the course. When the course is over he was expected to sign several documents and give an oath of loyalty to Soviet Russia.

When he refused he was instantly transferred to the Don valley with two years hard labour. An out of control rolling wagon took both his legs off.

From my window I can see the plennie cemetery, it has nothing which makes it look like a resting place. Just a dumping ground for the poor souls they couldn't put back together again.

One day I am witness to one of those burials. Four plennies try all morning to dig a decent grave. Once they have hacked through 50cm of frozen earth they reach sand. Then they collect the body. Without much ceremony the poor dead man is dumped in the hole, not even a hint of a prayer, nothing. Quickly he gets buried with sand and soil and soon a little mound takes shape, but that's absolutely it.

No cross, no nameplate, just a stake with a number on it. What a way to end a life. I hope what preceded it was better than the lonely end.

Once more the rumour of a transport takes place. 1000 men this time inclusive of hospital inmates. The Pony arrives full of smiles.

"Zimmerman and Schmitt, you go transport."

She gets really cross when we don't show the expected delight. 100 men from the hospital are part of the selection, we are getting our travel clothes and one after the other we are lifted onto trolleys. We are carried downstairs and I am almost beginning to hope. The senior doctor stands at the main door but next to her is Captain Semjonow with his list.

Both Horst Zimmerman and I get sent back.

2

When we return to our room, one good thing has come out of it. We now trust each other implicitly and I also realize another thing. The Russians don't consider a person's degree of invalidity. What is a one-sided limp compared to a man with no legs?

Home which was almost within reach a few minutes ago has once more disappeared in the foggy distance.

Now I have to concentrate on a much closer threat. How do I avoid the training course?

On my way to the loo one day I get talking to a plennie. As we watch through the window a new group of course participants turn up for their day.

"Must be nice," he muses. "Decent clothes, better food and preferential treatment for the next transport home."

"But at a price," I add.

However he thinks signing papers and making promises doesn't tie anyone down if done under duress.

He remembers having to give his oath to Hitler seven times and look what happened to that?

I want to stay as I am, but that doesn't get me one step nearer home. My new acquaintance is called Heinz Kuhnert. He of course is an activist which gives him an easier life, but also makes it possible to help some of his fellow plennies.

His work is in the hospital and once a month he has to give an educational talk which no one listens to, but who cares?

His real responsibility is in checking any outgoing mail. Together with a translator he has to go through all our mail. He offers to send one of my letters without it being censored. I just can't believe that this is a real possibility. My room-mates are regular correspondents, if Zimmerman and I need writing material he offers to supply it.

I mention this exciting offer to Von Lewandowsky our Luftwaffe man.

"Flash jack," he grins and says. "Ah, you have met flash jack."

Yes, it is possible through *flash jack* who steals the writing material from Anjuscha the translator. Otherwise there is always the night nurse who will buy the necessary things in Moscow for roubles.

We are both excited at the thought of being able to write a straight letter home, instead of a few words on the back of a card.

However, we both know to write nothing incriminating. In Russia it is paranoia that keeps you alive. I am just writing to Charlotte my wife, and once more I remind her of our holiday in 1939. I was as fit as a fiddle and no doubt she is concerned by the contact she has had from some of the returning plennies.

Before I have finished an orderly comes to collect me for an audience with the MWD Captain, Semjonow.

Without much ado he swings me on his back and carries me to the lower floor.

For once the Captain's face is wreathed in smiles, in a way he looks more frightening! In front of him are three packets, not little packages. He comments on all my friends in the west who send me these riches. One is from the Lutheran Church, one from the Workers Social Aid and one from my wife. We go through the familiar process of checking the contents and signing a receipt for each one.

My beast of burden gets a sizeable piece of chocolate and a piece of sausage for transporting me to and fro.

Then it is party time! Von Lewandowsky organizes the hot-plate from the night nurse, and the four of us celebrate right through the night.

Next morning I finish my letter and indicate all our heartfelt thanks for the parcels.

During my next massage Krawzyk the masseur tells me that Captain Baecker will be his next patient. The old lady doctor does not speak a word of German, but caution is advised. This man he says, was a big cheese in the National Committee and then a top functionary in the anti-fascist training course (usually referred to as the Antifa).

When I get moved to the therapy room I get joined by Baecker, he quite obviously wanted to talk but the treatment area did not seem a safe place to him. I suggested that he should visit me in my room, but he feared the airman would throw him out.

We finally agree on a meeting in the top floor thirty minutes after lunch, when the doctors are having their rest period.

He is a patient in the surgical ward. Two thirds of his stomach had to be removed. That's why he looks like a skeleton. Even in my worst time I did not look as bad as that. His skin tone is yellow and his eyes are unsteady and watery. I am curious what he wants to talk about.

When I get back to my room I decide to tell my room-mates about Baecker's approach. I want to keep a good atmosphere in our room. The airman understands that I have to accept this man's plea for a talk but advised absolute caution.

Baecker somehow fell from grace and as rumour has it, is doing his utmost to get back into Semjonow's good books; maybe he has been sent to soften me up in regards to the Antifa school.

A little after lunch I get one of the messengers to carry me to our rendezvous point. We are in a corner and no one can overhear our conversation.

Baecker offers me a cigarette and comments on my latest misfortune with the last transport and I tell him that's my third time. I am almost getting used to it.

The doctor in charge has spoken to him about me, for some reason she is keeping her protective hand over me.

I agree that it is something good to know, but the last word will always rest with Semjonow.

Baecker suggests he might be able to help me, but I tell him his price might be too high. Now I am intrigued. How would he benefit from helping me?

He wants me to be an intermediary with his family. Everyone knows his sellout reputation and hates him for it, but my good reputation and my profession within the church makes me standout as an honest man.

He freely admits that he has met the German communist big shots like Pieck, Ulbricht and Plivier. He was a tutor at the Political Academy in Moscow, so the other plennies mistrust is fully justified.

He is also considered guilty of betraying his comrades (an untruth according to him). He had to move out of the officers' quarters and is now living in a room with other ranks.

Nobody there ever spoke to him, his removal from the officers' quarters was preceded by a hunger strike by all the officers. To avoid any involvement by the MWD he was moved by the Chief Surgeon.

He has never been just a plennie, he has always lived in comparative comfort and signed many papers without realizing that he had condemned many of the plennies to work totally impossible inhuman quotas, which have cost lots of lives.

On a much broader scale it was people like him who signed, in the name of Germany, that infamous treaty to cede East Prussia to Russia and to set the border at the Oder-Neisse river. So it's no wonder, no one wants to have anything to do with him now.

He assures me that until just recently he had no idea how plennies existed, but these facts he only knew from hearsay, not real experience.

He was taken prisoner after the fall of Stalingrad. From 900 officers taken prisoner, there are only 300 alive today.

He still finds this hard to believe as Ulbricht, Pieck and General Seydlitz had assured everyone that the prisoners' treatment would be 'humane'. Maybe their definition of humane is slightly different from that in the dictionary.

Only now Baecker is finding out what being a plennie means. But I still don't know what he wants from me. He tells me he has had it from a reliable source that I will be on the next transport and would I contact his wife for him and try to persuade her to act for him through Ulbricht? He is now part of the East German government.

I wish his sources were correct, but I do not believe in my speedy repatriation. This may be so he says, but I should still reach home before he does.

I still have to find out why he is in Russia's black books. I am not surprised that he was actively involved in recruitment of Russians for counter espionage in Stalingrad.

When he was captured in Stalingrad and showed his willingness to swap paymasters he was given to understand that he would get an influential position in the rebuilding of the German economy; he was only to hold his tutoring post for a few months before being repatriated to his new post.

Such optimism.

Hadn't he worked out that the Russians are users of people, their own as well as anyone else's within their reach. A promise given even in writing means nothing, if it is no longer deemed useful.

I want him to keep his thoughts very much to himself regarding his past, he should really find out what it means to be a plennie.

Any plennie would consider it a 'deed of honour' to tell the Russians of his change of heart and the rest of his comrades would approve it.

It still doesn't explain his loss of favour with our masters.

The name 'Plivier' should have given me a clue. Baecker was one of his circle of friends and when Plivier escaped from East Germany to the west all his friends were in the soup.

Baecker had developed stomach problems, in other words he had outlived his usefulness and was unceremoniously dumped into the nearest PoW camp. From there he was transferred to this hospital and the only thing the MWD are interested in now is his time with the intelligence corps.

I remind him that part of his job as a tutor had been the assessment of his German PoW pupils. He assures me that he had been as lenient as possible, but I just don't believe him.

The Russians do not do lenient.

I just hope he never comes across one of his former students. He still doesn't understand that he ever did anything wrong. He was a committed communist and that makes everything right. Any sacrifice was worth it, especially if someone else was the sacrificial lamb.

This group of idealists, or traitors depending where you were, also produced a newspaper called *'Free Germany'*. He told me that they couldn't print all the articles sent to them – there were too many to choose from. It included reports from General Von Lenski, who said the Russians were entitled to annex East Prussia for historical reasons. Another article from General Meuller who couldn't do enough to prove his communist convictions. He still recalls a typical German Corporal walking past Gen Meuller and giving him a resounding slap on his rear-end and saying 'how are you doing my old mate. Oops sorry, comrade,' and all the General could do was give a forced smile. Just imagine that happening five years ago, he recalled how quickly some of these Germans change their allegiance. Ardent Hitlerites one day, and all for Papa Stalin the next.

Some of them even complained if their ardent communist outpourings had been watered down a bit. Of course, there had been many Generals whose behaviour and loyalty to their troops had been beyond reproach, but it's the others Baecker remembers. He is firmly convinced that these traitors will never make it in the new Germany, should they ever be repatriated.

I have my own thoughts, fat in soup and badness among people always floats to the top!

Some of these Generals misjudged their troops, usually the General comes straight after God in the common soldier's mind, but some of them pushed the borders of decency beyond what was acceptable.

These Generals of the changeable persuasion will, once home, get a pension from the state which will make a widow's pension, for herself and three children look like pocket money in comparison.

Of course they will recant everything and claim to have done everything under duress.

I have to laugh at his optimism and faith in the right thinking German people, nothing will happen to these men. They will have their reunions, smoke their fat cigars and laugh at the childishness of the Russians.

To get back to himself, Baecker is convinced the only way out of Russia for him is with the help of his East German connections; his wife has a flat registered to her in East Berlin, but spends most of her time in Luebeck with friends.

Again I am surprised he trusts me so totally when he doesn't know me at all, but he says he has everything to gain and nothing to lose. Poor deluded man – he should take a trip up north then he would realize how much he has to lose.

I intend to keep our meeting to a minimum as I do not want to be tarnished by this contact, with the other plennies. He gives me his wife's address in Luebeck and when I ask him how he knows that my family lives in the "golden west" I gather that word of my three parcels have done the rounds. I do promise to contact his wife should I be fortunate to be on the next transport.

When I return to my room I can quickly see how much the airman and the doctor disapprove of me seeing Baecker. I tell them I was obliged to listen to him and I felt he had been misguided rather than genuinely evil.

Dr Schmolk tells me he couldn't bring himself to even shake hands with such a man. I tell him it's easy to wash one's hands after a handshake, but that I have to consider poor Baecker's struggle with his conscience, when you weigh it all up he is a betrayed traitor.

Horst Zimmerman has a more objective view of Baecker. He tries to do him justice, his own ill-fate has made him much more tolerant towards others.

Christmas is once more approaching and rumours of another transport are again rife. The thought of home brightens everyone's life. Hope is ever present. There is a festive mood everywhere because everyone's thoughts are on the usual question. 'Will it be me this time?'

For a personal treat I receive a four page letter from my wife through the kind help of Heinz Kuhnert. This is the first long letter I have had since Christmas 1944 and its all good news, they are all well and waiting for me.

The Pony visits us regularly, she intends to discharge me to the camp as a semi-invalid but I have to avoid that at any price, because once I am considered a regular plennie I will have run out of my main valid excuse of not attending the Antifa course.

The next time I hear the approach of her clicking heels I hold my breath and I am on the point of suffocating as she enters the room. Contrary to her usual custom she comes straight to my bed. Her hands shake as she uses the stethoscope, I must be a lovely shade of blue.

She disappears and returns with the medical chief Dr Elisabetha who prescribes four weeks of strict bed rest. Another four weeks before they even think of my transfer out of the hospital.

Schmitt and Zimmerman's names are on the new transport list, we both hope of course, but our fears are soon realized – we are not going.

We owe it to Dr Elisabetha that we are not being dragged down to the main gate, only to be sent back by Semjonow, and all that on Christmas Eve.

Her bad news was made easier by the news there was a parcel for each of us from Germany.

It's amazing that I can get over my disappointment by the mere arrival of a parcel from home. I must have developed a really strong protective shell. Dr Elisabetha comes personally to tell us that being taken off the transport is none of her doing, a stronger hand then hers pulled the strings.

Towards evening Anjuscha the interpreter arrives with the activist to hand over our parcels. Even Semjonow cannot call me to his office this time as the doctor's word overrides his.

Dr Schmolk gets transferred out of the hospital, so Semjonow got his way – to ruin whatever festive spirit survived within our party of four.

3

1949

The January transport has gone, but I now receive regular letters from home, I find out about their flight from Silesia.

My family were taken to Pilsen where they spent four weeks in the most primitive conditions, from there they were taken to Amberg in Bavaria.

Initially they were dumped by the roadside and much shouted at and vilified by the locals. All good clean living Catholics on their way home from church.

Rumours once more abound. Von Lewandowsky our Luftwaffe pilot has heard that the whole barracks is to be cleared of plennies who are of no special interest to the MWD.

The camp is already overcrowded but the MWD had cleared a whole barrack dividing it into small rooms - they mean cells, with a central passage running the whole length of the building. When we find out that this particular building is now surrounded by barbed wire we speculate that they might be transferring women here.

A lot of nurses and other female members of the forces fell into Russian hands. So far we have no facts, plenty of rumours though.

In the middle of February I have another in-depth medical examination by Dr Elisabetha. I am relieved to find out through the interpreter that I am to stay in hospital for the time being and massage and heat treatment are to begin again. She reminds me that I have to stay clear of any major excitement and disturbances as she cannot be responsible for any consequences. *Tell that to Semjonow*, I thought.

I get carried to and from my treatment. The masseur Krawzyk is glad to see me again as is the elderly doctor. She very much approves of my Russian studies, but I'd prefer if this knowledge stayed here.

I am sure Semjonow wouldn't believe me if I were to tell him that my medical progress is strictly due to more recent efforts – the good lady however enjoys her role as a teacher as she becomes a living dictionary.

Every item in the room gets translated and I have to repeat it again and again till she thinks I have got it. Occasionally I tease her, I ask her what one of Semjonow's favourite expressions means. She blushes furiously and after a bit of thought she tells me it means that he is not happy and expresses it in this way.

I feel quite ashamed to have tricked her this way and it is also the end of today's lesson. She is back to learning her communist tract word for word for her next lesson – her way of telling me I behaved badly.

On my way back to my room we come across Baecker, but today I want peace and quiet so I am prepared to meet up with him the following day.

To keep peace with my room-mates I tell them of my planned meeting. Once more the pilot warns me - a communist sympathiser is always a communist – rarely does a leopard change its spots. Baecker couldn't do that in public it would cost him dearly.

He does seem to genuinely regret his involvement in the Russian anti-German activities. I wouldn't like to be in his shoes, his conscience must weigh heavily on his mind. With no one speaking to him, his life is a very lonely one.

The airman had been in a similar position, but unlike Baecker he refused to co-operate and had spent time in prison and punishment camps, and has scars to show for his refusal to join the easy road. He must have a very strong character.

That's why I am prepared to take his advice as to my behaviour in my dealings with Captain Baecker.

I take my time in keeping my appointment – I do not want to appear too eager. He was relieved to see me as he suspected I had thought better of it.

Before I agree to any further discussions I want a few questions answered and in detail.

He describes his life. He was a farmer and lawyer. The farm he acquired as a gift with his Nazi membership and he became active as an examiner of agricultural premises. So he lived the good life in the Third Reich. At the same time he was appointed supervisor to a large

Jewish business. He claims to have transferred money for Jewish owners, but he would say that now!

He had been a social climber very much egged on by his wife who saw herself as one of the upper-class, while he came from an ordinary working-class background, but his wife came from a military family.

He claimed to have actively helped Jewish families until a colleague betrayed him.

He had no choice – either to go in front of a people's court with the predictable result (concentration camp) or join the Army as a volunteer.

His wife was horrified when he had his first home leave and turned up as a mere Private. That did not fit her social status plans at all. As she had also been party to all his illicit actions she couldn't even get a divorce if she wanted.

Every letter from home was dripping with accusations and ill will. She was quite happy to live off the fruits of his actions. I tried to stem his confessions by saying that he couldn't possibly blame all his actions on his ambitious wife.

Even the decorations he received once he joined the army didn't pacify her, so he volunteered for the Russian front, a long way from home and his wife.

When Baecker had first met his wife his own star was already rising in the Nazi Party and she saw him as a good partner regardless of his working-class roots.

He tried to get straight to the year 1943 when he was taken prisoner but I wanted to hear more about his time before that.

He had been promoted as an ordinance officer and posted to a division, achieved through his wife's connections. He acquired medals, and citations came aplenty and he was right at the source.

Then came Stalingrad. Against my better judgement I can feel a small amount of sympathy for this man, but I am so glad we lost the war, if he is an example of what could have been our New Germany! The Thousand Year Reich.

He complains bitterly about their continued mistrust and rejection he encounters from other plennies.

He really is caught between a rock and a hard place. Whatever he says is wrong.

If he complains about the Nazis, he was an active member. If he calls the Communists for their misdeeds, well he worked for them too!

When Baecker attended the Antifa course he had to give a detailed life history, no holds barred. He felt it was absolutely amazing to hear some of the true life confessions.

In spite of all this he could still not see that he is in the wrong, he feels everyone is entitled to do whatever it takes to save their own skin regardless of the cost.

When he had to give his life history at the Antifa course he had admitted to membership of the NSDAP (National German Socialist Workers Party) and working in the intelligence corps.

That's as far as we get with our talk for the day.

Enough for me to think on. Baecker looks much relieved as we part company.

On my return to my room, my friend the airman comments sarcastically

"The moral ablutions must be tiring, you look worn out."

Lewandowsky remembers, when forced to attend the Antifa course, the way some were perfectly happy to air the dirty private and political linen in public, some just don't seem able to stop once they have shed their first inhibitions.

It is amazing how much incriminating information you part with once you have a receptive audience.

As Von L had been captured early in 1942 there had been no punishment and special camps for plennies then. They all ended up in the regular camps, he was under the impression their name and number were all that was required.

He soon found out to the contrary and after ten days isolation with standing room only and no food, any man would talk.

Lewandowsky admitted he then told the Russians he had flown for Lufthansa in the Spanish Civil War – that was perfect for the inquisitors. They had him there and made a real meal out of it. Even the most intensive interrogation and duress to persuade him to join the Free Germany Group failed, instead Von landed up in hospital as a consequence of his discussions with the MWD.

I felt that just because of his own experiences he should be more tolerant towards the likes of Baecker. We both decided that politics is a filthy business and we will keep clear of it.

Neither of us think there have been dramatic changes in the new Germany, East or West. The slogans changed but their unwritten rule is – 'I am aboard jack, pull up the ladder.'

Zimmerman had listened to our discussion with great interest, he still believes there is a decent well-intended group amongst all politicians. There are idealists hidden away in the back benches everywhere. Usually people who don't need other's goods and chattles as they were wealthy already and often born and brought up to govern.

That was one of the reasons the Russians did away with the old 'Prussia.' They were honest solid citizens not *for sale*.

It takes me all my time to win over the old lady doctor as she still has not forgiven my swear word. In my best Russian I ask her to forgive me, I really didn't mean to insult her. Instead of forgiving me she nearly collapses with laughter. She wouldn't tell me what I said wrong but 'nitschewo' and the ice is broken and we are back on friendly terms.

She even promises to obtain a simple Russian book. The dictionary is more difficult to obtain for me, as it would be looked upon as favouritism towards a PoW.

When I suggest a book by Dostojewsky she said that would be difficult. Somehow the writer is hard to find at present, others could be more easily obtained.

She tried to explain why Dostojewsky is not on everyone's reading list, she tells me that he describes conditions in the prison at the Tzar's time too well and little has changed. That kind of reading matter is considered undesirable at present and with that she turns away, she is probably scared she has said too much.

When I return from my treatment I find we have a new patient: Hartmut Kraft. He looks semi-conscious, desperately thin and yellow.

When Dr Elisabetha comes to examine him I see tears in her eyes, that poor man is only skin and bone. She treats him very gently and strokes his face with a motherly touch – the man is at death's door.

We feel the presence of the Grim Reaper in our room. Dr Elisabetha requests morphine injections to ease his journey to the other side.

That evening Hartmut wakes for the first time and the airman runs off to get one of the doctors. The Pony gives him another injection and once more he drifts off into sleep – he is so young, only 24.

I find out from our helpful activist he was a member of the SS and has been transferred to us from the Lubjanka. This is why Baecker should be present. He would see the result of his handiwork, it would cure him of communism for life.

The nurses take good care of the young man, he can only absorb very little but whatever he needs is available to him. Sadly he vomits most of the food. His poor body shakes with the effort.

He has been with us for a few days now, but so far he has not said a word.

Today I have another meeting with Baecker, I managed to put it off for a couple of days. I have also had another parcel from home and a letter from my wife.

I tell the old doctor my wife sends her good wishes. How is that possible with only 25 words?

'Sometimes the censors are generous and don't count the individual words,' she says. Then I tell her I have a little gift especially for her in my latest parcel, with that I hand her a small bar of chocolate. I hope she will accept it and I see how her sad prematurely aged face changes and big tears run down her face.

"Oh Schmitt, don't make a joke of an old woman's misery."

It's years since somebody thought of her. She just exists on the line, always worried in case she offends her new masters.

Always lonely and here I come, a plennie who has even less than she has and I do her a kindness. With almost a look of reverence she touches the chocolate. I feel really embarrassed to have caused such an outpouring of emotions with my gift. It once more proves that old saying. It is better to give than to receive.

I prepare to see Baecker. He is not someone I like, there is something about him I find difficult to accept. He finds himself in such an awful position that I feel I must at least listen to him. I am really the only person apart from Semjonow who he speaks to.

He had never acted independently, he was always a creation of other people's ambition. First his wife, then Plivier and I think he was more scared of his wife – she knew everything about him. Which Jews he had helped, but also the families he refused to help.

She seems to have created a monster which eventually ran amok and in the end was hoisted by his own petard, but however much he may hate her he will now do anything to get back to her, at any price.

The power he had was like a heady poison. He remembered the time when he was of the 'lower order' always depending on someone else's whim. Now it had been his turn both with the Nazis and then the Russians and had Plivier not taken refuge in the west, his calculations would have been just right!

Here too he would have been in a position of power, but alas, there is always that little bit of something which ruins so often the best laid plans of mice and men.

He expects me not only to write to his wife, but also to persuade her to visit some influential people on his behalf as they own a flat in East Berlin and also in Luebeck. They really had planned for all eventualities!

In 1943 he could see the Nazi star was waning and he did everything to ensure a successful *come back* once the Germany of the Nazi persuasion had ceased to exist.

He had no illusions as to the division by the allies. Things got a bit complicated but he had put his money on the rising of the Communist star in East Germany. As he was on the point of giving me further insight of his mixed up life one of my room-mates came tearing up the stairs to get a doctor.

Our young SS man was on his last breath. The Pony arrived with an injection at the ready.

I noticed Baecker's expression, he had gone even paler and kept repeating "I didn't want that to happen".

On my questioning he admitted that he knew the youngster. He had stayed behind in 1945 to be trained as a professor for the Antifa course and there were a lot of German applicants for attendance. The men had to pass several levels of screening before they were deemed suitable.

One of those aspiring young communists was Hartmut Kraft.

He had hardly had time to test his SS knowledge and training, so he thought of hitching his ambitions onto the communist wagon.

When it was his turn for a full and total confession as repeatedly advised by Baecker, Kraft admitted being part of a liquidation commando of Russian Jews in Minsk.

Baecker had thought about persuading Kraft to withdraw his incriminating confession but it was already too late.

The powers that be let him finish the course and he passed with distinction and then he was arrested. This is the first time Baecker had come across him again, as a dying 24 year old victim of Russian in-depth interviewing and punishment.

Hearing about Kraft doesn't effect a feeling of guilt in Baecker. Almost the opposite, he is pushing all the blame on the Russians. They made him do it with promises of a quick release and an influential position in East Germany.

That he had made a pact with the devil only became obvious to him when he was admitted to hospital. His hard work for the party was totally ignored and he was judged by his membership of the intelligence corps and up to now he had not been arrested. It was just the treatment from the other plennies which he had to endure.

When I was just about to give him a detailed account of what being incarcerated in Russia meant the Pony arrived and chased me back to bed. Hanging about in corridors was bad for me!

I suggest to him he should come and say a prayer for Kraft. He decides against it. Wise man, the other two patients would beat him to a pulp.

My room-mates cannot understand why I waste my time listening to him and both are convinced that Semjonow knows about these meetings. I really do not know myself why I agreed to listen to him, it's just that somebody has to listen.

Young Kraft died quite suddenly unbeknown to any of us.

The cemetery is full of little hills, the last homestead for so many of the patients. Zimmerman who was close to death many times feels that it is his sheer bloody mindedness which keeps him alive. No way is he doing the Russians a favour by passing away quickly. He has no intention of ending up as a stick with a number on it.

All these men who died will be added to the big count of victims on both sides. I know on our side the Russian PoWs had a hard time.

They fell under the collective term 'Untermensch,' which meant they got the worst and least of everything.

Hartmut died with nothing to cling to, all his ideals and icons proved to be false and valueless.

We are standing at the window watching Hartmut's journey to his grave. A feeling of sorrow at this lad's death must have become known. The plennies remove their hats as does somewhat hesitantly the Russian guard and we hear the sound of the Lord's Prayer coming up and we join in. I bet young Hartmut Kraft never thought his life would end like that.

Before long we see the arrival of young firs and birches. The cemetery is beginning to look like one, not just a grey area full of large mole hills.

I turn down repeated requests via the masseur by Baecker to see him. I just cannot see him. My frame of mind is such that I would prefer to thump him rather than listen to any more of his self-pitying drivel.

The old lady doctor however treats me like her lost son. I do not think its just gratitude for a bar of chocolate. It was probably the first time someone thought of her as a human being.

Wouldn't it be a wonderful idea if people the world over were kind to each other regardless of race, creed or colour?

The old lady offers to give me daily lessons in Russian. I must talk more, which is the best practice. To increase my vocabulary she offers to lend me Tolstoy's *War and Peace*. It is not a regular book, but a school book and it has explanations in German and Russian. I thank her profusely.

When I return to my room I find Lewandowsky standing near the window with a face like thunder. He has found out our young man was beaten so badly in prison he was literally beyond repair. Here in the hospital he was under the special protection of the chief doctor. Should he ever have recovered she would have protected him from Semjonow.

I have to be very careful not to betray the actual person behind his deliverance to the Russians. If it would make him a happier man is doubtful, but should Lewandowsky ever find out I think little of Baecker's chances of survival.

I try to get him off this personal subject of hatred of an as yet to him, unknown person.

I point out to him that in Germany, once the Nazi's demise was an accomplished fact, the extent of revenge of the former oppressed towards their once powerful oppressors must have been terrible. I feel that until somebody stops this tit for tat all our lives will be destroyed.

The airman cannot accept my idea that humanity towards our neighbour would be a world-wide panacea.

What a change of reputation for the world-wide hatred of Germans it would be. Would they carry out the Lords commandment of *Love Thy Neighbour*?

He appreciates the ideology but lacks the faith, he is too disillusioned with life. He wants to know if I hate the Russians, but I have to say I don't.

They too are subject to a higher evil power which makes them act under duress. It's people like Ilya Ehrenburg who appealed to the most basic instincts of the Russian soldier with his propaganda leaflets.

Von L describes me as a fatalist. If I am prepared to endure the excesses of the MWD, what effect would my hatred achieve?

Quiet suffering is what marks the Russian people. It's the only way they tried to survive the ever present threat of the Tzaristic ruler and now the Communist equivalent.

For my own moral well-being I have to believe that God, our father, will be the victor one day. If I live to see it is another question all together.

Before God, 1000 years are but a day.

Von Lewandowsky now understands why I have such patience with Baecker and he too has been opening up and talking more than he normally does.

My Russian studies are progressing in leaps and bounds with my conscientious teacher.

4

My postal connections to home are still functioning well and I have a lot more details about my family. They seem to have got over the worst of being homeward bound and they are living in two rooms on a small farm. The children sleep in bunk beds, their food rations are increased through CARE parcels from America. A Jewish school friend of mine who had emigrated to the USA before the war managed to contact them and supplies them with regular parcels.

My two fellow patients also receive parcels from home, the mood seems to have lifted and I am getting used to being on the transport lists and being taken off again.

Zimmerman shares my fate and we are both proof of the saying that a worry shared is half the worry. I am still full of admiration for the persisting sense of humour Horst displays.

He is firmly convinced the Russians have something evil up their sleeves for any former intelligence corps members. He also feels that there is little they can do to him now.

One day he gets measured for his artificial legs, it's supposed to take four weeks to get them made and fitted. Horst has mixed feelings about this. All three of us are pessimistic about the trip home. Semjonow makes no attempt to hide his intense dislike of Lewandowsky who doesn't help the situation by greeting him with "How are you today your lordship?" It's obviously the hatred of the peasant for the nobility. Zimmerman does not make any effort to ease the strained relationship. He often simply ignores Semjonow's vicious baiting, which earned him three days arrest for ignoring a senior Russian officer.

However as there is no holding cell within the hospital, he is confined to his room and bed for three days, when he uses the commode instead of going to the toilet as normal this is against doctor's orders, so Semjonow had to rescind his punishment. That really did not help Lewandowsky's case, it just made Semjonow even angrier.

This is how we spend our days with summer halfway through, once more a transport is being prepared. Patients from other areas are being put up in the corridors ready for transport.

Both Horst Z and I are as usual on the list and get supplied with our travel clothes, but really have no realistic hope of going.

I ask if anyone is going to Bavaria amongst the returnees, to ask them to call on my wife as no notes are permitted, everything is confiscated at the last minute.

Tonight all the medical staff are in the hospital, there is a concert for all the plennies that are leaving us. I can vaguely hear the music but it doesn't really move me. I am staying.

In the morning the loading of the plennies begins and it's the sort of summer morning you can only see in Russia. The sun is not up yet a light grey sky is draped over the Moscow silhouette of church spires and houses. A fresh wind blows away the humidity of the night and brings a pleasant coolness. The lorries pull up in front of the hospital and all the patients are called by name to be taken down to the waiting lorries.

Suddenly from one lorry a wonderful clear and resonant baritone sings the famous song of the *'Linden tree next to my father's house.'* The melody and the words touch us all, especially those left behind, we are almost ashamed to show our emotions.

Elisabetha the chief medical officer enters the room and listens at the window, tears run down her face and she just touches me with her caring hand.

"One day, one day," she whispers as she leaves us.

I have long realized that my plan regarding the stroke has not had the desired effect of a quick ticket home. Especially with the red MWD stamp on my papers.

I have as yet not recovered much movement on my left side. Dr Weigert visits from time to time but has little to add, we talk about many things, rarely about my physical fitness or lack of it.

I feel I have put Baecker off long enough, my masseur Krawzyk tells me he has been asking for me. Apparently he is being seen quite frequently by the MWD, so I agree to see him today after lunch in the usual place.

When I see my Russian tutor, the old lady doctor, she looks very pleased with herself. She arranges the curtains round my treatment trolley and then produces a little white bread roll. I feel really touched and tell her how much I appreciate her gift. Secretly I feel that the plennies are often better fed than the Russian population, but she just strokes my hand and tells me that she knows that plennies are always hungry. She asks me to eat it there, as it could cause problems for her. She had tried to find something, but that was the best she could think of.

When I come across Baecker after lunch I am almost frightened by his appearance. He looks absolutely dreadful, he looks like a man who can see death waving at him. He is chain-smoking, where he gets his endless supply from is a mystery.

He does not seem to understand that he and he alone caused young Kraft's death. He too was under duress 'only following orders,' the age old excuse. I have a question of my own to ask him before I was prepared to listen to him. He was initially transferred to a dacha outside Moscow. There were other German officers there, but he was not allowed any contact with them.

All the Russians were interested in was his knowledge of the German economy and agriculture in the Third Reich. In July 1943 he was then transferred to Krasnogorsk where the original 'National Committee of Free Germany' was created. A lot of well known influential Germans were part of that group, including quite a few authors, Theodor Plivier amongst them. But it was a very precarious position according to Baecker, a careless word could cost you dearly. Not even the good food made up for that all prevailing fear. The aim of the group was to topple Hitler and to persuade the troops already in captivity to change their allegiance and help with the rebuilding of Germany under the "Hammer and Sickle".

This existence seemed preferable to the fate of an ordinary plennie in 1943. Everyone in Russia was on short rations so quite obviously the plennies suffered most. The Geneva Convention didn't get a look in, if the indigenous population were starving.

As far as he likes to think, conditions in the PoW camps were fine – conscience was never his strong point!

But as the Red army were more and more successful in their battles with Germany, the 'National Committees' main task was to re-educate German PoWs. Baecker's special task was to pick out and train camp leaders.

He claims not to know the effect of their reports and encouraging calls for higher production within the camp.

The already awful camps changed into hell-holes, one plennie denouncing another for a piece of bread or bowl of watery soup. The activists were beginning to be known as 'cashavists' (casha is a porridge type mash). The Russians didn't need to act the bad guys, the German committee did it for them.

When we get back to his own fate he still persists in his plan that I will contact his wife on my release. I try to remind him of his wife's character, does he really think she is the least bit interested in the return of a human wreck? But he insists he wants to die in Germany, it's really much cheaper here, but he is not amused.

Theo Plivier wrote an infamous article once he escaped to the west. 'My twelve years as an actor in Russia,' with the publication all the closely associated men fell from grace.

We are still deep in conversation when Semjonow suddenly turns up. Baecker turns even whiter and when asked why he had left the surgical ward he stutters that he felt the need to air his problems with another human being.

"Nix problem," shouts Semjonow. "Go back!"

I also achieve a quick getaway and once in my room I get one of the runners to fetch Krawzyk the masseur. Somehow I trust this man and know I am justified when he returns from Baecker's ward with the message that he still wants to continue our meetings. He wants to discuss the Confessional Church and German Christianity. Clever chap.

Baecker knew not to mention the real subject of our conversation. I knew it would cause problems for us both were it to become common knowledge. All I can really do for him is listen, I cannot offer forgiveness especially as he still feels justified in everything he did.

After a few days I get the predictable call to Semjonow's office. I am beginning to be able to climb the stairs with the orderly's help, being carried everywhere was getting to be a nuisance.

Before I am even properly in the room, the translator shouts at me.

"Why do you see Baecker?"

I explain that I met him in the treatment room, they want to know whether I have come across him before in Germany. They want to know exactly what we talked about, I am able to say that we so far have only discussed the position and development of the Lutheran Church in Germany. I have to weigh up every word, no way do I want Baecker to fall even deeper in the mire. I can tell them honestly that to the best of my knowledge he doesn't belong to any church. That seems to be the end of the Baecker questions.

Now once more I am asked about my decision to join in the Antifa course, as always the possibility of release home is added to by my attending their school. They need intelligent anti-fascism in Germany. I am quite ready to admit my anti-fascism frame of mind, but I am not ready to join in with their communist way of thinking.

Once more I tell them that I would not be able to commit myself in writing to perpetuate their teachings in Germany. What does a mere signature mean? The Russians could quite happily do without it, but the German tutors would feel they had to insist on it.

My obvious mistrust of the German teachers amuses Semjonow, he wants to know my reason for my mistrust. That's simple to do. Everyone should mistrust a traveller who has just got on the tram for his own good. Could I give him an example for that?

How was it possible for a former Silesian landowner to become overnight a backer of the Stalinist idea of land reform?

Again I am told they are only interested in a person who will genuinely act with the people for the people to create a new free Germany. I ask him once more to give me more time to consider the proposal. Again on my way out I am handed two parcels from home. One from my wife and one from the Lutheran Church. I had heard on the usual reliable grapevine that there had been a delivery of parcels. So Semjonow must have deliberately kept mine until we had our little chat.

We once more plan a prasnik in my room. I also intend to tell the others exactly what was said at my recent interrogation. The airman Lewandowsky decides to quickly go and tell Baecker about my questioning, much as he dislikes him he still wants to warn him.

He made it just in time. He met Baecker on the stairs as he was on his way to be interviewed. He was able to tell him what I had said to Semjonow, so I was reasonably safe for the time being anyway.

I know he cannot delay my decision for too long, it's now October and the course starts in December. Whatever I say is wrong for me. I have to try once more to use my state of health as an obstacle for non-attendance at the course.

After our meal I put my half empty tins between the double windows to keep them fresh for another meal.

5

October 1949

Next morning there is a lot of excitement all round. A commission of very high officers and officials are coming to visit the camp today. A big spring clean is the order of the day. Shortly after lunch several limousines drive into the camp.

The most senior officer is a Colonel. There is the usual excitement on the corridors – doctors, nurses and orderlies are rushing about. Our Ward Sister comes to check us over and finds everything in order.

"Attention!" can be heard getting closer and closer as we all stand to attention as best we can when the Colonel enters our room.

He is small built and very smart in appearance. He greets us correctly and asks if we have any complaints, he actually *asks* us, so Horst Zimmerman tells him we want to go home!

Not his responsibility he tells us. When he sees my tins of food he smells each one carefully and pulls a face.

"All Marshall Plan rubbish stinks!" and all his minions laugh obligingly.

When they leave, Zimmerman who is an expert in Russian insignia tells us that they were all administration people, no medical experts.

We find out later that the main interest in this inspection is directed towards the remodeled barrack. This cost more than the whole hospital. We are none the wiser as to the barrack's purpose.

Next day the orderly arrives with the Pony to try on Zimmerman's artificial legs. They get attached to his stumps with leather straps and bits of webbing. It's torture for us to see the anxious concentration and effort. He has one arm around the medic and one round the orderly and he is also covered in sweat. He knows that he will never walk again without crutches and the Pony promises to get a pair from Moscow. His stumps are burning like fire due to the friction. After a short supported walk from his bed to the window and back he collapses with the exertion, but with his usual sense of humour he compares it to trying to walk on stilts as a youngster.

The prostheses are very heavy which makes any movement doubly difficult.

In the evening our friendly activist pays us a visit, not only does he want to find out how Horst got on with his new legs, he wants to ask a special favour. He knows how much we all treasure our illicit letters from home. But could we all hand them over so he can destroy them safely in the incinerator.

The celebrations of the day of the Revolution are taking place shortly and before that a big general search will take place.

We would all be in trouble were those letters to be found and it would also be a sudden end to our more detailed postal link with home. We all part with our letters. So far I'd had eleven, they are a piece of home. The translator is our secret link to the local post office, so she would have incurred the wrath of the MWD for her humanitarian act.

All of us are very sad. Von Lewandowsky's wife works for a butcher so he knows she has enough to eat. He had only been married for six months. Horst Zimmerman's wife works as a cleaner for the occupying forces so she and her boys are reasonably secure.

We are allowed to keep our photos which is a consolation.

We survive the search without any problem and the big official party passes us by with just the usual fireworks and the drunken singing of the guards. Our poor activist has to give a speech about the blessing of the October Revolution for the Russian people! He has to do it twice. Once for the 1st floor and again for the 3rd floor. The German orderlies job is to break out into a 'spontaneous' cheer at prearranged points.

As we want to indirectly thank our activist for many past favours we assist in the clapping and cheering. Our orderly is a bit of a joker, so occasionally he cheers at the wrong bit of the speech, but it all takes place without any major incidents.

Moscow is covered by a thick cloud of smoke once the fireworks are over.

6

A few evenings later after lights out, Krawzyk the masseur pays us a surprise visit. He apologises for the late hour but it is very urgent.

Baecker has been taken away in handcuffs in a police van. Before he was taken away he sent his regards to me via one of the dormitory's plennies.

Apparently he had cried bitterly when he was taken away. Semjonow and the medical chief had been present.

To us it looks like a transfer to the Lubjanka. All three have at one time been guests in that infamous establishment.

At the back of our minds is the fear that he might admit to the contents of my discussion with him. All I can do is hope that he manages to keep schtum. After all, I am his last hope to get him out of the clutches of the MWD, or so he thinks.

Before long we have other things to talk about. We too are beginning to adopt the 'Nitschewo' frame of mind of our captors.

One day a lorry load of desks and chairs arrive at the hospital. All our rooms are to be fitted out with a new desk and a couple of chairs. So far we have no idea what's in store for us, so we carry on with our daily routine.

Horst Zimmerman, with the help of Lewandowsky and the orderly, persist with his daily walking attempts. He learns to balance his body weight differently to normal walking and now manages from his bed to the window and back successfully.

The highlight of his walks is an attempted trip to the toilet. It takes him half an hour and we are possibly just as pleased and exhausted as he is!

Horst is sweating profusely and his hands are shaking and he just about reaches his bed before he collapses. Both his stumps are red raw and the Pony promises to bring a piece of lint to ease the friction.

When Horst complains that his toes are very painful we get concerned. The orderly explains that the nerve endings at his stumps are causing the pain and the connection between his brain and toes is still functioning.

Lewandowsky is particularly patient with Zimmerman. He is usually very quiet but to distract Horst he tells stories of his time as a pilot.

He is a born storyteller and before long we are all laughing and Horst is more his usual self.

In the evening just before the work brigade returns to the camp a group of 100 MWD officers and 10 young women move towards the mysterious barracks, but before long they march out again.

The German camp leader is called and is severely taken to task, as to why there were no stoves in the redesigned barrack.

Next day it is rectified and the MWD return. Before long officers and their translators return and the interrogations start.

We are able to watch the proceedings from our windows, we are not surprised to see curtains being put up by the evening. The cross-examinations are not done in the usual manner. No beatings, no threats, just polite questions. How many chickens did you eat while in Russia? How many trees did you cut down for firewood? Such questions were the norm.

Our orderly keeps us informed through his various sources in the camp. The interrogations continue and everyone has to sign afterwards, but no further action has taken place so far.

November 1949

Towards the end of November, rumours abound regarding the closure of the Antifa school. The participants are all mentally preparing themselves for well set up positions either in East Germany or in another school in Russia.

The furniture gets collected along with the mountains of paperwork.

The day after the closure of the school brings a nasty surprise for all the hopeful course attendants and instructors. They all get transferred into the normal camp where only the next day they share the life and fate of an average plennie.

Work brigades which had been decreased due to the frequent transports were now back to full strength. Many of the high and mighty activists are back to being just a PoW stranded in Russia.

I personally am greatly relieved to find the threat of the Antifa school is removed. It is doubtful whether they have another school of this kind attached to a hospital.

I have to maintain my present status quo. No improvements, no relapse unless the situation demands it.

Both Horst Zimmerman and I go for regular 'walks' in the corridor, two ruins supporting each other. We still keep a careful eye on the goings on in the interrogation barracks, but so far it all looks very casual.

The activists are still having a hard time readjusting. Their better clothing soon loses its shine and I am sure they badly miss their extra rations and cigarettes, as they are expected to perform hard labour.

On top of that, they have to undergo interrogations just like all the others. One of them was told by the interrogation officer "you nix anti-fascist, you big fascist now"

It was hard for the youngsters who had quickly changed their allegiance from Nazi propaganda to the Communist teaching.

Now they had nothing. They were rudderless in the big maelstrom of plennie life. It will take some time before the MWD have seen every inmate.

Winter is with us again but our room is tolerably warm, but for the camp plennies it's a time of cold and hunger. Their rations are just enough to keep them alive, but the hard labour is not calculated into their daily needs and many suffer greatly.

One of the former activists had not given up hope of once more rising to the top of the heap. He was working on a building site and after an encouraging speech to his fellow workers he suggested they should raise their quota of daily work.

Everyone listened politely without comment, but 24 hours later he was admitted to the surgical ward with multiple fractures. Accidents will happen.

He now keeps quiet – no further raising of quotas, he had learned a useful lesson.

Four days before Christmas, Krawzyk comes on a flying visit just after 9pm. He was our reliable link to the camp and always kept us well informed.

30 plennies had been arrested and transported to prison. There were 27 plennies, 2 course participants and one tutor at the Antifa.

All had been warned, any escape attempts and they would be shot. What a disappointment for these men just before Christmas – not at all what they expected.

The oh so simple questions at their interrogation were full of traps, the men like soldiers everywhere had lived off the land and had stolen Russian goods and food, so that's enough to land them in prison. There are no doubts, definitely not innocent until proven guilty in the Russian process of law.

Before long it has to be our turn, and there is nothing we can do to prepare ourselves.

For many nights the transporting of arrested men continues. Christmas has been and gone. My whole energy is aimed towards home, my only real goal.

At present my biggest obstacle is that of possible arrest and once more a transport to prison. Semjonow is not my number one fan.

There was only so much the medical chief could do for my protection. Our own German doctor is not very effective, he pales into insignificance next to Dr Elisabetha. This lady has noted how many times my name has been taken off the list. As a small gesture she makes sure that neither I nor Zimmerman have to go through the stupid performance of getting dressed and being taken to the main door, only to be returned to our room by Semjonow.

Dr Elisabetha knows in advance of any lists, so if the night nurse hands me two sleeping tablets I know I am once more off the list.

Throughout the Christmas and New Year period the interrogations and arrests continue and we are glad that we have safely reached 1950 without being arrested.

7

1950

My imaginary illness has become second nature to me. Originally I had thought fourteen days would be enough to get me home. Yet, here I am two years later still trying to stay out of prison.

My room-mate Horst Zimmerman is getting more daring by the day. He refuses to be escorted by the orderly, he can manage fine. One of his madcap plans was to visit a friend on one of the lower floors. After a few minutes the most unearthly racket can be heard from the area of the main stairs accompanied by a volley of typical Zimmerman swear words.

Before long he is returned to us on a stretcher. An open wound on his forehead, his nose is bleeding and his left shoulder is bruised. The one positive thing is that his legs survived.

The Pony arrives to check him over and severely tells him off, but once he's cleaned up and bandaged he looks like a brigand of the old days.

In retrospect he can laugh at himself and his exploits, but as a concession he promises to take the orderly with him next time.

My improved Russian knowledge allows me to talk to the old lady doctor. She listens carefully, correcting or adding missing words. I always bring her something when I get a parcel from home.

At Christmas my wife had sent me four red candles and a small golden Christmas angel. I gave the old lady the angel and a red candle and a bar of chocolate on the 5th January, Russian Christmas (Epiphany).

I secretly placed the gifts in her large handbag. The next day she reciprocated handing me a holy picture and a small packet of ground coffee. I feel a bit guilty as I have two tins of Nescafe in my room, but no way could I upset her by refusing her gift.

In the main camp the general morale is probably as low as is possible, no one is safe.

They have had to appoint a group of watchmen in each barrack to prevent suicides. The worst time is about 9pm when the runner comes from the Budka with a list of names of those to be transported that night to an unknown destiny.

The hospital too is touched by this atmosphere of fear and uncertainty. Zimmerman continues to exercise regularly so he can "walk when they cart me away to prison".

Von Lewandowsky hopes the opposite might be true – he shouldn't get too good on his wooden legs so that the Russians will get rid of him because he is useless. Some hope - the Russian reasoning works different to our European logic.

By the end of February, 800 men have been sent to prison. By the middle of March it's our turn and both Dr Elisabetha and the Pony are very anxious. As they both know what can happen to us and up till now they have stood between us and Sonjonow, but now they are powerless to help us. Even the old lady doctor gives me a hidden warning.

She compliments me on my good progress in Russian studies and she says our will is of no importance, only the big boys will decide what is to happen to us 'little people'.

I think now is the time for me to act up. Up to now, no one has been arrested and they are just playing with us, keeping us on tenterhooks.

Lewandowsky is the first to be questioned. Our friendly activist has already had his turn and he comments that he was only asked very simple questions.

When Von L returns he is absolutely furious. He was asked whether he had dropped bombs on Leningrad. Of course he had, that was his job. What had he been told? To aim for military establishments? Did he know if he killed any non-military personnel and people?

He could not give them a satisfactory answer, he was in his plane, not on the ground.

We are gradually putting together a lot of information from the East German papers and Pravda. It is no longer considered acceptable to keep PoWs, but war criminals are a different story all together. So, for example, Von Lewandowsky dropping bombs on civilians automatically makes him a war criminal and they can do with him what they like.

A name keeps popping up in the East German media as well as in the Russian papers. Pastor Niemoeller. He had been a naval man at the beginning of the war who supported Hitler. But when he was pursuing his career as a pastor he soon became aware of what was happening in Germany. He and his supporters suffered greatly and he spent time in prison as well as concentration camps. When he was liberated he put all his energy towards trying to create a better image of the ordinary German people abroad.

It was thanks to his strenuous efforts that prisoners of war from all the occupying forces of Germany were expected to be returned at once.

So to keep up an appearance of goodwill, the Russians are doing their best to change the status of many of the plennies to one of being a war criminal.

I try to be prepared in as much as I can for their questions. Von L was asked to sign their protocol after his interrogation. When he refused he was told that it did not matter. Both the translator and MWD would under oath confirm the validity of the document. So he signed.

Horst Zimmerman too faces the same questioning and he finds it impossible to stick to the old proverb 'if in doubt keep your mouth shut.'

I try to persuade him to answer questions with yes or no and little else. But he plans to tell them what he thinks of them, but the Russians care little about his thoughts and will only use them against him.

Zimmerman appears determined to dig his own grave, maybe literally. The Russians are quite obviously under pressure from their allies to release all PoWs, so if they want to hang on to any of us they must prove we were war criminals. Why keep us?

Once they have succeeded in branding us as war criminals, but still send us home, they hope to gain an international reputation of goodwill.

When I next go for my massage, Krawzyk awaits me anxiously. It had been his turn to be called to the MWD, the previous night. One of the main questions concerned the events at a German clearing station for battle wounded soldiers. He had helped to check over and bandage not only German but also Russian soldiers? And had any of the latter group died? He had acted only as an orderly, the decision whether or not to treat had never been his.

That soldiers of both nationalities had died was true, so in the eyes of the interrogators it was a simple fact. Russians died and he was there, so he was guilty.

Looking at it from a logical point of view, this was utter nonsense, but the MWD didn't consider reason. Russians died, so he was guilty. The horror of his situation seemed to hit him hard.

I feel guilty by adding to his problems, but I have to once more use my tried and tested method of needing urgent medical attention, that is to be "unfit for questioning".

I stop breathing for as long as I can with obvious results. Krawzyk panics and races off to fetch my friend the old lady doctor. She checks my pulse and tells me to lie still. Dr Elisabetha and the Pony also arrive. A new stroke is Dr Elisabetha's diagnosis.

She tells the doctors that she is not surprised at the recent turn of events. She feels the treatment by the MWD and the transport lists was bound to have that effect on an already weakened system.

She promises to contact an influential friend of hers who will hopefully put an end to Semjonow's dirty deeds. I am certainly grateful to my Russian teacher, had it not been for her I would not have understood this whispered conversation. She tells me in her careful German that I am to be returned to my room and she will see what she can do. Dr Elisabetha knows she has the support of her colleagues.

On our way back to my room we come across Semjonow who obviously wants to know what is going on.

"Ah well then, I will just question him at a later date," he says when he is informed about my recent stroke.

When Dr Elisabetha notes that another more severe stroke might be fatal, Semjonow replies that would be an ideal solution and save everyone a load of hassle.

He is not prepared for Dr Elisabetha's response, for as long as she is in charge of the plennies health, she will not tolerate inhuman treatment of her charges. Semjonow has never come across any open opposition to his cruel treatment of prisoners. Whoever dared to do that must either be a fool which the doctor obviously was not, or have some very strong support from someone more powerful than the MWD. He decides caution is now his best way out.

Zimmerman is horrified. He never considered that I might die at the last hurdle and the Pony gives me a powerful injection which sends me off into a dreamless sleep. I don't really surface until the middle of the next day

I find Von Lewandowsky sitting next to my bed, he has been keeping watch over me since I returned. Zimmerman is pleased to see me back in the land of the living.

Semjonow has continued his questioning and arrests throughout the camp, but seems to stay clear of the hospital. Some of the arrested men include Home Guards who had been working as guards in the German PoWs camps for allied prisoners.

Zimmerman is not open to any persuasion about his own behaviour at his interrogation, he is convinced he could reason with the MWD. Surely the absence of his own legs should prove my point to stick to simple answers and never argue.

The next evening when the hospital inmates are back on the list of visits to MWD, he too is called.

It takes some time until we hear the clip clop of his wooden legs. He was absolutely furious. Contrary to our advice he argued with his questioners and had given them his own version of humanity towards PoWs. He had however noted that the officer had put a red cross next to his name.

I am only too aware of the meaning of the red cross on one's notes. Mine too carries that sign which means 'Not to be repatriated,' but wisely I keep that information to myself.

Dr Weigert at long last comes to visit. He assures me that Dr Elisabetha is still protecting me so no interrogation for me in the near future. We are never too sure about Dr Weigert, he has a reputation of a very thorough medical knowledge and is very popular with the other ranks; he must have had some bad experiences with the officer patients.

Our connection with our families has re-started, we receive frequent parcels and regulation cards.

Up to now 1200 men have been arrested and the camp is down to 2200. Everyone is scared and waits for his number to be up. We are all cold with the feeling of fear and uncertainty. My two room-mates are thoroughly decent characters but as I am not totally honest with them, I feel there is a bit of a wall between us. I know they wouldn't betray me but why burden them with this knowledge of my self-inflicted illness.

Every night we are tense and anxious. Whose turn is it tonight? In some ways not knowing is as demanding as actually waiting to be arrested.

One night, both my companions are asked to get ready. Their clothes were brought to them, not by our usual starski as he too was going away.

Von Lewandowsky gives me his wife's address just in case. The Pony arrives and tells Zimmerman to delay as long as possible. Dr Elisabetha is on her way, she also asks him not to attach his wooden legs. We too say our farewells and suddenly a dreaded silence engulfs the few of us left behind. We all feel guilty and glad at being spared. A lot of time passed, I turned off the light when the door burst open, the light is on again and a stretcher containing the grinning Zimmerman returns.

"Hello mate. Nice to see you again!"

Dr Elisabetha had acted for him, she waved a piece of paper at Semjonow's nose and he had to release him for the time being.

I am so pleased for him, but I am equally pleased about the positive intervention by the chief medical officer.

Both doctors come to see us before we settle for the night, we are reassured that we have the personal protection of a Guardian Angel whilst we are within these walls.

Both Horst and I are given sleeping tablets to ensure a good night's sleep.

There were 50 hospital patients on the transport so we realize that something will happen. This hospital is too big for just 150 patients. For tonight and a few other nights no further calls to MWD officers or transports, but we know better than to relax and our mistrust is justified.

One Sunday morning we observe a troop of Russian soldiers lining up outside the camp. All are carrying shotguns aimed towards the camp, the whole place is surrounded by MWD soldiers.

All the plennies are lined up carrying their backpacks. The Russian Camp Commander arrives with a long list. The men he wants are all lined up in rows of five, anyone who is a bit slow gets kicked by the guards. Semjonow joins the commandant, he too carries a list. Our names.

Zimmerman decides to remove his artificial limbs. The Pony chases every patient back to their bed, but Semjonow has arranged to have all the belongings brought to us. Both Zimmerman and I smoke an illicit cigarette, but of course Semjonow has arrived whilst we are smoking. He wishes us a pleasant journey. Zimmerman cannot resist another chance to be rude to him, just one last time.

Anywhere would be better than here with Semjonow. And I assure him that we will always remember his humanity. He is surprised by my sudden knowledge of Russian, something his spies have not told him.

Krawzyk too gets told to collect his gear, just a few are left behind and we are mentally preparing ourselves for yet another journey into the unknown.

But just as we are ready to be carried through the gate Dr Elisabetha arrives. She is running as fast as she can until she confronts Semjonow. Both get very heated and I am able to hear the whole argument. The upshot is my return to my room, but Zimmerman is still going.

I shout farewell to Horst through the window, but the battle is not lost. Dr Elisabetha can be heard on the phone to whoever her powerful friend is.

Semjonow orders the plennies to carry Zimmerman's stretcher as the orderlies' names have been called and they are now part of another group. The Pony runs as fast as she can totally ignoring all the mud and puddles. She then faces Semjonow and shouts at him. Once more Zimmerman is dumped whilst Semjonow races back to the phone call.

Sharp commands are heard, the plennies have to put down all their belongings, even the canvas bread bags, and then they have to form new groups of ten, away from their belongings. One man who was a bit slow in depositing his bread bag was helped along by a sharp push from a Russian soldier, and when a man objected the Russian fist lands on his face.

Once more everything comes to a halt. Semjonow and two helpers run across the courtyard and Zimmerman gets picked up and returned to the hospital.

I wait for him at the door of our sanctuary. He is pale and shaking, his face is drawn and all signs of his usual humour are blown away. I greet him full of feelings, but we both know it is just a question of time, without realizing it we drop the 'Sie' and use 'Du,' all these experiences have brought us closer together and done away with the unimportant things.

The orderly undresses him, he is still shaking with cold and I too can feel myself shaking with exhaustion and fear. The Ward Sister arrives with two cups of steaming tea and she sits with Horst and tries to comfort him. The hot tea does its bit to bring a bit of life back into us, it feels as if the tea had a sleeping draught added to it as I no longer have the strength to keep my eyes open.

When I awake it is spring outside. Yesterday and all the cold and nightmarish occurrences seem just like a bad dream. Horst is still fast asleep, he looks absolutely drained.

When the Pony arrives I make an attempt to thank her, it was she who alarmed Dr Elisabetha who was unaware of the events, but she laughs and says "Nitschewo."

Horst too has joined the land of the living and he too wants to thank her, but she just puts her fingers across his lips to silence him. And leaves us.

We know we owe our stay here to two doctors, but we are desperate to find out how the other plennies fared last night. Horst puts on his legs refusing all help, it takes him some time to get ready. His legs creak as he stumbles along. I tell him to oil them next time. He can cope with humour but not with pity.

I must have fallen asleep again because I awake with Horst sitting next to me.

His news is very distressing. 1150 men have been arrested, added to 48 men from the hospital and with us two it would have been 50. The hospital inmates were all crammed together in one lorry. Pushed, shoved and beaten with the butts of the Russian soldiers' rifles. On the roof of the driver's cabin two soldiers sat with cocked weapons.

First the other plennies were marched out, then the hospital lorry followed. A company of Russian soldiers went ahead and another company followed the lorry.

As to what happened to the back packs, they were thrown onto the back of another lorry and driven away all in the direction of Moscow.

There is another bit of news. Most of the plennies and guards have gone and only one man is stationed in the Budka.

The few remaining plennies are hopeful for transport home. We might – but then why hope?

We all know about the unpredictability of the Russians. Another miracle occurs, The barbed wire is being rolled up by some plennies. All the remaining plennies were requested, *not ordered*, to stay within the confines of the camp by the Russian commandant.

The few remaining guards were for our own protection. The 'war criminals' have been taken away for their deserved punishment, the remainder would be sent home.

But Horst and I know we won't be going home. The doctors cannot protect us forever.

The red stamp on our notes makes us the property of the MWD and all we have gained so far, is time.

We live for the moment, enjoy what there is to enjoy and tolerate what can't be enjoyed.

We decide to avoid the subject of home, but we both receive parcels from home so we have to talk about our families. Horst has told his wife about his legs, but knowing about it and living with it is a different thing. He used to go on long hikes with his sons, he had good fun with his lads but what will it be like now?

We both produce our family photos, whole stories are attached to each one. On the next day all evidence of a former PoW camp has been removed. We hardly see Dr Elisabetha and my own teacher is gone. The number of nurses shrinks daily.

13th April 1950 is the day everyone receives their going away outfits, including us. The cemetery is tidied up by a group of plennies, everything points to a general closure.

15th April we are all called to the Chief Medical Officer's office – we are being sent to another hospital.

As far as we know we will then be sent home, as soon as we are fit enough to cope with the rigours of a long journey. That's all she can do for us.

Before we can thank her, we are whisked away by some medics. We are carried past all the other patients, we ask them to contact our families for us.

Semjonow has the last word. You are going to another hospital, soon you will go home too, but he is smiling whilst he is saying it. We are filled with mistrust.

As we are placed on the lorry, well covered in blankets, all the remaining plennies in the hospital wave and wish us good luck.

The two doctors Dr Elisabetha and the Pony wave till we can see them no more. To add to our confusion we see Semjonow waving too.

What a way to go!

PART FIVE

1

**Another PoW Camp Hospital
Near Moscow
April 1950**

Our lorry drives straight through Moscow. I could stand up and enjoy the sights of a busy city, but I feel very low and just cannot be bothered. I am beginning to feel resigned to my fate. In spite of all my efforts I haven't moved an inch nearer home.

I just seem to go round and round in ever diminishing circles. Dr Rachmanova was quite right in telling me about the red stamp on my papers. So far I have managed to avoid ending up in prison, but the threat of a repeat incarceration hangs permanently over me. I love life too much to be able to keep up my role as a semi-invalid. I am pretending to be someone I am not, both in my dealings with my compatriots and the Russians.

Should the latter ever find out, I would disappear into the depths of Siberia for ever.

As far as the Russians are concerned anyone leaving their own country of their own free will, must do so purely to act as a spy. No one will ever believe that my wife and I drove across to Czechoslovakia purely to drink beer and eat cream cakes in the early years of the war when I was on leave. The Americans realized far too late that the concession they had made to the Russians would cost them dearly one day.

The same Germany not so long ago destined to be populated by agricultural workers by Morgenthau, had overnight turned into a valuable asset in their battle against communism.

The Americans too have had a few black spots in their dealings with German PoWs. The camp at Kreuznach was one of the worst places. Many German soldiers died from starvation and ill treatment.

Now the Americans as well as the Russians are busy trying to win the Germans over to their camp.

We decide to change the subject, it is too depressing, but we have learned one valuable lesson. Not every plennie is necessarily our friend and not every Russian is automatically our enemy. We have paid dearly for this lesson.

In the meantime our lorry has come to a stop, our guard wakes up and rewards us both with a cigarette. He even lights them for us. He doesn't look too bright but he is friendly, so we start chatting as we both speak passable Russian, so we thank him for the cigarettes, but are not too sure when he tells us there will not be any lunch.

We also want to know why we have stopped in the middle of a forest, once more we get to see how the Russians manage to survive.

As usual our transport is not without its problems. We somehow spend a whole night in a forest. Guards, drivers and ourselves dead to the world with the after effects of two shared bottles of vodka, acquired in exchange for some of our petrol.

I just manage to see the headlights of a car in the distance. I wake the guards and driver and within seconds they had the bonnet up and were tinkering away with their tools. Luckily the SIS (Russian staff car) didn't stop.

We decide to move but before long our lorry has made an unscheduled halt in a ditch. When we have managed to persuade a passing lorry to pull us clear, the driver is persuaded to tow us to our destination.

Horst Zimmerman and I are both quite relieved when we are handed over to the hospital.

It is wonderful to be able to get into a clean white bed after a good wash and all the excitement.

We know we have once more a roof over our heads. The odd thing is everyone speaks Russian.

When we have recovered from our journey we find that the orderlies are Poles from a part of the Ukraine that used to belong to Poland. The majority of the Poles in the camp belonged to a volunteer brigade of the Waffen SS and were all automatically condemned to 25 years hard labour.

Zimmerman and I are the only two men in the camp who as yet have not been to trial, which makes us a bit of a novelty to our medics.

We feel from the general look of the camp that it seems to make little difference to the inmates, whether they are under sentence or just plennies, but we will see.

The highlight of our discoveries is a flush toilet that actually flushes – what luxury.

We have to go to the barbers after a short rest as the doctor doesn't like to see unshaven men. We also have a radio in the hospital. It broadcasts from East Germany and Horst is thrilled to bits by the luxury of a tiled washhouse, a flush toilet and now music!

I am eternally grateful to Maria and the old lady doctor for insisting that I learnt Russian, it makes life so much easier. How often have I noticed that the appointed translator rarely translates what might in any way upset the Russians.

Our breakfast gets served in white earthenware bowls; its barley soup, there seems to be even a hint of fat and a few bits of meat in it. Our spoons are Russian made and we have to hand them back after the meal.

I cautiously check with the other patients about any activists and a general camp privileged section. I wish that was the same in all the other camps, the name Schneider reminds me how one lazy activist cost so many plennie lives.

Two orderlies arrive after breakfast to make the invalids' beds and then a real clean-up starts. It reminds me a bit of my mother's spring cleaning, not just moving the dust around a bit, but damp dusting and polishing – the works!

After the cleaning is finished an older nurse comes to get us ready for Dr Suslowa. At 9.45 as the radio is turned off we hear a report being given: the number of sick new arrivals.

A slim older lady enters the room and I mean 'lady' – an aura of calm efficiency emanates from this doctor and she speaks excellent German and is accompanied by a swarm of doctors in snow white coats. First she visits her regular patients, then it's our turn.

First she speaks to Horst and he gives all the required information when she asks him how he came to lose his legs.

I see a shadow of anger crossing her face as she closely looks at the reddened inflamed stumps and promises to supply him with protective socks. When she asks Horst how he is coping with his legs he tells her they are still managing him! As yet he has not managed to find a proper balance on his walking tours. She then tells Nicolai, a huge man, to be with Horst as a support every time he is walking.

When it's my turn the Polish doctor gives her all the details. I listen carefully, he is well prepared and misses none of the particulars. She orders continued radiation treatment and massage.

Jan, a tall young man, a medical student, as I find out later, is responsible for my treatment.

For the time being I am to have bed rest, but Jan is to commence my treatment straight away. After she has taken my blood pressure and checked the degree of muscle wastage on my left side, she leaves us.

I get transported across to the treatment area which is very well equipped. There are four treatment bays separated by curtains; Jan explains that there are women in this camp, about 40 of them, nurses and wives of German Jews. To my amazement I find these unfortunates originally emigrated to the Baltic then went over to the Russians.

Instead of being welcomed they were interned initially but then just thrown in with the other PoWs. Their fate is no different from that of a captured German soldier.

My conversation with Jan is somewhat stilted as he tries to speak German and my knowledge of Russian is still limited, so we decide to use Russian as it will be easier for both of us.

Jan is a good looking young man and were it not for the bitter twist of his mouth one would never know that he had already gone through a war. We are talking to each other the way plennies do, carefully but not giving anything away.

He is in the process of repairing, or trying to, the electrical measuring gauge for nerve reflexes. It's an old broken down appliance but Jan is trying to repair it himself, not the Russians. This last bit makes me think he's all right, he won't want to do me any harm because one correct measurement with a fully functioning measuring device would automatically show me up as a fake.

So I take a chance and ask him not to be too quick with his repairs for the time being as I am quite enjoying my little holiday in the hospital.

He seems to understand my hidden message and no dangers will threaten me from his corner.

He is a wonderful masseur, he is so gentle that I almost enjoy the massage. When I ask him if the treatment room is a good place to have a cigarette he says yes, but he has no cigarettes. As all the officers are under sentence their cigarette supply has been stopped. I produce a packet of tailor made and his eyes light up. He produces a home-made lighter made from bits and pieces he acquired from a broken down Mercedes on the camp.

I see by the way he smokes how much he's missed his nicotine, as I have a good supply of cigarettes I know I am a wealthy man in this camp.

When I invite him to a cup of coffee he agrees but feels it is better to drink coffee in his room. The doctors finish at 4pm and then the coast is clear, he will provide the hot water, I will bring the Nescafe.

When I return I find Horst absolutely raging. There are 50 Generals in the camp, destined for a propaganda transport home. His old divisional General is amongst them.

He is trying to control his fury and Horst knows - were he to see his General now he would beat him to death for betraying him and his men to the Russians. I do my best to persuade him to keep his distance from his General.

I know there are some decent men amongst them, but the 'new' Generals had no tradition of loyalty to their men. They often consisted of men who got to their status not through effort and good management, but through contact, 'whom they knew, not what they knew.'

He has some upsetting news for me. Friend Baecker is also part of the transport. I who so calmly talked Horst out of his fit of fury, suddenly feel even more furious.

I yell for Nicolai, Horst's helpful orderly. He is bribed with three cigarettes to go and search for Baecker. Nicolai is back within a minute and tells me Baecker is waiting outside.

If it's possible, he looks thinner and paler than on our last meeting. I congratulate him on his forthcoming trip home. How did he manage to stay out of prison? What or rather who paid the price of his ticket home this time?

If he wasn't such a coward he would hit me, but he doesn't.

His release was requested by the East German government, because of his extensive knowledge of Agriculture and Economy. He was collected from the prison by a Russian General with an apology for an 'official error'.

He looks terribly worried and hopes that he can count on my discretion. He knows that once in East Germany he is still not safe from the Russians. I assure him that I have no intentions of writing any reports concerning people, especially people like Hartmut Kraft.

He cannot say 'goodbye' quick enough, but this time I manage to avoid his outstretched hand. I just wish him a pleasant journey without any accidents.

Horst has been listening to our conversation. He really begins to worry whether there is any point in going home if its people of Baecker's calibre who are running the show.

I am glad he is going, he was once more on top and could have been dangerous for me.

Most of the chronically sick patients keep themselves to themselves. The fact that Horst and I have not been sentenced forms a dividing wall. Most of them had been arrested and thrown into prison, where they were all sentenced without trial to 25 years. Some even have a triple sentence but that seems to make little difference. The state of their respective imprisonment in the various prisons cost them their few belongings.

As we see it, it was a carefully executed plan by the Russians. To retain efficient and highly qualified workers under the guise of legality for the rest of the world, these men are all sentenced criminals.

It comes across quite clearly when we read between the lines that the brother allies are anything but united. There is definitely a wall growing between the east, headed by communist Russia and the west headed by capitalist America, but the focal point is Germany and the border.

We feel almost reluctant to go home. Hopefully we will be considered too old to be soldiers again.

Horst is still planning to go and see his old General. When he returns from his visit he is in a predictable rage. I gauge his temper by the way he bangs his sticks.

The General denied everything in spite of Horst having seen his signature under an incriminating piece of evidence against himself. In fact the General threatened him with a complaint to the Russians - harassment he called it.

At 3pm another minor miracle occurs. The orderly enters the ward with cups of cocoa and two white bread rolls for every patient.

Every camp gets these goods, but only here thanks to the medical chief they get to the intended people. Elsewhere they stay firmly in the hands of the Russians. Now I understand why it's possible to buy ground coffee for 7 roubles. In a previous camp it was meant for us anyway and as a rule the Russian people prefer tea to coffee.

After lunch we get to watch the 50 Generals getting ready for a trip to Moscow. Posh suits, hats and beautiful shirts and ties. Oh, what it is to be a General! Especially one who changes loyalty like other people change their underwear. A few younger very elegant Russian officers join the group, delighted greetings all round.

Two buses drive in and everyone politely climbs aboard, strictly according to rank. The Russians first of course. Baecker is in full flight, no doubt he is one of the organisers of this cultural tour of Moscow. The gentlemen, so our source tells us, even receive some spending money to buy a little trinket for their lady wives at home.

Unfortunately the plennies surrounding the buses watching their former superiors' behaviour don't hold back with their none too complimentary comments. It just glides off the Generals' backs, they are going home so what's a few negative words from the ugly plebs!

Around 4pm I take my tin of Nescafe and cigarettes and limp across to my masseur. He is well prepared for our coffee meeting. A clean white sheet is spread across a table. Two white cups are ready for use. It's like old friends meeting. In PoW camps you quickly get each one's measure.

True, there are failures from time to time, but my instincts serve me well. Jan wants to improve his German and in exchange he will correct my no way perfect Russian. He wants to know why I am so intent on learning the language, so I tell him it's always wise to know the language of one's enemy.

We both agree it's the system we consider to be our enemy, not all the people. Both of us have met people who have treated us with kindness and goodwill.

As Jan has already been sentenced to 25 years he only stands to lose his present post, but I am stuck with the status quo of waiting to be sentenced.

Jan was the link between the Germans and the Poles when Warsaw was first occupied. All his family felt sure in their decision to throw in their lot with the occupying forces. They believed in Hitler's promise that in the New Europe every nation would have a voice.

Of course they found out the Poles were only considered second class people; before the family could do anything to rectify their situation the war was over as far as Poland was concerned. Most of his family was briefly employed by the Germans; but as things developed they remained in Warsaw as the Russians fought and won the town.

Most of the Germans disappeared and Jan had some months previously joined the Polish resistance movement, when his group tried to join their Russian liberators they were taken prisoner. His family fared worse, his father tried to protect his wife and daughter from the marauding Russians and was shot trying in vain to protect the women. Both were gang raped, then they too were shot.

He himself was sentenced for collaborating with the enemy, the fact that he had joined the resistance movement and had witnesses to prove it made no difference. He states that only the hatred for the Russians kept him alive, as it was with so many of the other Poles. They all waited for the day when they could take revenge for their lost families and ravished country.

I tried to warn him that hatred often blinds us to the issues in life, but for the time being that's all that keeps him going. He does however agree that like me he hates the 'system' and not every Russian he meets.

I now tell him a little of my life, about my family and home. I include a little bit of military life and describe my illness as a fact and how Horst and I were rescued by Dr Elisabetha.

I also tell him that I shall be sentenced as soon as I am fully well, so my fate is in his hands and his electrical appliance. If he repairs it properly I shall be cured, if not I shall be able to exist in this quite pleasant no man's land.

Jan just grins and explains that he makes the apparatus work and at the same time not work. It sounds highly improbable to me but technically I am gifted with two hands of left thumbs.

Jan however enjoys a challenge, especially if he can put one over the Russians at the same time. So once more I am safe for the time being.

2

April 1950

On 18th April the Generals' transport is taking place, the night before a big party celebrating the event took place.

The Polish doctor passes all the details on to Jan. Only the best drink and food is to be served, the public at large are of course excluded, even the windows are covered with blankets to keep any nosy parkers away.

Next morning just before 9am we stand at our windows and observe the departure. All their luggage gets packed onto a lorry, after all Generals need so much more than your normal plennie who makes do with a toothbrush, spoon and soap dish.

In a see-through bag the gentlemen are well supplied with food for their journey. The buses are surrounded by guards to protect our Generals from their former troops, but as there is not a single plennie in sight, only our Medical Officer and the Head Nurse, there was no need for the armed guards. Some of the Generals wave to the two women but instead of waving back they turn their backs on them and return to the hospital.

I'm sure there are some decent men amongst the departing Generals who will, once home, tell the truth about the situation of the plennies as it really is.

Jan is in a brilliant mood today, his fellow Poles served at the tables at last night's party and managed to stash away one or two things, so he is providing vodka and cigarettes at our 4pm get together.

I ask him to spare me the details about last night's party, it's embarrassing enough to know it's my countrymen who are selling out.

Jan did tell me that Dr Suslowa had been seen crying, crying with shame at the spectacle of these 'Gentlemen.' A Russian officer was heard to comment that one had to be drunk to be in the company of such men.

There are new patients expected in the hospital, after some time our door opens and the orderlies carry in a stretcher followed by three worn out and ill looking men.

One sticks out from the other two due to his height and almost skeletal thinness. I realize there is something vaguely familiar about his face, we have met before. He too stops and stares at me, but then moves on.

Now I know it is Captain Merk. I greet him like an old friend, we had met in Paris when we were both stationed there.

'My name is Beauclair,' he quietly whispers in my ear. Sounds good, so why not? Beauclair it is.

Everyone has their secrets.

The other two have spent time in the Lubjanka, it's cold there at any time of the year. One is not a plennie, but from East Germany.

The first government is already doing its first purge. He was one of the informants who no longer fitted into their frame of things.

When Dr Suslowa visits the new patients she asks Merk or rather Beauclair whether he is French.

"No," he explains how his wife came from an old French family and as she was the last member they decided to keep her name. He does not like being the centre of attention, and our Polish doctor stands with a grin on his face. He knows more than he's telling us.

But we soon know. In the treatment room at the rear of the ward is Beauclair's wife, she suffers from a heart condition.

They were married a few days before the war ended, his in-laws had emigrated from France around 1681 - they were nobility.

I tell him I am not owed any explanation, it's strictly his own business what he calls himself.

But he and his wife had been sentenced to 25 years.

The newcomers are surprised when our usual afternoon cocoa and bread rolls arrive and another 10 patients are being admitted. To get away from all the noise I visit young Jan.

He is busy with some technical looking diagrams but is happy to stash them away to hear my latest news about 'Wonder Woman'.

So far he knows more than I do. As far as he has heard she is an 'Angel in human form.' An accomplished Major in the Luftwaffe with the Knights Cross, she is also a double doctor but in what he doesn't know yet.

The rumours are everywhere about this beautiful addition to our humdrum plennie life. Jan had only one swift glance of her, but is absolutely over the moon with his very Polish enthusiasm for a beautiful woman. But Jan is a little bit annoyed with the Polish doctor who just grins every time Madame Beauclair is mentioned.

This makes me wonder. The doctor is no fool, he must have a good reason to distrust our Madame de Beauclair. I decide to find out for myself what's behind all this mystery.

So far I have found out that she reacted quite unexpectedly when addressed in French. Madam had no idea what the doctor was saying.

Very much to my surprise I find that all the Poles have put money together to ease Madame's lot in this plennie camp, only the doctor refused to contribute 20 roubles.

I have to cool Jan's ardour a bit and bring him down to earth by mentioning Mr de Beauclair. When I leave Jan I meet up with Horst. He wants to know more details about the Beauclairs, as far as he knows there were only three known female air aces and Mrs B certainly isn't one of them. The only woman who ever received the Iron Cross first class was Hanna Reitsch – so another made-up story.

We do not really mind people trying to pull a fast one, but do they really have to overdo it to such an extent? For all we know she is little Lilly Mueller from some little village who decided to live the high life, had she not overdone it she might have been safely home by now.

My neighbour starts chatting to me after our evening meal. His wife has to suffer so much as she needs a special diet for people with a heart problem, but of course he cannot buy anything, as he is not receiving any plennie pay as a sentenced man.

I am genuinely touched by his concern for his wife and before I realize what I am doing I hand over my last 20 roubles. All my good advice went straight out the window, a new sucker is born every minute.

Horst taps me on my shoulder with his stick.

"What the hell's the matter with you?" but all I can do is laugh at my own stupidity.

However next morning after our doctors' visit my neighbour handed me a little card.

'Ellen de Beauclair, Major Luftwaffe requests the pleasure of Mr Schmitt for tea at 4pm.'

Well there you have it. Amazing what 20 roubles can do for you. I hope Jan is not going to be jealous.

When I think about the good lady, 40 roubles in 24 hours is not bad going.

Jan is madly envious but persuades me to have a haircut and shave for my tea time appointment. That costs me five cigarettes! I hope she is worth it.

Jan's enthusiasm knows no bounds and I have to keep reminding him of the existing husband.

Piotr the hairdresser has been able to offer his services to Mrs de B. He is still in seventh heaven thinking about it. I wish he would concentrate on my head and face. I am seriously worried about his scissors and his shaking hands. Still in memory of that angel!

He would fetch the stars from the sky for her. He made do with stealing some Eau De Cologne from a Russian officer, he gave her a free manicure and pedicure just to please her.

"Anything else?" I asked, but he just ignored me.

The poor lady is totally worn out and she nearly fainted after her assorted treatments and the lucky hairdresser was able to hold her in his arms for a few minutes, to stop her falling of course.

I am beginning to think they are all drunk, this lot! I cannot wait to meet the origin of all this excitement. The hairdresser refuses to take my 5 cigarettes as payment, anything absolutely anything for this woman.

In spite of my built-in sceptical attitude I find myself getting more and more nervous as the clock moves towards four.

"Just look at you. You are as bad as the rest," Horst teases me.

So far she has managed to get 70 roubles by just batting her eyelids. Next time I want to be a woman, if I am to be a prisoner – it's more profitable.

Mr Beauclair opens the door and tells me that I am expected. When I enter I am face to face with a very healthy looking beautiful young woman. She holds out her solid little hand obviously expecting to receive a kiss, so I oblige and thank her for the invitation.

She wears the usual plennie shirt but it's so tightly done up that her bosoms are clearly visible. She sends her husband off to get the tea. She now gives me all the details of her illness. She is supposed to be suffering from Oedema.

"Look at my thighs," she pouts. "Swollen all the way up."

With that she throws her covers off. I get a full frontal (all for twenty roubles!) she tells me to touch and press to see the indentations, but caution and the thought of her husband returning with a pot of hot tea restrains me, so I bend over and cover her up. I want to enjoy my tea.

I have got her measure. If she is prepared to show me all for 20 roubles I dread to think what she would offer for a higher contribution. I initially intended to leave straight after my tea, but now I intend to stay for a while and enjoy the whole performance.

As we are enjoying our tea, there is a knock at the window. A plennie is looking into the room and waves his hand. Madame de Beauclair asks her husband to relieve the plennie of his gift.

A white loaf, some sausage and 10 roubles are handed in with good wishes for the lady. I see how she adds the roubles to a well filled wallet.

In all my time as a plennie I have never seen so much money.

This woman is a gold mine, a never ending source of income, but I still cannot understand why he is desperately thin. But Ellen, as I am encouraged to call her, just pulls a face.

"Just sausage and bread when I ask for salmon!"

For once I am actually stuck for something to say which is a rare event, but now I am going to get my money's worth.

"I hear you have been to university."

"Why, what made you ask that?" she replies.

"Well, two doctor titles would seem to make one draw that conclusion."

She obviously isn't comfortable with the way the conversation is going, but I am going to stick with it. So she carries on, not suspecting anything, to inform me that a Major in the Luftwaffe gave her sufficient time to attend lectures at Milan, whilst she was flying there regularly.

She claims to have a doctorate in Meteorology.

"No, nothing to do with meteors just about the weather," she says when I use that exact term.

When I want to know where she completed her Rigorosum, she says that the Milaners were fine but she did have to re-sit her degree in Berlin as they did not recognize her Italian degree.

Poor old Merk, he has realized that I have tumbled to his wife's lies, bit by bit she drops the lady and becomes quite ordinary, if not to say, common.

As always we must never judge a book by its cover. She starts to get a bit louder and more demanding in our slow moving conversation, she asks her husband to bring some vodka that some plennie had given her for a 'quick flash at the window.'

As we have not got any glasses we drink straight from the bottle and the alcohol has the expected effect. She throws her covers off saying she is too hot. Her husband is sinking into himself with embarrassment. Poor man, he really suffers from his addiction – love is not the right word here.

I cannot watch any more of this. I've had my fill and I say my goodbye. Deliberately ignoring her outstretched hand. Her shrill laughter follows me to the door.

Horst has been listening at the door.

"What a woman, certainly no lady," he says with the rest of the patients who have also tried to listen in as best they could.

She has suddenly become Ellen, no longer Madame.

When we return to our beds for the evening meal, Ellen's husband tries to explain her peculiar behaviour. She was spoilt at home and all the adulation from the plennies doesn't help.

She has become dependent on alcohol and on morphine and yes, the doctors started her on that.

The more I see of Merk the more I feel sorry for him. He pays dearly for his continued infatuation with this woman. I can't wait to see Jan. I went across shortly after breakfast to put him out of his misery. He is very quiet when I tell him about my tea date. He has already heard all about it from another source, so his enthusiasm has already been quashed and he was back to normal. Now he tells me how he found out about our femme fatale.

Last evening the Polish doctor had asked him to accompany him on his evening walk, as if by accident the walk took them past the 'Lady's' window where a queue of plennies were waiting to hand over their gifts. From time to time Ellen would appear to flash bits of her anatomy, so Jan was truly cured. Word had spread to the other Poles so Lady Ellen's supply of Polish goodies has now run dry.

His repair of the, to me dangerous appliance, was progressing well but as Jan assured me would never be of any real problem to me. I could rely on him to fix it in my favour.

May 1950

The season is once more changing dramatically. May in all its glory has come and the countryside around us was bursting with new life and colour .On the other side of the lake were birch trees, firs and pines. Sometimes the wind brought the scent of the trees to us in the camp.

If it wasn't for the barbed wire and guard towers one could think of oneself to be in a Swiss Sanatorium.

There had been no post or parcels from home for ages. One day we heard a broadcast from Tass, the Russian broadcasting service. The Soviet Union has repatriated all their prisoners of war. At the moment there are 9000 German PoWs still in captivity and these people are serving time for war crimes. There are also another 7000 PoWs who are still to be questioned. 14 other plennies are too sick to be transported for the time being.

So, Horst and I will fall under the 14 sick plennies, as this is the exact number of unsentenced patients in the hospital. I get picked to ask our doctor on her next visit. When I see her she promises to get details from Capt Kusmin the Operatiwnik in our camp.

An hour later she returns and confirms that the number 14 refers to us in the hospital. We all have to improve before we are fit for a long journey. Horst jokes that maybe they are waiting for his legs to grow again.

Doctor Suslowa is not amused, he must become more skilful with his prostheses, but the doctor also mentioned us by name which causes us great concern. It means she has been studying our papers in detail. We are the only former members of the hated Intelligence Corps left. What can we do? So we wait and we have much experience in that.

In the next few days I begin to feel unwell, neither our precious cocoa nor the cigarettes taste nice. I also have some pain on the right side of my abdomen. Jan persuades the Polish doctor to have a look at me. He prescribes strict bed rest and regular observation.

Jan assures me the operating theatre was on stand-by. But Doctor Suslowa likes to avoid surgical intervention if it can be avoided, but 10 days later I am still in pain so everything is prepared. Dr Wizner the German surgeon visits with Dr Suslowa and decides that my appendix has to go. For once I am not dreading the operation but only anything I might give away once I am under or coming out of the effects of the anaesthetic. However when I hear that Jan will do the honours I am reassured. Hopefully my secrets are safe with him.

Everyone is talking about my impending operation. Camp life on the whole is very routine and sometimes even boring. Anything out of the ordinary gives cause for talk and speculation.

Just when the party was about to start there is the most awful racket and commotion. The roof of the operating theatre collapses and for the time being the theatre is unusable.

The sudden release and shock of this event seems to have achieved a minor miracle. My pain has gone, my appendix saved for another day. I am told by the surgeon that he could, should an emergency arise, operate elsewhere in a few days. Even my temperature is back down to normal, a bit like going to the dentist, my toothache automatically disappears when I sit in the dentist's chair.

Horst and I make good use of our permission to walk in the grounds. We are only in the hospital for the doctors' visits and meals. The camp is empty during the day as all the working brigades have left.

Summer here is very hot even at night and we long for the early morning hours.

Life around the lake becomes very busy and it's quite amusing to watch the new social regroupings, obvious through their mode of transport out of Moscow. Only the privileged arrive by car, the rest come on the bus or on a little train.

One group is particularly outstanding. Every day about 3pm a black limousine drives into their always empty parking spot under a tree. The chauffeur is a tall slim but very fit man. He wears a snow white shirt, a perfectly creased pair of trousers and a chauffeur's hat. He drives very carefully, parks and dashes to the other side and opens the door for his two passengers.

A very young pretty girl about seventeen and her babuschka (grandma). The old lady is dressed in the old fashion of the early 30s. Grandma carries a large umbrella with her that the young girl changes behind into her swimming outfit.

Everyone is trying to catch a glimpse of the youngster during her change, but grandma's umbrella hides it all. We notice the guard on duty on the watchtower uses a pair of binoculars, but no luck there either.

Once our young nymph reappears from the protection of the umbrella dressed in a red swimsuit, she quickly dives into the lake. Poor grandma keeps watch and shouts for her to come back, but Maria as she is called, has no intention of returning until she has had her swim. It looks like a mother hen with her young duckling.

When Maria is back under the protection of grandma, the chauffeur gets his turn in the water – talk about showing off! One time he comes close to the camp and the guard fires a couple of warning shots. He too is showing off and when the chauffeur considers himself to be at a safe distance he turns and shouts at the camp guard. He of course returns the unprintable compliments and before long all the visitors to the lake can enjoy the swearing competition.

Young Maria ignores the two men's verbal battle and waves to us, impartial observers behind the wire. This greeting across the wire becomes a regular event and we two elderly gentlemen quite look forward to it. The guard gets quite annoyed and attempts to chase us away, but as we are well away from the dead man's zone he has no jurisdiction over us.

Jan and I meet regularly as we now have established an aura of complete trust. Sadly my Nescafe supply has run dry so we are back to tea and smoking.

Jan dreams of a free Poland one day. A Poland no longer attached or lorded over by another country. He keeps telling me that I would make a perfect Pole, we are blood brothers. His pet hate are the Piasten – a Polish group of noblemen who encouraged German settlers to come to Poland. He feels that this is when the rot set in, he cannot see that this successful mixture of races made Silesia into the pearl of the Prussian crown.

Now he has news of a different kind, his measuring appliance is repaired, the scanner is back in action. So much for being blood brothers I tell him, and he just laughs and tells me we will have a trial run.

He explains the functioning of the gauge, it reads from 0 to 10. A healthy man can take up to 2 or maybe 3 but no more. He fastens one of the probes to my leg and turns it on. The gauge points to 1, the other probe is attached to my right hand, a slightly prickly sensation occurs on my hand when he turns it up to 2 and my arm and leg begin to jerk but nothing happens to my left side when the probe touches various points. When he turns it up to 3 I can't stand it anymore on my right side, but on the left side it's just a very muted sensation and when Jan touches me with his fingertips he gets a shock.

It's his secret how he managed to repair and arrange a scanner in such a way and his secret it will stay. I do not need to know.

Jan reports to Dr Suslowa that the apparatus is now ready for use and a time is planned when I will officially be scanned. Jan and I once more repeat the performance.

Was Jan not my friend, I could count on packing my gear and being transported straight to prison as a fraud and a malingerer.

Before the electrodes are applied Dr Suslowa checks my heart and blood pressure, she can see I am nervous but she just smiles.

"No cause for concern," she says. "It won't hurt a bit."

Jan repeats the whole procedure, the reaction is the same as before. Nothing on the left side, mild to severe jerking of the right side of my body. When Jan pushes the gauge up to 4, 5 or 6 Dr Suslowa tells him to stop at once.

As from tomorrow I am to have regular electrical stimulation on a daily basis as the damage is much worse than expected.

When Dr Suslowa has left, Jan looks at me with a satisfied look on his face.

"Am I a good technician or not?" he asks.

I can just nod. I am still bathed in sweat of fear and Jan tells me through the Polish doctor what Dr Suslowa has written in my case notes.

3

August 1950

Our daily life in the hospital changes very little, but still no news from home. No news, no parcels.

Maria and her friendly wave has become part of our daily routine, we miss her on Sundays as it is probably too busy for her at weekends. Horst wonders how we shall fill our day when our ray of sunshine no longer comes for her swim.

He now has become proficient on crutches and prostheses – he is now in charge.

The heat has been all consuming this month. There is even fear of a very bad harvest because of the persistent drought. On one of the last evenings this month we can see the sky darkening, the lake looks totally still, flat and grey. Suddenly we notice an absolute silence and not a breath of air. After a few seconds a strong wind breaks out gathering strength every minute. The sky is covered by jagged clouds being blown across the horizon.

The visitors down at the lake are making a hasty retreat and a mad dash starts to get transport to the safety of their homes.

A flash of lightning lights up the landscape, followed straightaway by a very loud clap of thunder. It is as if the evil spirits are doing a macabre dance in the trees on the other bank.

The lake has changed to a midnight blue colour and foam capped waves crash against the lake shore. A few heavy drops fall and once more there is total silence and then the real rainstorm starts as if the heavens have opened. One of the trees has caught fire but the downpour quickly extinguishes the flames. The rain flattens everything, the flower beds are just a sea of floating blooms.

We feel as if we are in the middle of an ocean of noise that surrounds us, the paths throughout the camp have turned into streams, the assembly place looks like a lake and the water is already seeping into the hospital, and before long it will have reached our ward. The orderlies try in vain to push the water back and suddenly the electricity packs in and we all sit in total darkness.

Just flashes of lightning illuminate the area and as suddenly as it started the storm stops. Before we begin to relax it starts all over again – the wind howling and causing damage. Part of a roof comes flying through the air and hits the wall of the hospital and then the storm is over.

The sky once more turns blue and the evening opens up a picture of devastation. Uprooted trees, the watchtower and the guard have been blown into the lake. Half the roof of one of the barracks has been torn off, even in our room there are puddles of water.

The boats are out looking for the drowned guard, so far he hasn't been found. As if to make up for all the damage around us, we see the most wonderful rainbow stretched out across the lake and before long a blanket of stars covers everything. It's become much cooler after the storm – the idyll of summer has passed.

Jan comes to tell me my therapy sessions will have to be postponed as the treatment room looks as if a bomb has hit it. He will come to me and do the basic massage. Dr Suslowa's only entry into my case notes states the extent of the damage will keep me in hospital for some time and declares me definitely unfit for work.

Horst and I pick our way through the shambles of fallen branches, roof tiles and other bits of flotsam. Our camp has suffered much, water damage is the worst. The actual water has gone but a horrid stench of dampness and decay is everywhere.

We have little contact with the other plennies and I have turned a deaf ear to more pleas by the Beauclairs', so no more invites to tea.

I intend to celebrate 15th September – my wife's birthday. I have saved a few roubles to buy tea and I still have plenty of cigarettes. Both Horst and Jan are invited, with my family pictures out on display. Family and home are a never ending subject for plennies. Unfortunately we end up with the other most popular subject of conversation: politics.

Jan is convinced that Horst is still an ardent Nazi, but he is just as incorrigible by trying to perpetuate a Polish national state.

Maybe encouraging these two to air their ideological differences was not one of my better ideas. After all Horst had been a teacher and no doubt well versed in all the Nazi theories and tracts.

As we were in the middle of a stormy discussion we hear a gentle knock on the door and Ellen B enters.

When she finds out it's my wife's birthday she disappears only to return with a bottle of vodka.

'But Madame we don't want to deprive you,' says Jan with a naughty hint at her weakness.

She ignores him and is quite happy to share the drink Russian fashion by passing the bottle round. I must say she behaves impeccably. No swearing, no sexual hints and her alcohol intake is controlled so we all spend a thoroughly enjoyable few hours.

October 1950

Before long our walks become a thing of the past and we have autumnal rain for over a week.

There is a niggling worry in our otherwise quiet plennie life; we haven't heard or seen anything from the MWD. Horst believes the tale of the 14 chronically sick waiting to be well enough to travel, but I can't quite believe it.

Middle of the month and the first snow starts to fall – another Russian winter to go through.

Dr Suslowa soon brings us back down to earth on her next visit. The hospital is to be closed down. All 24 patients including the 14 not sentenced men will be transferred south. There will be plenty of fruit and vegetables to speed up their recovery.

This news was like a bolt from the blue, the very fact that we get advance warning gives us food for thought. Horst actually believes the idea that they want to feed us well before sending us home.

Maybe the last transport home told the western press about our continued confinement and general poor state of health? In Russia you never know, everything is possible.

Next day we receive laundered padded clothing, we are able to take off in the morning. Six young soldiers and a lieutenant arrive to act as our escort. They are wearing their best uniforms and they are quite excited about their change of routine. The search before we leave is quite casual.

A big Pullman wagon is waiting for us well-padded with cotton mattresses to avoid the usual draught. Everyone has their own stretcher and in the middle of the carriage are two beds, one for a very sick man and one for Ellen.

The usual little stove is there to provide the necessary heating. There is plenty of wood, even an axe for chopping kindling and for food we have dried fish, tea and a tin of fish for each person. It all looks too good to be true.

The lieutenant promises that we will have fresh water at each major station, then the wagon is closed but we are not locked in.

I still cannot conjure up any positive image of home. I sometimes have nightmares of what home will really be like. My children don't know me, my wife has coped very well without me.

She has been doing laundry for some Americans stationed in the barracks close to them. She has done office work for a small factory and quite a bit of tailoring. What will she make of me when I return? Only a shell of a man she used to know.

By the afternoon our wagon is attached to a larger train and we start to move.

Early next morning we stop at a large station, our guards are delighted to find us all present and correct.

"Good, very good, nix running away, nix shooting."

We are all allowed out onto the platform to visit the toilets accompanied by our guard.

It is Autumn 1950 but the station still looks as if it was war time, the police screen our wagons from the rest of the train.

When we are all safely back on board we receive a big bucket of hot water, we fire up our little stove then brew some tea.

Dr Suslowa has been telling the truth so far, we are definitely heading south. We hope the rest is true as well. We have a few more stops where we get out and receive once more our promised hot water. Our guards are decent chaps, no pushing or shoving. After two more nights we stop around lunchtime, now things change dramatically.

We see a lorry backing up to the wagon and a different group of guards enter the train and everything has to go at speed, dawai, dawai!

The driver of the lorry is an older plennie who gives us a friendly wave. Horst is first to be loaded onto the lorry lifted by two plennies. His legs get thrown in after him.

There are a lot of raunchy comments by the new guards when they see Ellen. The first news we hear from the orderlies, this is a camp for sentenced plennies run under a very tight regime.

This is our first disappointment. We are told that we are going to be admitted to the camp hospital, in camp language referred to as Hell.

4

Russian Prisoner of War Camp
Away from Moscow.
Autumn 1950

We drive around the town and hit every possible pothole or so it seems to the very sick.

This camp contains 5000 men, half of them are German and the rest of them are Hungarians, Romanians and Italians. There are only ten men in the camp who have not yet been sentenced. Five of those are in the hospital. Everyone else has been given a minimum of 25 years, some even 75.

Our hopes sink deeper and deeper and Horst in particular is getting very angry.

"We were told we were the remaining 14 patients."

So thought many others our orderly tells us. He doesn't care, he knows we all have to go home some day.

Our driver, so he tells us, was a German General, we have never had such a distinguished driver. Our orderly points to a low stone building.

"This is Hell, your hospital."

In front of the Budka a bulldog faced Sergeant is waiting for us, he grins as he opens the gate for us and our new home receives us. A scruffy looking nurse stands in the hospital door her eyes fixed on Ellen.

"What does this whore want here?" she asks of the plennies. Ellen gets her reply in first, most of it unprintable. The nurse turns her back to Ellen lifts her skirt and wiggles her bottom at her. The nurse has to do her bit for Russian femininity, so she slowly does up her suspenders!

"Very nice, but only after eight days of scrubbing!" Horst laughs as he says it.

Everyone laughs and Horst has made an enemy. The nurse did not understand his German comment, but everyone laughed at her.

When we enter the ward we are absolutely horrified. We haven't had a bath and now we know why. All the beds are occupied so we have to double up. My bed mate isn't exactly thrilled to bits. He has a kidney infection but it could have been worse. There are plennies here with TB and others with syphilis. Horst shares a bed with a man with severely swollen legs. Ellen draws the worst straw, she gets separated from her husband and even on the toilet she has no privacy. Luckily the starski suspends a couple of sheets around her bed.

When we get our evening soup the impression of being in hell gets even more so with stinking soup of sour cabbage in dirty bowls. My bed mate sees the look of disgust on my face.

"That's it. This is all you get, there is no special diet for hospital patients." The whole camp gets this disgusting muck.

There was no need to leave Moscow for this, where are the fresh fruit and vegetables?

Rumour has it we get a small beaker of plum juice daily, but all it is is water with the occasional pip floating in it. The Italians in the kitchen eat the plums and then spit out the pips into the water.

About 8pm our scruffy nurse arrives carrying a syringe, and the orderly with her carries the ampules. That's what they call dessert here! The nurse fills the syringe with the contents and injects six men with the same needle, then repeats the procedure.

She really is a filthy woman, her hands haven't seen soap for some time; her nails are painted bright red and dirty. I contemplate refusing the injection but one of the other patients warns me that the nurse will fetch reinforcements from the guard room, so I give in.

Ellen too doesn't want to co-operate in spite of the orderlies attempt to calm her down but she too has to give in. Nobody knows what we have been injected with. The labels have all carefully been removed and we get told it's to keep us calm. Why?

We all pass a dreadful night and at long last we can go and attempt to have a wash and use the toilet in equally dirty surroundings.

We wait for the new doctor, but before he arrives we newcomers get a warning not to complain otherwise we could end up in solitary, that's even dirtier than the hospital.

There is no attempt to clean or air the ward, it all stays filthy. When the doctor arrives I find he just fits perfectly into this place called Hell.

A small wide shouldered man, totally bald with huge ears, clad in a filthy white coat enters the room. Everyone reports loud and clear and failure to do so means missing a meal.

"How many dead?" he shouts. There is a meticulously clean Hungarian with him who quietly points out there are new patients.

Horst and I are pointed out to him and its Horst's turn first.

"Nix sick camp," the doctor shouts when he sees his stumps.

Then it's my turn and I say I have post-stroke left side paralysis, but the answer is predictable.

"Nix sanatorium, out."

The Hungarian doctor tells us to report to the Sick Bay at 10am.

"Thank god," shouts Horst. "Anything to get away from this hell hole."

Unfortunately we faced the same doctor in the Sick Bay. He tells Horst to forget about his wooden legs, he can learn to slide on his behind. I get told to take my clothes off and walk. I do my usual 'stroke walk' using my left leg as a prop.

"You Work Group 3"

Beauclair is also waiting to be seen. He has chronic gastroenteritis and he too gets Work Group 3, and he will also get medication from the Sick Bay.

When he asks can he stay close to his wife he gets told the camp is not a cathouse, He is a broken man, all we can do is advise him to try to get his wife out of the hospital so they are together.

We are barely back in the ward when the orderly hands us our belongings. We can't wait to get out of this hellish place. By 11am seven of us including Ellen, who has declared herself cured and well, are ready for transfer into the camp.

We are taken to the German camp leader Georg Meyer a former Major in the Luftwaffe. He greets and welcomes us without much ado and we are sent to existing free places in the barracks; being presented with a married couple gives them a few problems.

Horst and I are in the same billet, but as yet not next to each other. We are informed that in general everyone refers to fellow plennies as 'Sie' it keeps some resemblance of civility alive. The more senior officers are addressed by rank.

It is 4pm and we have to report to the camp doctor to be properly graded for work groups.

The camp is run under very strict lines, it is necessary with so many sentenced men. Any problems we have Georg Meyer promises to do what he can.

The Beauclairs are asked to wait in the bath house until he is able to arrange a place for them to stay. The rest of us are taken to our billet with a note that the orderly carries.

It has started to snow and the orderly takes Horst and I to a shelter under a billet roof as we can't move as fast as the others. He promises to return for us as soon as he has placed the others in their quarters. We are both impressed by the camp so far. The camp leader seemed efficient and organized. Before long the orderly is back and takes us past the Hungarian and Italian barracks. Each nation has their own administration and tries their best to co-operate with the others and not to differentiate too much regarding discipline and cleanliness.

They too have had no mail for six months. That makes life difficult in regard to food, if one has to depend on camp food.

The German work commandos all work in a factory; with their earnings of 180 roubles they buy extra supplies in the camp shop. So the Germans manage, but the Hungarians and Italians work on building sites where they earn less. On one occasion there was nearly a riot and jobs were swapped. The Italians took over the factory, but there were so many complaints from the factory management that the swap had to be reversed.

By then we were in Barrack 3 occupied by 250 Germans, 20 of them were Generals.

The Generals have their own allocated room and sleeping space separate from the men. General Von Geyersberg has decided not to bunk in with them. He is to be my neighbour and everything looks very tidy and neat.

We are both given a small card, mine is 171. Horst has 68, we have to add our names then tie it to the bottom of our bed.

Once we are settled in we have to report to Colonel Bischof the billet leader.

It was nice to have our own beds and I go to join Horst who muses what Dr Suslowa would make of these latest developments. We are sure she would do her utmost to get us out of here, we are also sure she too was a victim of deception.

We report to the billet leader Colonel Bischof. He is a tall slim man, one of his arms is missing and he uses a prosthesis. His room contains just the bare essentials – a bed, a small table and two chairs as well as some shelves. He promises to get us beds next to each other as soon as possible, the only problem, in this camp everyone has to work.

When Horst points to his missing limbs the Colonel says it's absolutely essential for everyone to be occupied, if for no other reason than to stop people brooding.

He feels once we have seen the camp doctor with the works officer something will be found for both of us. He realizes that we are not sentenced but it's still not possible to get our usual officers extra rations of cigarettes, fat and sugar.

But life in camp is bearable and everyone works well together.

One bit of good news, it looks as if the mail service will be re-established before long. It could be just a rumour, but everyone is hopeful.

Everyone including the invalids work – they keep the courtyard tidy and wash up in the kitchen and maintain cleanliness within the barracks.

I go and pick up our spoons, something we plennies always carry with us and join some of the others in the day room. A big stove at both ends keeps the room tolerably warm.

Our dining room is a few minutes walk away, a big room with rows of rough tables and chairs that fill the room. It is spartan but clean. We all line up to receive our bowls of cabbage soup, what a stench! We meet up with Ellen, they have a bit of space partitioned off in the wash house, so far it's lovely and warm. But she dreads to think what it will be like in the summer. After we finish our soup we return to our billet, it's still snowing but the paths and road have been cleared.

My neighbour is there to greet me, he is a small thin man with snow white hair and bushy eyebrows with piercing friendly blue eyes. He is also pleased to have a new neighbour and he knows the camp leader is always very careful who he allocates to this space.

It's one of the few concessions for being over 70 years old. He has been sentenced to two terms of 25 years, due to some time he spent in Russia during World War 1. He has of course appealed against the sentence, but it made no difference. He works in the snow clearing group so he has to take a rest to recharge his batteries now and then. I am very impressed by this man, he exudes an aura of calm and dignity.

He is an impersonation of the old ideal of being an officer, a real German of the school of Potsdam. He no longer wears the red stripe on his trousers and he sleeps peacefully.

I too fall asleep and only wake when called to the Sick Bay. I meet up with Horst who is having a hard time with the snow, so much so he accepts my help! The Sick Bay is close to the camp entrance near the hospital, but quite separate. It's the same group of seven men and Ellen, all recently discharged from the hospital. We all get allocated a number and get called accordingly.

The lady doctor is older, a small solidly built woman, very fond of bright red lipstick and fingernails. She speaks with a very deep almost masculine voice and she smokes. A papirossa is stuck in the corner of her mouth when she asks me do I speak Russian? I decide to do my old teacher proud, I admit to slightly faulty Russian.

She compliments me on my ability and becomes more animated and her slightly Asian face becomes very friendly. I note she has my case history. After a very thorough check-up she decides that my status will be as an invalid. But I have to work. When she finds out that I can read and write Russian she offers me the post of the journal keeper for the Sick Bay.

I have to record the times and dates of visits, treatment and therapies ordered and any other changes.

Dr Gebert the German doctor should really keep this journal but has managed to avoid it wherever possible.

My working hours are 6 to 9 in the morning and 5 to 9 in the evening and my place of work is the ante-room of the surgery.

The next patient greets the doctor like an old friend, he needs an extra hour to fulfil his quota of eight hours, so he gets allocated an hour fire watch at night. When it's Horst's turn he too gets a job he can manage. The works officer will have a special chair made for him and he will become our Librarian. Two older invalided plennies will assist him.

Tonight I will do my first shift as the recorder, it's about time I had something to occupy my mind.

There are many men in the camp who suffer from nightmares. One in particular shouts for help and assures someone that he doesn't know anything. He repeatedly goes through a cross examination by the MWD. When he gets too loud, I wake him up.

Dr Gebert the Tatar's assistant is a conscientious doctor. He is very generous towards many a plennie when he sees they are at the end of their tether and need an additional rest day. Everyone knows his reputation and so far no one has abused his kindness.

He also has a very nice way to keep any exaggerated illness in check. A young man arrived claiming he had a high temperature; its part of my job to take temperatures, so I give him the thermometer and leave him in the waiting room. When I check, it reads 39 which to my limited knowledge seems quite high. Somehow it doesn't compound with the general appearance of the man, but Dr Gebert takes his pulse and repeats the temperature check, only rectal this time, and the reading is 36.

The doctor never says a word just hands him a headache tablet. I doubt he will be back unless he is genuinely ill.

There are also the usual tablet hunters who turn up regularly with some complaint or other. They need their daily visit to the surgery like others need their daily bread.

But our doctor Tatar has obtained large supplies from the former German medical depot and keeps the group of pill addicts happy.

The Tatar turns up every morning at 6.30 and she is genuinely concerned for her plennies. A total opposite to the doctor in the hospital from Hell.

One morning two medical orderlies carry in a very sick man, reluctantly the doctor admits him to hospital and one of the orderlies carries him across on his back, but returns within minutes.

The hospital doctor was present and threw him out as a simulator. The poor man went off to work with his brigade and when they return at night they bring a dead plennie with them.

Another success for that awful Major who calls himself a doctor!

Our Tatar is deeply upset when she gets told of the day's events and explains that only very few Russian doctors have such poor medical ethos or lack of it. Unfortunately this Major works closely with the MWD so he is always safe.

Now we know where we are with the Tatar. I also know her better through my daily contact as the journal keeper. She usually leaves a couple of papirossi at my desk.

She loves to talk about Germany. She herself got as far as Upper Silesia in a fighting group and while there had taken careful note of everything she saw. She remains cautious through our talk – the MWD is never far away. But she looks after the plennies in her care, she has managed to ease many a plennies burden.

Horst Zimmerman enjoys his job as well. His library contains 500 books and he gets on well with his co-workers. We miss our frequent chats, lunchtime is usually the only time we can meet. Ellen Beauclair is one of Horst's most regular clients as she fills her time reading.

The one thing that depresses us all is the lack of contact with the outside world. My neighbour is usually resting when I return from my morning shift, today however he is still awake.

"Tomorrow we get post," he whispers. He had the good news from Colonel Kuckof.

As General Von Geyersberg is not a man given to spreading rumours, I feel ashamed to have asked him where he got his news from. I should have trusted him, but he seems fine about it, like all of us he cannot wait to have news from home.

One of the other types of General made in the Hitler school was our divisional commander; he managed to get away safely on our retreat from the Don to the Donez in 1942/43 and left the remaining group encircled by the enemy. Only the good command and leadership of a Colonel got most of us back to our unit.

We came across our General again near Poltowa. He made the mistake of sitting with some soldiers in a film show where it showed a carefully planned and executed retreat under the General's leadership. The soldiers' memories were quite different, like us they remembered absolute chaos and had it not been for the timely and professional takeover of duty, many more of their comrades would have joined the ranks of wounded, dead and frozen.

Only the presence of the 'chain-dogs' (Military Police, so called for wearing a chain and a metal disc round their necks) prevented the General's lynching.

Next day ten men from the billet report to Colonel Kuckof. Two big lorries arrive accompanied by twenty guards. Once the lorries are emptied they go off and return two hours later laden with parcels.

They have used four large store rooms to sort out all the mail and as usual it's all perfectly organized by the German leader. The plennies who went with the armed guards told us that the latter were needed to protect the van from the Russian crowds who were watching enviously as the mail was transferred from the holding depot.

In the morning after working all night, the men are ready to deliver the mail to the plennies staying in the camp. The work commandos get theirs when they return from work in the evening.

As expected the Sick Bay is having a quiet morning and once finished I go and queue up for my packages, the usual routine of unpacking and comparing the contents with the enclosed list takes time, but everyone waits patiently.

The officer overseeing the checking couldn't contain his amazement at the variety and quality of goods he saw. I receive seven parcels, two from my wife with the remainder from charitable organizations. I can hardly carry all my gifts as my left arm is out of use.

Horst too received five parcels that another plennie carries for him. We are going to have coffee. The hot water is supplied by the Hungarians in exchange for two cigarettes and a piece of chocolate, and we sit and enjoy our new riches.

General Von Geyersberg has also received several parcels and invites us later to join him for coffee.

Now I take my time to admire the beautiful things caring hands have packed for me. Of course, every bit of paper had to be removed by the sender, so sometimes it was a bit hit and miss when a tin was opened. Luckily my wife had taken the trouble to scratch the name of the contents on the tins with a nail.

The other contents apart from the food, contain warm socks, a tracksuit and a pair of gym shoes…all fit.

In the afternoon we have our get-together with Von Geyersberg. He provides the coffee and I the Ryvita with meat paste and Horst sweets and cigarettes.

It's fascinating to listen to our old General, he makes old times and places come alive. He talks of a time before the First World War where the upper classes and the nobility were the recognised leaders. They were born and bred for the job of governing.

What happened later really was a free for all, for anyone without breeding and conscience to get to the top, so clearly displayed by the Generals who live separated from the common herd in our barracks.

We can fully understand General Geyersberg's reason for not living with them; there is one General who sticks out among the rest due to his obnoxious behaviour.

This man obviously had a few parcels from the west and he is busy admiring the contents – lovely salami, wonderful ham, superb cheese… choices, choices what shall I eat first?

Next to him is an older man who comes from East Germany and has not received any parcels. He looks pale and under nourished and all he has is a tin mug full of hot water and a piece of black bread that he cuts into small pieces to make it last longer.

Both Horst and I watch the General boast about his riches and he even asks the man to smell the salami, but he doesn't part with a single bite. So much for comradeship!

Time now passes quickly as life is a bit more pleasant with the aid of friends and family from home.

So it comes as a bolt from the blue when I get ordered to present myself at the MWD office and have to go right away. They intend to alter my status – I am to join the ranks of the sentenced plennies.

5

The MWD occupy a department which is separated into several interview rooms, with the usual padded doors, desk, separate table for the translator and a chair for the plennie facing the desk.

There is a Captain Ludanow, the full light falls on me whilst the Captain sits in the dark.

I state my name and then I am asked to explain why I am limping. Then again I am asked to give details of my personal and army life. I hear everything twice as the Captain speaks a very cultured Russian and the translator speaks a very clear high German without any emphasis.

After about an hour we have completed a resumé of my private life as a civilian. The Captain is not happy with all my answers. Next time he will cover their favourite subject – introduction of Russian agents into Soviet territory.

Next in is Horst and I am not able to tell him much as the translator calls him in. He spends a long time being questioned and when he is still not back after two hours I get really concerned. I know what his temper is like, he finds it hard to keep calm.

The snow is falling very heavily so I go to meet him and just as I get to the MWD billet he comes out. Straight away I see the danger signs. Bright red face, flashing eyes and before we are even half way back to our billet he starts shouting.

"How dare they question my party membership, how was I to teach and keep my family?" and of course he gets into a shouting match with the Captain. He gives away his good knowledge of Russian. He quite rightly feels he paid a heavy price for all his misdeeds, both real and imagined, by losing both his legs while being employed in the Russian industry.

The Captain replied that the Soviet Union was in no way at fault, had he stayed at home and not joined the aggressive army he would still have both legs.

Sadly, this initial interview will affect all future questioning. Horst doesn't seem to care – just as well to get rid of the uncertainty and get his 25 year sentence. One day he will go home.

December 1950

There are only ten days before Christmas and with any luck there will be some mail. My latest news from home was all good. My three older children are all in high school with the financial help of a doctor I met in my early years of imprisonment.

My wife was able to buy a flat in a newly built complex on the outskirts of Amberg. Thanks to the never tiring efforts of my wife the family's living standards have improved no end. Out of every letter and card that I read there is the reassurance that I am still part of the family. My photo is part of every family occasion.

Next day I get called for another cross-examination. This time we get straight to the hub of the problem.

"What tasks did you have on the Eastern Front in January 1945?"

Before I get a chance to reply the MWD Major calls the Captain out of the room. This gives me time to gather my thoughts, and after he returns I once more go through the history of being ordered to the Intelligence Corps in Tilsit which was still in German hands then.

It was a time of retreat and sending Russian agents across was the last thing on anyone's mind. As always they are not prepared to believe me and he tells me to go away and think about it. There is a definite threat in there but we will have to wait till next time.

With Christmas approaching preparations are afoot to celebrate as best we can. General Von Geyersberg has invited Horst and myself to a get-together.

Three days before Christmas the Sick Bay is not busy and I am exchanging a few words with our lady doctor when two guards arrive with orders to collect me.

Both guards, a Lieutenant and a soldier are carrying machine guns and once they confirm I am Schmitt they try to handcuff me. When the doctor objects as I have left-handed paralysis he just puts the handcuff on my right wrist. I ask can I collect my belongings and get told there is no need. I shall not be away long.

Dr Gebert promises to inform Horst and the lady doctor lights a cigarette and puts it between my lips and at the same time pushes an unopened packet in my coat pocket. As we leave the Sick Bay a new commando with General Von Geyersberg notices us and tries to bar our way. The lieutenant looks very uncomfortable. They are not allowed any contact with me, the General promises to look after my belongings and tell Horst.

When I get taken off the register in the Budka (Guardroom) we leave camp. Outside there is a police van waiting for me. I am still handcuffed to the Lieutenant and I feel like a serious offender. Before long we both relax and smoke a cigarette together. The Lieutenant wants to know whether I have murdered somebody. I assure him that I had been a soldier just like him, to get the usual reply.

"Nitschewo!"

We drive through the streets of town and I can see very little through the barred windows. Before long we arrive at our destination and the rattle of chains tells me I am once more in prison.

Prison

We drive through a large gate and after leaving the van we enter a large reception room. Another lieutenant takes over and my handcuff is removed. I sign a short form giving my particulars and then my escort leaves.

I am asked do I speak Russian and when I confirm I do I get told that according to prison regulations I have to take a bath and have my hair shorn off. When I object to the latter as I am an officer, I achieve little. Regulations are regulations.

After my haircut and bath I get my own clothes back minus belt and laces. I receive a small wooden token with a number. I get rubbed down again but get away with my cigarettes – not much good without matches, but you never know.

Then I get handed to a prison guard, we walk through a lot of corridors until we stop in front of a reinforced door.

"You are going to have very refined company," he tells me. He opens the door pushes me inside and quickly shuts it again.

I find myself in a dusky cell where only a little bit of light comes in through a small opening near the ceiling and it takes a while for me to see anything. The cell is large and stinks to high heaven. The contents of a bucket and the sweat of many men conspire to make the air almost unbearable. On the other side of the wall I can see a row of men sitting on the floor.

They all stare at me, I cannot think of anything else to say so I say "Good evening."

Total silence is the reply, so I sit down near the door and wait for whatever will happen next.

One of the men opposite me gets up and comes across to me.

"Who are you?"

I give my name and tell him I am a plennie, but before I am finished speaking he hits me in the face which gives me an almighty kick, then another man gets up and lands my attacker with a right thump and puts him down and out of action for a while.

"Are you really a Fritz?" he wants to know, and what had I done to end up in jail.

When I tell him that as far as I know I haven't done anything, everyone laughs and say they know just what I mean.

The man who defended me told the others to leave me in peace as I was under his protection. This man belongs to the Blatnoi – an organized gang of professional criminals like a Mafia who live and die by very strict rules. Once a member there is no get-out card, no place is safe from their long arm of retribution. The man who hit me has to empty the bucket for the next few days, to learn who is boss.

Michail, my protector clears a space next to him. The heating is on full blast and I try to take my coat off and Michail helps me. I tell him my left side is useless and feel it best if I hand over my cigarettes. He accepts them without a word, the customs and behaviour amongst criminals are still a mystery to me, but obviously that was the right thing to do. When I speak to him I can understand him, but the other men's slang is more difficult for me.

Now the problem is fire. Someone stands in front of the inspection hole, another man produces a bit of cotton out of his jacket and another has a thin splinter of wood.

By twisting the piece of wood at high speed he produces a spark that catches the cotton wad and catches fire and the first cigarette is lit.

Michail is first, then me, then the others.

A small bit of smoke is clearly visible which unfortunately the guard notices as well. With reinforcements of three other guards we all undergo a careful search but nothing is found. After the guards had strip-searched three of the gang they give up as it was too dangerous for them in our cell.

When the guards leave we take up our old positions. Michail laughs and says to me:

"Fritz fetch the papirossi," and I make for the door where there is a hidden recess. No luck and everywhere else I look the same thing – nothing! "Oh Fritz what an amateur you are," he comments and with that points over my head to the ceiling – the guards like me looked everywhere else. He explains to me what had taken place.

Whilst I was being searched one of the men chewed the lid of the box then stuck it on the ceiling.

The food we get is the usual disgusting fish soup and sometimes porridge at lunchtime. Time passes quickly, the men have many questions about Germany that I answer as best I can.

They themselves are somewhat reluctant to answer any of my questions. It's considered bad manners to ask personal questions in their fraternity, but I have found out they are all doing 10 to 25 year stretches and are waiting to be transported.

When they ask what a German prison is like, Michail tells them I would not be able to answer their question as he doubts whether I have seen a German prison from the inside.

After three days there I have to go for an interrogation. It's the morning of 24th December. It is a nice surprise to be handed a Christmas parcel rather than have to answer questions. The translator of the camp had taken the time and trouble to deliver the parcel. What a kind thing to do.

I have to undo the parcel but find it difficult with just one hand, the lieutenant assists me with his pocket knife.

The contents are wonderful, I can see his eyes getting bigger with every item I unpack. There is liver sausage, black pudding, salami, a packet of margarine, a bag of sugar lumps, sweets and a bar of chocolate and two packets of cigarettes as well as Ryvita.

He tells me I have to empty the tins as metal is not allowed in the cells, so with some difficulty and help from his (made in Germany) pocket-knife all the contents of the tins are carefully placed in the empty package amongst the wrapping paper. I manage to hide the cigarettes up my sleeve.

The guard kindly helps me pick up my goods, so on the way back to the cell I offer him half of the sliced sausage. He opens the door to the washroom and gives me a bit of soap to wash my sticky hands.

He thanks me for the piece of sausage – he could never take a gift from a criminal but as I am a plennie he will accept it gratefully. He only cut off a tiny piece, he will take the rest home for lunch.

He checks the corridor to make sure it is clear and he also warns me about my cell mates. I tell him I have a protector.

When I offer him the other half of the sausage he refuses but asks for a bit of chocolate instead. He has a little boy at home who has never tasted chocolate.

With a friendly pat on my shoulder he lets me into the cell, not without handing me a few matches and promising to turn a blind eye to our smoking. When I enter the cell, everyone looks at me and my package; without a second thought I hand it over to Michail. The contents are all mixed up but we soon sort them out. He comments about only having half a sausage and I produce the matches and to make him even prouder I shake my sleeve and the cigarettes tumble to the floor.

"Welcome to the fraternity," Michail compliments my swift action. To smuggle cigarettes into a cell is highly dangerous but very profitable. He decides that it's time I had some basic survival lessons whilst surrounded by experts.

Piotr is to give the first lesson by stealing our guard's pocket-knife. I prefer to go without the lesson, but I do not want to cause offence, however he produces the upper half of a kitchen knife, where he had hidden it during the search is a miracle to me.

But as Michail said, they are experts. The knife is handed to me so I can sort out my foodstuffs in some sort of order. Once that's done I hand the knife back to Michail. He proposes that we should eat the sausage tonight as they won't keep. He doesn't want to die of food poisoning, he wants a proper gangster's death.

When the midday soup gets handed in the knife blade disappears. We eat our soup and look forward to our treat at supper. We will all have a smoke after lunch – cigarettes with a proper match.

"I knew the Fritz had more culture," jokes Michail.

The men do not really enjoy the German cigarettes that much, compared with the Russian smokes they are very mild.

I am busy dividing the sugar lumps and sweets. The men hand in a slice of black bread and Michail spreads it with margarine topped with liver-sausage and black pudding. The sugar lumps and sweets complete the evening meal.

Piotr jokes about the food being such good quality but lousy packaging, before I can explain he smiles.

"I know, I know. I have seen how they do it."

Michail suggests one more smoke. I tell him that today is a very special day. It is Christmas Eve where at home we all go to church and then receive a present.

After a moment's thought he hands me the half of the salami that was left as a present from them all. If my family and friends knew that I was spending Christmas Eve with a gang of criminals they would probably not wish to have their own celebrations. But as it is, I feel safe and sheltered by the men.

Suddenly Michail starts to sing quietly and bit by bit the others join in, by humming a background harmony. It's a song about the hardships of being a prisoner who is longing for home and freedom.

The night guard tells us to keep the noise down and before long a snoring chorus is all that can be heard.

Alas, all that good food has caused chaos in our innards. There is a mad rush to the bucket, and before long there is a terrible stench in the cell. We politely ask our guard could we empty our bucket but no luck, we will have to wait till morning. The thick air gives me a headache and night seems interminable, never was morning so welcome.

We all can't wait to get out into the fresh air. Our usual guard has left the cell door wide open whilst we are enjoying our ablutions. On our return to the cell I hand the other half of the sausage quickly to the guard.

Speedily it disappears in his uniform pocket, he gives me a big smile and pushes me back into the cell.

Before long there is a rumour that all criminals are going East in a transport. Michail gives them directions for the move as he knows that they will be separated for security reasons.

He doesn't think I will travel with them. Again I am surprised how much he knows about me – he is already saying goodbye to me. He tells me to remember his name should I ever find myself in prison again.

All ten men are serious criminals who have offended against the laws of this country in a most serious way. They simply refuse to bow down to the system, that their own system is worse in its ultimate punishment they accept without question.

They only tolerated me in their midst because I accepted their rules and customs without question.

I also realize Captain Ludanow quite deliberately had me incarcerated in this particular cell. He hoped it would give him a solution where he could keep his hands clean.

I get ordered to the interview room. On our way there the guard whispers you are going back to your camp, I hope you enjoyed your stay. I have to see the funny side of the remark. Enjoy it maybe is overdoing it a bit! But it has certainly widened my horizons and taught me even more how the other half lives.

The lieutenant who brought me in here is waiting for me. The guard hands me my belt and laces. No time to put them on, but I am used to coping without them now.

I have to sign another document. It's 7th January 1951 so I have spent seventeen days here. I sign without argument as there would be no point in asking why I was there, it would be pointless. But I have to play the piano (i.e have my fingerprints taken) this gets added to my record which contains two pictures of me. I was never aware of having my picture taken, it must have been done whilst I was being questioned.

I am now a fully fledged member of the Russian criminal system.

6

**Back at the Russian Prisoner of War Camp
Away from Moscow
January 1951**

When I get back to the camp, I go through the Budka at double quick time straight to Captain Ludanow's office.

He wants to catch me whilst the impression of the prison is still very much alive in my memory. When I enter his office I greet the translator with a friendly nod which she accepts with a smile. It's only thanks to her and the delivery of my parcel that my stay was easier than originally planned by the Captain.

He ignores me totally – well as much as he can as I still have the smell of the prison on me. He tells me I look ill but I reply that I have no reason to complain. However, he still thinks I had a bad time with the criminals and threatens me with spending the rest of my life with people like that if I don't tell the truth now.

However, I have to disappoint him when I mention my 'friend' Michail.

I can see I have hit on a sore spot. Did I know Michail belongs to the Blatnoi and what reputation this particular gang had?

I could have told the good Captain that I had been treated well by the criminal world, in fact better than by many so called upright citizens, but that was pushing my luck a bit.

The Captain looks totally perplexed.

"Here I am trying to frighten the life out of this German and what happens? He comes back and tells me he made friends and had a good time."

I also learned a bit about the legal system from Michail. After all this was 1951 and I had not been sentenced, so I had rights. With Michail's help I had written a letter of complaint to the head of the Soviet prison system.

That was the last straw for the Captain, he thumped the table and told me this letter would cost me dearly.

"Not me," was my reply and with that I made a hasty retreat. The translator whispered that I had really riled the Captain this time.

When I am walking to my billet I notice there is a lot of activity. The plennies are wearing new quilted outfits, they even have fur hats and new gloves.

I hurry to see General Von Geyersberg and Horst to get all my news. To his surprise I haven't been sentenced but I can see he has bad news for me by the expression on his face. I automatically think there is bad news from home but no, it's much closer at hand.

My long suffering friend Horst who has been my companion through much adversity died on Christmas Eve.

He died quite suddenly of meningitis. It started in the morning with a bad headache and high temperature, by lunchtime he was unconscious and by early evening he passed away quietly.

Poor Horst. He had no inner and physical resistance to such an infection, he was always scared of going home. How would a lively family cope with a man with no legs?

It is now my sad task to bring the news to his wife, as both our wives had been in regular contact and in such a way we were able to get more news home about our lives in captivity.

It is one of the many sad facts of a plennie's life that friendships cannot last. Mine and Horst's had lasted longer than most.

The rest of the camp has seen a lot of changes. The Italians, the Hungarians and Romanians have all been transferred to other camps on the eastern side of the Urals.

The Germans ceased working on 5th January and they too are waiting to be transported, but where to? There have been hints that it's going to be Siberia.

So at the moment the plennies are spending all their hard earned savings, in spite of being told by the camp leader to hold on to it. If it is Siberia they will need every rouble. I too find a new outfit on my bed and I change into it and take my old clothes to the store. As always I keep my old coat, it's been with me throughout my plennie time.

On my way to the stores I meet Ellen, she looks well as always, compared with that poor wreck of a husband.

Then I go to visit the Tatar and she is delighted to see me back in camp. We sit and enjoy one of her cigarettes and she wants to know all about my time in prison. I thank her for her gift of cigarettes, which opened the way for me to make life more bearable among the criminals.

She says that I am turning into a proper Russian by accepting life as it is, not as I would like it to be.

In the evening I spend a lot of time talking to General Von Geyersburg. Horst is still very much on our minds. I tell him of my dream of him on Christmas Eve where he is standing waving to me at the camp gate.

Next day I report as usual but alas, no customers. A messenger arrives for Dr Gebert, he has to report at once to join a transport of 900. Ellen and her husband are also part of that transport.

There is a lot of noise and confusion at the meeting place, the searches are very thorough. Most of the plennies are still under the mistaken impression they are going home!

They will not listen to common sense. The absence of any armed escorts strengthens their hope. As they leave the camp they break into song. 'At home we will all meet again,' but the song suddenly stops when some jeeps turn up with armed guards and dogs to join their convoy.

The disappointment and disillusionment set in and must have hit them hard. For once the Russians told the truth but nobody wanted to listen.

Even the General is hit hard, he too had hoped for home. He gets called up the next morning to join a transport of 800 – a quick goodbye is all we have time for.

I join the Tatar for stocktaking in the Sick Bay. She tells me it will be my turn tomorrow. I would have preferred to stay, but my wishes do not count. She tells me one day I will go home.

Next morning I return to the Sick Bay to say "Thank you and farewell," to the Tatar. She tells me it's a special transport with destination unknown but definitely not home. She shakes both my hands, both the orderly and I receive a packet of cigarettes.

My goods are all packed in my rucksack, it's amazing how little we have, and how much we treasure each individual item.

At the general meeting place all the names are called out, except six of us. When the others leave, we form a sad little huddle. We are the ones who have not been sentenced yet.

A Russian officer comes across and takes us to a building that used to hold the German administration. We can help ourselves to anything we want from the empty barracks, as we shall be here for a few more days.

It's really weird. The camp is empty apart from us and two guards stroll casually through the camp.

The Russian cook gives us rations for five days. Barley, bread, salt, tea, potatoes and lard. Now all we have to do is decide who is to be cook!

I take over as head cook and bottle washer. Tonight we will have a hot meal for a change.

The officer comes to see us and tells us that we have to move all the shelves out of the barracks and move them to the courtyard. I am excused because of my status.

My first night's meal will be Goulash. When I return to the kitchen to search for herbs and spices I find the rats have already moved in. Luckily I find some paprika and some laurel leaves and even a bundle of onions. When the others return a lovely aroma of food meets them at the door. I have even managed to set the table after a fashion, so after a quick wash up we all sit down together and enjoy our meal. We round off a pleasant evening with a game of chess. The Russian officer comes and watches our game for a while and tells us that work will start at 8am the next morning.

A few days pass in this fashion, the horizon is still covered in mist and fog regarding our future.

When the fifth day dawns we know something has to happen today as our rations were only for five days. Just as we are sitting down after lunch our Russian arrives and tells us it's time to go.

The search is easy, we all found some mess tins and we are allowed to keep them. We put out the fire, take our luggage and walk across to the Budka. It's bitterly cold outside after our well heated billet.

We get our travel rations and stash them away, then we leave the Budka and on the outside we are faced with a prison lorry and several armed guards.

We drive through the town and once more towards, to me, a very familiar prison.

In the courtyard we see large groups of men and women sitting in the snow and they are all loaded together into large lorries, helped along by kicks and pushing by the guard's rifle butts. I suspect Michail and his lot are amongst this sorry collection of humanity.

A captain looks in our lorry. "Room enough for nine boys."

Youngsters of varying ages climb in and sit at our feet. One wants to speak to the officer but he just gets threatened and told to keep quiet.

When we leave we find we are at the tail of a convoy followed only by an armoured car. We come to a stop at the goods station where the security measures surpass everything I have ever seen.

Everybody is loaded at top speed, anyone slacking gets the usual kick or rifle butt. Punches, kicks and rifle butts are falling at every lorry. Dante's picture of hell must have been dreamed up here!

When it's our turn to leave the lorry it's quite a different thing. We are asked quietly to step down and marched to our rail wagon. As I am not as quick as the others one of the guards is about to give me a swift kick when he is pushed to one side by the officer.

"Are you mad? These men are prisoners of war!"

The compartments are separated in such a way that there is no way communication is possible, one guard is in the corridor keeping watch over several compartments turned into cells.

Compared with other prisoners we travel in reasonable comfort. There are six of us in one compartment. The others have about twenty-five in the same space. Two officers walk along the corridor and they inform us that we have different rights compared to the jailbirds.

We have to go to the toilet together, but apart from that we can tell the guard if we need anything.

A bit embarrassed, one of the officers asks if we mind having the boys with us again. It's an order dressed up as a request so we give in gracefully. The boys climb up to the top bunks with clear instructions not to stray anywhere else.

The young guard looking after us is not very keen on his job. He hates to listen to the suggestive talk of the women who are in the next compartment.

I try to involve him in conversation and when I ask can we smoke he says yes but only one at a time. That is as far as I get with him.

As I light up I hear a little whisper from the bunk above.

"Please Fritz give us a smoke!"

A dirty little boy's hand takes the lit cigarette out of my hand. The boys sit totally naked in the heat of the upper bunks. They are all Besprisornyis (neglected homeless children) from Odessa. They were caught when a group of them attacked a man with the intention of robbing him.

Unfortunately they had picked on a MWD officer who was armed and shot their ringleader. The rest of the gang were arrested and were now on their way to a youth education camp.

These camps are the breeding and training grounds for criminals. There they teach each other survival skills of the criminal world.

Everyone seems to have settled down. The many changes, the warmth and sound of the train makes everyone sleepy. Even the women seemed to have quietened down.

Next morning we arrive at a major station. We have no idea where we are. There is no way we can look out of the tiny barred window.

A wild fight starts amongst the women and only with the help of other guards and their whips are they able to quieten them down.

When the guard comes to us he looks totally unmoved by the recent battle with the women. He opens our door and lets the boys out to go to the toilet. They climb down and line up in the corridor hands on their heads. Once they have finished it is our turn.

We have to go past the women. We can see they are the scum of Russian society. We are very glad they are safely tucked away behind their locked and barricaded door.

Two of our officers start a game of chess. Russians are great admirers of the game. The boys watch very carefully from above and the guard too watches with interest. I feel very thirsty so I ask the guard for water. On his request I hand over two mess tins. Two other guards fill the tins with ice cold water. We were contemplating our salted fish but on trying them they were found to be much too salty for our consumption.

The thirst would have been unbearable shortly afterwards but the boys, always hungry, eat our fish and before long have a raging thirst. When their gang leader asks for water he gets told to shut up and wait for lunchtime.

The lad persists in his quest for water and finally the guard has had enough and opens our door to give him a good hiding.

The youngster moves with the speed of a monkey to the top bunk where he is out of reach.

"You can't touch us, we are Papa Stalin's boys!"

When the guard has locked us in again I ask for water and two more mess tins are filled again. The guard knows what I am doing but pays no attention. We drift off to sleep again only to be woken later at night when we realize our wagon has been shunted and then stops.

I take a chance and ask the guard and surprisingly he answers. We are to go to a camp for plennies in this area.

The prisoners are going to a dispersal camp.

With the help of the sunlight we have figured out that we have first moved in a northerly direction, then headed west.

PART SIX

1

Another Russian Prisoner of War Camp
1951

The night passes without incident. I am a bit curious what the new camp will bring. I do not realize that I am gradually adopting the Russian attitude of *we will see* - you live longer that way.

To get to worrying about what might happen is just a waste of mental energy and I just concentrate on what's directly in front of me.

More than a year has passed since the mass arrests, I can see what the world at large thinks about these by very occasionally getting to see a Russian paper.

They defend the state's action against war criminals but you have to learn to read between the lines in Russia. If things hadn't changed since the spring I too would be amongst the sentenced plennies.

Morning begins and with it the stirring of life all around us. Everyone gets taken to the toilet and we get allowed to have a quick wash.

The unloading of prisoners starts as usual and nothing is done as fast as the guards would like. Our nine young boys are ready to go and they carry nothing except what they are wearing. They have to be quick to avoid the usual slap round the ears. The youngest lad begs for a cigarette and quickly hides it in his pocket.

Our Captain arrives and wishes us "Good morning."

He chases the boys out of the compartment as we hold on to our worldly goods, otherwise the boys would steal them.

Outside the noise and shouting continues until we hear the sound of the lorries driving away. A blessed peace surrounds us as the doors open and fresh air enters the wagon.

The distant noises we hear make us sure we are near a major town and station.

After a short while the Captain returns with our guard, we take our belongings and leave the train. We are expected. A small police van is there with two new soldiers who carry their guns across their shoulders, a sure sign they do not consider us dangerous.

Their hands are buried in their fur coat pockets.

When I say "Doswidania," (Auf Wiedersehen) to the Captain he laughs.

"I hope not!" He says and wishes us all the best.

The guards sit in the front part of the van, separated from us by a metal mesh. One very tall lanky chap cautiously asks if we have smokes. I offer him my cigarettes and he takes one for himself and one for his mate. We are allowed to smoke as well.

We are aware of driving through a big town and then the suburbs and eventually we stop in front of a Budka. A lieutenant comes out to meet us. Our clothing has to be handed in before we are allowed in. He takes off and comes back with two plennies who are carrying old greasy looking outfits for us.

When one of the group objects, the lieutenant says that's fine, I will just get the guards to assist you.

Yuri the tall Russian guard who collected us from the train begins to look worried. He cannot understand these Germans, how can they not obey an officer's command?

The police van has left, so the two guards must belong to the camp. With no other option we start taking our clothes off in the freezing snow, but then the lieutenant notices our new underwear and he puts a stop to the proceedings and the plennies have to go and get new underwear for us.

They returned with laundered but used underwear and once more we take our clothes off.

Corporal Yuri can see that I cannot manage very well, so he helps me with taking both my new travelling clothes off and putting the camp clothes back on.

It must be -20° but none of us even catches a cold; at long last we are allowed in the lovely warm Budka and gradually we can stop shivering.

The main means of communication in this camp is Russian. A Yugoslav who is the Starski in the banya (bathhouse) gives us a quick rundown of the camp.

There are no sentenced German plennies in this camp. The main contingent of the camp are 300 Poles, they had joined the SS in a Polish legion against the Russians. They are Polish but their part of Poland is now part of Russia and they are likely to be summarily sentenced.

There is also a big Yugoslav group as well as people from Holland, France, England, Norway, Denmark and Finland. Also a few Jewish people who had emigrated from Germany at the beginning of the war. The majority of the above nationals had volunteered to fight in the SS during the war.

The German contingency only counts twenty so far, so we must be a welcome addition.

The MWD was very active. Two Lieutenants Mirow and Andreitsch, the translator was called Tonya.

The spy system within the camp was highly organized. Now for our quarters. We report to the camp leader who is a Yugoslav and he welcomes us and lets us deposit our belongings in his office. After lunch, when some of the work detail returns to camp he will see to our quarters with other Germans.

First we have to see the doctor and her assistant, a doctor from Argentina. The main jobs are taken up by locksmiths, carpenters and mechanics, the pay is the usual 180 roubles a month and the camp canteen provides the necessary extras for sale.

On our way to the Sick Bay we meet a young blonde woman with a baby. She is part of the Polish group who met and married their Polish husbands and now live in the camp.

We sit in the waiting room and one by one get called in. Then it's my turn, Dr Giessler the Argentinian assistant speaks accent free German. The Russian is Dr Onissimowna who notices my limp and asks the reason for it, so obviously my case history has not yet arrived.

My Russian knowledge turns out to be very useful once again and I give her a fairly detailed run down. She listens carefully and then gives me a thorough physical examination.

When she has completed this, she asks whether I am very susceptible to emotional influences. I confirm this and she tells me to avoid this at all costs. I laugh and ask her to pass this message to the MWD.

She carefully changes the subject and tries to convince me that the Germans in the camp are waiting to go home soon.

She puts 'invalid' on my papers which means I do not have to work. So far so good, neither the doctor nor her assistant are a danger to me. Six of us wait in the warm banya until lunchtime. When we go for lunch we are pleasantly surprised. Apparently everyone contributes a few kopeks for the cook to purchase some extra herbs and spices.

The sour cabbage soup contains nice pieces of potato and something which almost looks and tastes like meat. Everything proceeds peacefully, everyone joins an orderly queue and sits at their usual table.

After lunch we get shown to our quarters. I share a bunk with Hans Wohlgemut, he is very pleased with himself as he has got a job as a carpenter in the factory. He really is a salesman by profession, but has a good knowledge of carpentry and has technical know-how. Sadly I have none of that. I am a fairly useless individual in the technical field.

I use the afternoon to find my bearings in the camp, while having a good nose around I enter a big room which mystifies me, but not for long. A Russian Lieutenant comes out of the one hidden corner and shouts at me.

"What are you doing here?" I get such a fright I answer in Russian.

"I am new in the camp and just want to get my bearings."

What followed was hardly a friendly conversation with questions barked at me and I have to be very careful to answer correctly and to remain polite.

I gather I have just met one of the MWD officers and I am on top of his 'to be questioned' list. He calls me a dangerous intellectual. That just about sets the tone for our future meetings. I could kick myself for letting my mouth get ahead of my brain, this man can make or break me.

I continue my camp inspection and just intend to be a bit more careful. There is an out of use railway wagon which makes me curious, it has little windows with curtains and all looks very mysterious.

Before I get to decide whether to look through the windows I get addressed by a tall young plennie.

"Hello. My name is Juergen Bachmann, I am the camp electrician."

After I tell him who I am he opens the security lock on the wagon and invites me in. It's a small room with a bench in the centre and shelves along the wall that contain an assortment of radios in various states of disrepair.

He has also got a good selection of hand tools and rolls of copper wire of various thicknesses. Under his bench he has a small radiator and in front stands a very comfortable looking armchair. A blanket suspended from the ceiling separates his workroom from his living space.

His bed is used as a couch during the day and two well-made armchairs sit next to a little round table. He even owns a few books, the whole impression is one of comfort and cosiness.

I take a seat and accept a cup of tea.

At first it's the usual careful getting to know one another, and more importantly 'can we trust each other'. I am always suspicious of Germans in privileged positions.

Juergen has a degree in engineering and the Russian administration has appointed him as camp electrician. He also repairs radios and the income flows into the coffers of the admin. But he also has a little sideline in speedy repair which costs extra and that is his to keep.

It's not always money, he often gets paid in kind and he manages to live quite comfortably amongst his books. He has the Elegies by Rainer Maria Rilke, he reads aloud to me and barbed wire and the camp are lost in the beautiful poetry.

"Conspiratia," suddenly interrupts our day dreaming, but more as a joke than serious. It's the younger of the MWD officers and he is the total opposite to the other officer. Whereas the other was squat and uncared for looking, this man is elegant to a point of foppishness. His perfectly fitting uniform is topped off by a silk cravat. His high boots are a symphony of beautiful black leather and he is surrounded by a hint of Eau de Cologne.

He accepts a cup of tea and asks Juergen about his radio. As far as Juergen is concerned it's a totally outdated model and useful only for spare parts.

I think it's time I took off, I shall have plenty of time to meet officer Mirow in his official capacity.

On the way back to my billet I see the Camp Hospital which is under the leadership of a German surgeon. The hospital only deals with minor surgery, there are ten beds and anything major gets transferred to the town's hospital.

There is a lot to tell on my return, my bunk mate's workplace is well heated so he is quite content, less happy are two of the other officers as they are working outside on a building site which is a great hardship in this weather.

Daily new transports arrive in dribs and drabs, even single plennies arrive and most are not sentenced.

The parcel post has been following me through several locations as I can see by the stamps.

I can well use the extra rations and I have been able to write home so my family know my new address.

Two weeks have passed and I still haven't been called to the MWD but one day one of my billet mates gets called to their office and returns very shortly just to collect his things. His escort will not even allow us to shake hands, he is off to prison.

The atmosphere is now at an all time low, everyone expects to be called next, whether guilty or not guilty is quite irrelevant. The regular influx of German plennies just confuses the issue. Some are already sentenced, some are not.

2

February 1951

Rumour has it the Dutch are going home, there are about thirty of them. But suddenly the MWD are very interested in them, there are daily interrogations but we cannot find out what they are being questioned about.

By the end of February the work brigades are staying on camp. One lunchtime a transport list gets posted and all the Dutch are on it.

Two of my colleagues attend their interrogations one evening and one returns severely distressed. He was in charge of a police regiment which was appointed to root out partisans behind the lines. He is accused of having ordered the execution of non-combatants.

The other officer returns hampered by an escort to collect his things and is allowed no communication. That only leaves half our group.

Not even the impending departure of the Dutch cheer us up as we too are likely to depart, but in different directions.

One of the remaining group, a chap called Klose offers to play chess with me. I put up five cigarettes and he stakes his life. I refuse such a deal but he stays adamant. He is generally a bit weird but a good player, so we start our game. I notice even from the first move he is not concentrating, his mind is elsewhere. After five moves I can call "Checkmate!" He just about holds himself together. He shouts at me to carry on playing and after my seventh move he gets up and tips the figures on the floor.

He refuses a return match as he is not in the right mood. Klose sits with his head in his hands and frightens us all by a sudden burst of laughter.

"Right you lot, stop looking so miserable! We are going to celebrate my wife's birthday."

He uncorks a bottle of vodka and drinks 'to life', when I suggest we should drink to his wife, he replies we are a bit late. She died in

1943 in Berlin during the bombing. Today was the anniversary of her death as well as her birthday.

A very uncomfortable silence hangs over us. Klose shakes everybody's hand and then walks towards his bed.

At night I awake quite suddenly and notice Klose's bed is empty, his blankets are neatly folded and his rucksack is on his bed, not under.

I wake up the chap above me and we start a search. First the toilets, then the washroom. No luck. A guard on the watchtower tells us to get lost, but when we ask him whether he has seen anyone he recalls an incident.

He had just come on duty about three hours ago when he had seen a German going into the Dutch accommodation on the first floor above the MWD quarters. We run up the stairs as quickly as possible with the ice and my limp, but still nothing. We are just about to come downstairs when we notice a ladder leaning against the wall and from it hangs the body of Klose.

We gently lift Klose off the ladder, he was frozen stiff and well beyond any human help. I get the other German to go to the Budka and get the corporal on watch. Whilst alone with him I say a quick prayer which is all I can do for him.

The plennie returns with Yuri the soldier who met us when we first arrived.

He takes one look and does the sign of the cross, he has no idea what to do. I tell him to go and inform the duty officer while one of the Dutchmen helps carry Klose's body down to the washroom.

Corporal Yuri, is dead scared he will get the blame for Klose's death. When we tell him that the guard had seen him earlier on he is visibly relieved, someone else can carry the can.

When I tell Yuri that we must fetch a doctor he is mystified.

"What for, he is very dead?"

We need a medical death certificate so Dr Giessler is called and they say the Lord's Prayer. We all join in and at the end the doctor removes his hat, makes a sign of the cross, we all follow suit as does Yuri.

We return to our beds but sleep is out of the question and 6am is very welcome today. I keep telling myself I should have prevented his death, but then I reason that had I been successful last night he was sure to try again and be successful.

I hope God shows more compassion to this man than we did.

When the work commando leaves, the Dutch contingency receive their new travel clothes, but there is no real atmosphere. Klose's death hangs over us all.

However, the Dutch say goodbye to us all and present us with a lot of their belongings and they march to the Budka. Nobody carries any written messages – the death of Klose is quite enough news to take back.

All but two of the Dutchmen have gone but where are the other two? The big lorries taking the Dutch to the station have gone but the police van is there and two escorts accompany the two handcuffed Hollanders. Their luggage gets thrown in the back after them – typical example of the MWD system!

How will they explain Klose's suicide? A number of senior officers have arrived to sort out the cause and effect of the man's death.

Our 'in house' MWD officers look very worried, they both dread being sent to the Far East or the freezing North.

Shortly after lunch I have to present myself at the MWD office. The questioning is directed by a Colonel. It's rare that a plennie's suicide causes that much commotion, but it is 1951 and the world news will now hear all about it from the repatriated Dutchmen.

I am asked about my thoughts on the death. What had persuaded Klose to kill himself? I informed them he was afraid of being arrested. When Lieutenant Andreitsch said he had not threatened him with arrest he was sharply told to shut up by the Colonel. Andreitsch seems to visibly shrink, his face turns grey.

Then I explained that a group of us had recently joined this camp and we were all plain plennies (not sentenced) and two of the officers had already been arrested and Klose had felt it was his turn next. I had similar fears as well as Wohlgemut.

The Colonel gives me his word of honour that I shall not be arrested. I shall go home as soon as my case is cleared. Whatever that means.

Once I return to our quarters there is a call for an assembly. The Colonel gives us a speech in which he says that Officer Klose tried to escape his trial on earth, but now he has to face superior judgement.

Officer Mirow looks all right but Andreitsch still looks worried.

Two days pass, the carpenter produces a coffin for Klose and I get called to Mirow's office and told to direct the religious ceremony. I have to write down exactly what I am going to say. No sermon, just the burial ceremony.

In the evening all the plennies gather, the coffin is put on wooden blocks in front of them.

After I have said my blessing the coffin is carried past all the lined up plennies with their hats removed. The four soldiers on guard are in their best uniforms. The Russian press is also present and the flash bulb lights accompany the procession into the graveyard.

A few days later I meet Juergen the electrician. He invites me to his place for a chat and some tea. I ask if I can bring Wohlgemut but he would rather I come on my own this time.

This evening thirty Germans move into the empty quarters of the Dutch. The move doesn't take long. We just pack our rucksacks and try to get to the new place quickly to make sure we get a decent space.

Wohlgemut races along with our two rucksacks while I follow more slowly with our mattresses. He is lucky to have secured two beds next to each other.

When I am about to leave for Juergen's place Wohlgemut gets ready to join me but I have to explain that I cannot take him this time as Juergen had specified I should come on my own.

Juergen has set up a melodic door chime. He laughs, it is a greeting as well as an alarm system.

I get offered a choice of tea or vodka so I agree to both – first tea, then vodka.

He hums and haws for a bit, but then he shows me how much he trusts me. He has been able to repair one of the old radios to such a degree that he can get a western station. In his workroom the official radio plays music, but we are both anxiously listening to Radio West Berlin. They bring an in-depth report from the repatriated Dutchmen and our camp is described in detail. The suicide of officer Klose is mentioned as are several names including mine and Wohlgemut, we are described as the two men awaiting arrest.

We listened absolutely spellbound. He had heard it first at lunchtime and we are aware that somewhere the Russians will have heard the same broadcast.

How will they react? At the present moment it would be very adverse propaganda was something to happen to either Wohlgemut or myself.

I wonder if it will be beneficial for us to be in the limelight of the international media.

To follow the news they play 'Homeland our homeland how our stars are sparkling like diamonds.' And that's all it takes to get me really homesick.

I ask him can I bring Wohlgemut next time, I trust him implicitly and that's enough recommendation for Juergen. As from now there will be three of us. The plan is to make it a three man chess game.

Yuri is the *sleeping partner* of the radio repair business, and supplied him with the chess set. Yuri also likes to play cards so his little abode is quite a casino.

I meet up with Dr Giessler a few days later and he invites me to visit him one night at the Sick Bay. When I ask if Wohlgemut would be welcomed he quite happily includes him also.

When we turn up in the evening we enter an artist's studio. Dr Giessler has erected four easels and they all display a similar picture. A Troika followed by wolves travelling through the Russian winter landscape. He tells us he is going into mass production as there is so much demand for his pictures.

He does slight variations on a theme, but more or less supplies the demand for romantic art.

His other subject is the three bears but it's not as much in demand. Every guard wants to give his girlfriend one of these pictures. Wohlgemut who has been studying the pictures suggests they should be framed, he could supply them at say 8 roubles a frame. A done deal.

We suggest a Greek friend of ours Erechthos could stain the frames or paint them gold or silver from odd items he rescued from his luggage. He was employed in the Greek Embassy in Berlin before he was taken prisoner. The paints were in his Diplomatic luggage and so far he had found no use for them.

He is happy to join the 'artists' and expected 10 roubles a frame, he will also supply all the necessary ingredients to prepare the wood.

My job, as I am totally unskilled, it to buy the necessary food to prepare a good evening meal.

Our parcels once more arrive with welcome regularity and this too helped to make our evening meal a veritable feast.

The Dutch had got in touch with my wife and I could read a lot of hope and faith in my return in her cards.

Business is booming in our kitsch business. Even I have found a job, our Greek friend prepares a mixture which I paint onto the frames. In about 24 hours it looks almost like a slightly green antique patina.

We are gradually running out of canvas. All our sheets have been considerably shortened, one day the business will have to end.

Yuri turns out to be our saviour. One night he suddenly appears in our 'studio'. At first he shouts and yells but before long he smells a good sideline. He is able to supply us with sheets and can provide a wider outlet in town. He is on duty four nights a week so we can work undisturbed on those nights. The other three nights we spend with Juergen listening to the German news and enjoying wine and other treats.

The canteen and I have a special arrangement by which I supply a shopping list and the lady running the canteen gets the things in town, but not without first getting her cut of course.

One of the Polish prisoners is allowed to go to the bazaar to buy milk for her child, she has seen a stall there selling our artwork!

One day I meet Officer Mirow who carries one of our paintings. There you are, typical Russian art, he proudly announces!

Our colony of artist members is beginning to look healthier and fitter, we are now in a position to help others. The Polish families have a very hard time. The men's wages are very low and the women with small children cannot work.

It's very lucky that Lieutenant Andreitsch is away at present, he would have found out about our activities. Mirow is too busy with his love life at night to bother checking up on us. When we try to find out about Andreitsch from him he just grins and says 'away on business.'

Carpe diem is our logo while we rake in the roubles. I have got to know Dr Giessler much better during our painting nights. I have my suspicions about his medical doctorate. It's not the doctorate I doubt but the medical bit. He strikes me more as a doctor of divinity than medicine, but we all have our secrets. I watch the way he treats plennies, he is kind and caring to everyone, much more of a healer of souls than I could ever be.

One thing is odd which in a way proves my point, he will not treat or examine women. The surgeon has to look after any sick women.

Spring has arrived. The snow has melted and the camp's roads have turned into a quagmire.

Late one evening I stand outside with Wohlgemut, the spring wind stirs the pine trees and a sliver of moon bathes everything in a pale unreal light. A tatar guard who is on duty in the watchtower sings a song full of longing and homesickness.

We have handed in our padded winter clothing and have received lighter cotton outfits.

The weather is turning warmer and the Poles sit outside their billets in the evening. One of them plays the piano accordion and sings clear and pure, his voice rises above all. His comrades accompany him by humming a background harmony to his song. You can almost see the vast flat areas of their homeland. The song builds up to a crescendo and then slows down till it stops. Total silence follows his performance, till a wild applause from the locals on the other side of the fence is heard. They come every night to hear the beautiful music.

The evening is always ended with a song in praise of Mary, mother of God. So much gentleness and purity stands in an incredible contrast to the rough and ready men.

3

May 1951

May has arrived in all its splendour when I get called to the MWD. It's Lieutenant Mirow I have to see. Tonya is there as usual. Juergen Bachmann has warned me about his methods, he likes to trap people with apparently innocent questions. His first question is true to form.

What do plennies think of him?

I tell him through Tonya that I am entitled to be questioned in German as a plennie. He replies that this is not an interrogation, it's a friendly chat.

However, I am not being done out of my rights. It's German or nothing. Mirow is terribly vain, so I intend to form my answers in this direction.

I tell him that most of us think that Officer Klose would still be alive had he been questioned by Mirow. What made us feel this way he wants to know?

So, I really put it on, he is known for his tact in his interrogation or so I tell him and he really laps it up.

Tonya seems to guess what I am up to but she sticks to her job and just translates. Mirow comments about Andreitsch, that he doubts whether he will learn manners and tact in his four weeks away. So much for his business trip!

That is the extent of my meeting with Mirow tonight and I am dismissed and only Tonya replies to my goodnight.

The next day I get a lovely surprise. The Polish Starski whose family I helped with chocolate, sweets, sugar and salami has carved a beautiful walking stick for me. He has no idea how much I treasure this gift, it authenticates my invalid status.

Once more I get called to the MWD office, I know Andreitsch is still away so what does Mirow want?

There is not only Mirow there, but two captains. One is Captain Woronjuk and the other is Captain Hirschfeld. They politely ask me to take a seat after the introductions, which is a novelty in itself.

Captain Hirschfeld has been appointed as my defence in my trial. As from today I am no longer under the jurisdiction of the MWD but under the MGB (State Security).

Tonya goes off to collect some tea, so that we can have an informal chat and my defending officer can get to know me better. The Captain offers me a cigarette from a silver case. He notices that I had had a good look at the case. Not made in Germany but from Tula he says. He must have read my mind.

Tonya returns with the tea things, Mirow gets to bring a tablecloth, he returns with half a torn sheet! You still have a lot to learn he gets told, then he and Tonya are politely told to leave.

One Captain produces a lovely packet of biscuits. They come from the shop where I order my treats, he tells me. Nothing stays hidden for long in this country.

His wife had lent him this beautiful china, just to give me a treat. We had used Russian throughout our meeting so far, I am totally on my guard as all this politeness could be just a cover.

I have been an invalid for three years and had I been handed over to their department earlier, I would have been home by now.

When I get asked about my family in Bavaria one of them says it's a pity. We need honest men in the eastern part of Germany to work with us to rebuild it. Sounds very familiar so I have to watch my step.

Once more we cover old ground of the reason I refused to become an activist. My personal beliefs and faith we cover until we come to the old stumbling block. Why did I join the army as a volunteer?

Then I once more explain that it was a choice between the army and the Nazi Party. I opted for the army.

Captain Hirschfeld confirms that from personal knowledge. The German officer corps was very traditional not to say reactionary until 1936.

Once again I get asked how could I agree, as a clergyman, to work for counter espionage?

Again I tell them. "Orders are orders", I was told to report to the intelligence corps in Tilsit which is now in Russia, but then it was in Germany. Again Captain H confirms this.

After I am dismissed, next in is Wohlgemut the picture framer. I have to warn him quickly, otherwise they might have him for theft of Russian materials. But he is prepared. His foreman had given him the wood from the pile of off-cuts.

He returns very quickly, apart from being offered some nice cigarettes they asked him very little. Nothing was mentioned about a court case, so it was just a cover. I have to be really on my guard.

Our artists club has run its course, we have to find other means to increase our rouble and food supply.

Next day I pass Andreitsch, I salute him as expected but receive no reply. He really hates the Germans now and I feel I am fairly high on his hit list.

The bazaar did a roaring trade, any prospective customers were told the artist had died!

A newsflash in the camp goes round like wildfire. Pastor Niemoeller has been in Moscow to try to effect a release of German PoWs.

On my next visit to Dr Giessler I find him totally immersed in his latest creation. Two armies of the Middle Ages facing each other in battle. He had started dreaming of the Troika and the three 'bears'. Just as we were settling down Andreitsch comes barging in and without a word he searches everywhere.

"Where are the pictures?' he demands.

'"What pictures?" Dr Giessler replies.

"Watch out you hooligans," he shouts. "I'm onto you!"

"We know that only too well, the death of Officer Klose is a clear example of your attitude to the German PoWs."

We are lucky it is 1951 and not 1945 or we would both be dead by now.

He tries to send us off to our billet but it's only 9.30pm and he has no right to do that. So he flounces out of the Sick Bay banging the door behind him.

On my way to my billet I drop in to see Yuri, but Andreitsch had the same idea. I can hear them both yelling at each other. It's no secret that Yuri is his sworn enemy. Yuri once caught him trying to rape one of the married Polish women, he did not report him but can have it hanging over him. Andreitsch knows when he is beaten and cursing loudly he leaves the Budka. Luckily he has not seen me.

A period of relative peace follows, parcels are arriving regularly and we have enough to share. On a walk I pass Juergen's cabin and to my horror I see him packing his belongings on Andreitsch's orders without any particular reason. We both know Andreitsch is trying to put one over on Mirow. Juergen is moving in with us and the radio will be set up outside Andreitsch's office!

Before we discuss further details of his move, Andreitsch arrives. He is shouting and swearing. I could finish up in the clink again as I'm not supposed to be in the electrician's cabin.

Poor Andreitsch, he obviously doesn't know yet that I am no longer under his jurisdiction, but the MGBs.

Mirow quite deliberately hasn't informed him yet of my change of status. I threaten him with a letter of complaint to his superiors and I was just about to pass him when he attempts to give me an almighty kick.

I saw it coming and managed to avoid it. He however ends up on the floor pulling the work table and everything on it with him!

Amongst the breakages of course is Mirow's radio, so it couldn't have been better. Juergen quickly throws the camp radio on the pile of breakages so chaos reigns and it's all Andreitsch's fault.

Corporal Yuri gets ordered to put me under arrest in one of the camp cells by a direct order from Andreitsch. Blanket, spoon, matches and cigarettes are all I am allowed to take.

Insubordination is the offence. Yuri keeps my matches and cigarettes and he will return them later.

Andreitsch makes me strip to examine every piece of clothing separately. I am not bothered, it's against regulations and it's a warm day. Andreitsch is just digging himself deeper and deeper in the brown stuff.

Tonya is passing and I call her over to be a witness as Andreitsch takes my wallet containing 400 roubles. She comes over fascinated by a naked plennie arguing with Andreitsch over his wallet!

Both Yuri and Tonya will speak up for me. So Andreitsch yells at them to disappear, but Yuri has the keys to the cell so he has to call him back.

He utters a lot of insults and uncomplimentary comments and Tonya once more turns up, she has a message from officer Mirow which she whispers in his ear.

Andreitsch has now passed the point of no return.

"Mirow can kiss my arse!" he yells. Which Tonya says she will pass on to Captain Mirow, but has her doubts whether he will agree to his request!

I deliberately take my time getting dressed again, but Andreitsch is still not finished.

By law he has to ask me if I have any requests and when I ask him for a pencil and paper to write my complaints he nearly bursts with fury.

"Take him away, lock him up," he yells at Yuri who has no option but to obey, but slowly.

Down in the cell which is in the cellar and very dark a voice welcomes me. It turns out to be a Finn.

He has been a prisoner of the Soviet Union since he was 16, he is now 40. He had formed a communist youth group in Helsinki and when Stalin invited the communist youth of the world to Moscow in 1927 he followed the call without having the correct papers. He was caught trying to get across the border and since then he has been going from camp to camp with the label *Spy* around his neck.

He is a good worker and saves his earnings and once a month gets hopelessly drunk. He doesn't get awkward or disruptive, he just has a tremendous hangover and misses work. Being thrown in the cells is his punishment for that.

It's lovely and cool in the cellar, lunch arrives and with it I receive my cigarettes and matches, as well as writing material as promised.

I briefly write a letter of complaint enumerating my troubles and describing my arrest. I want this letter to go to Captain Woronjuk via officer Mirow.

Tonya has obviously informed him of all the details as Mirow arrives in double quick time.

When I tell him about his radio's fate through Andreitsch's hasty action he promises swift retribution for him. But for the time being I decide to follow the Finn's example and have a sleep.

Suddenly all the lights go out, no doubt Juergen's act of revenge. Our guard Piotr brings us a big candle as he knows we will not abscond, so he sits on the stairs and has a smoke.

Once more everyone blames Andreitsch as he was the one to sack Juergen from his job. I live dangerously, just for a while anyway!

My game with Andreitsch versus Mirow is working well, so far Mirow is winning.

Next morning Yuri comes to pick me up. Two strange officers (my Captains to go by his description) are here to see me in Mirow's office.

First I get handed my wallet with its contents correct and my cigarettes and matches. As it's normal to send in a complaint, after 24 hours have passed I get a chance to be magnanimous. It's enough that the MGB know what happened and with that I tear up my letter to the great relief of all.

4

The Forest Prisoner of War Camp
Ukraine

Unfortunately I get transferred to the forest camp which is an extension of my present camp. Corporal Yuri is waiting for me outside and I persuade him to take me past Juergen's place, who is busy trying to restore a semblance of order. He is assisted by two electricians from town in his efforts to restore the electricity back to the camp.

Juergen has been to the forest camp. The MWD officer there is Captain Lerner (another German immigrant) and a totally decent man. Juergen will keep me up to date throughout. He frequently travels between camps, he is also working on a hot plate for Yuri's mother.

I have to say "Farewell" to Wohlgemut, another passing of ships, also part of the Russian system to break any friendships.

Neither Mirow nor Andreitsch are around when I take my departure the next morning.

Yuri is my escort which suits us both. On our journey we drive over a beautiful wooden bridge across the river Dnepr – I was here many years ago in 1942, it seems a lifetime ago.

The bridge had been built by German soldiers in World War One. And has been added to in the second war and now German plennies are repairing and completing it.

Smoking is prohibited on the bridge, the guards on the bridge are very hot on making sure everyone obeys this order.

On the way out of town I invite Yuri and the driver to a beer at an inn.

"Great," says the driver. "You are my kind of Fritz!"

We get a bottle of ice cold beer each and 200g of sausage with a roll. The bartender fills four little glasses with vodka and in broken German tells us he was a prisoner for four years in Germany in the first war.

Many a time he has regretted coming home, but homesickness brought him back. He suggests that we should visit the grave of a

German soldier. An old farmers wife whose husband died in the First World War and her son in the Second War, now looks after the grave in the hope that someone far away will do the same for her men.

Our driver says we must make a move, otherwise we will be here all day and Yuri cannot hand me over blind drunk.

It is very hot, this is typical for this part of Russia with its expanse of ripening cornfields. We see a village from a distance and as we come closer we see it was once part of a collective farm.

Every house has masses of flowers in their little front garden. Yuri points to a garden just in front of us. In the shade of a Jasmine bush is the grave of the German soldier. It has the double cross of the Russian Orthodox Church and suspended from it is the helmet of the young dead man, shot through on both sides. The grave is a mass of forget-me-nots, surrounded by the white river sand.

When we leave the village we soon turn off out of the heat into the welcome coolness of the forest. Before long we reach the camp which is unlike any camp I have seen. No watchtower, very little barbed wire and when we drive past the Guardroom (Budka) the soldier on duty salutes us in passing without getting up.

Yuri hands me over to one of the camp sergeants and I ask him to give my regards to the 'artists' and Andreitsch! He tells me he is happy to do the first but will skip the latter.

The camp consists of seven barrack blocks, the inmates are mainly German but also *red* and *blue* Spaniards co-exist peacefully.

The German camp elder is a bit of a nonentity who is busy doing nothing, also my favourite occupation. He told me little about the camp so I shall have to find my own way round.

About 5pm the work commando returns, they look healthy and suntanned. For the time being I intend to keep myself to myself. I hope my stay here will be only a short one.

On my first evening there a tall good looking Spaniard addresses me in perfect French. Manuel grew up in Ceuta, Spain and he was a 'drawing room' socialist. When Spain collapsed he and like-minded young men immigrated to Russia. The theory of a classless society appealed to them.

First they enjoyed a relatively free existence, but around 1941 they ended up in a camp. Their fate is now identical to the *blue* Spaniards who fought on the German side. They are all plennies.

Spain is a country of horrendous contrasts, there are nobility and the Catholic Church who own vast tracts of land and fortunes. On the other side are the majority of Spaniards who are incredibly poor.

But Manuel tells me he is well and truly cured of his youthful dreams and enthusiasm. The bleak reality of communist Russia soon saw to that.

Poverty in Spain was bad enough but nothing compared to poverty in communist Russia.

If the *red* Spaniards ever get home they will once again be imprisoned, still it would be preferable to being a plennie in the socialist heaven.

Next morning I have to report to officer Lerner of the MWD. Apart from giving me a parcel from home he doesn't want to have any further discussion. The Spaniards are the only ones not receiving parcels so I share my riches.

Yuri frequently comes to the camp and always stops off to see me. This time he brings me a letter from Juergen Bachmann, the electrician. We meet up in the dining room and get all the news, no doubt the same news Juergen has put in his letter.

New plennies arrive daily and among them is one who is not allowed out to work as he repeatedly tried to escape, on one attempt he got as far as the border with Romania, before they caught up with him.

Then I recall Hans Schubert who had been trying to persuade me to join him on an escape back in 1947. To meet up with him again would be strange, but all is possible in this country.

Yuri has kept his best news till the end. Andreitsch had had a terrible hiding from the Polish Starski, he was once more caught trying to have his evil way with the Starski's wife.

The Starski had returned to the camp early because of a minor accident and caught Andreitsch red handed. The good thing is he cannot do anything about it, he was the guilty party.

When I read Juergen's letter it confirms Yuri's story. He also conveys greetings from Hans Schubert.

I write a few lines to Juergen, but I don't write to Hans as Yuri doesn't really know him. Hans is the only plennie from my very early days as a prisoner whose path has crossed mine.

5

July 1951

Early one morning in July I get called to the MWD office to meet up once more with Captains Woronjuk and Hirschfeld. They have all my personal details confirmed, but want to go over my military details from January 1945 onwards.

Before I start Hirschfeld asks if the name Niemoeller is known to me. I have never met the man but his history is known to me.

Initially a supporter of Hitler he became an ardent opponent of the Nazi regime. He spent time in prison and concentration camps. In the post war period, he was very active on an international level to do as much as he could to prove not all Germans had been active Nazis. Some were now suffering severe hardship. He had also helped my family personally by passing their address on to American and Scottish aid agencies.

Then a very in-depth questioning followed regarding my last posting in Tilsit. I had been employed as a Quartermaster for a while as I was not fit for active duty due to the wound I received.

After my transfer to Koenigsberg I was meant to join a ship leaving the harbour for safety, but my place was given to a woman refugee.

Once more we go over the recurring question. Had I instructed Russians to become spies?

When I tell them I never had occasion to do that it seemed to be it for the day.

When the Captain asked me have I any requests, I asked whether Hans Schubert could be transferred to the forest camp. They both laughed!

"Ah, our escapee! You're not planning a quick getaway are you?"

I decide to look at it as they had. A joke.

"No, I had met him many years ago and would like to meet up again."

One night a longed for rainstorm brings relief to the all pervading heat, it's beautiful and cool once the storm has abated.

In the morning I receive a larger than normal parcel, my wife has sent me a suit but of course it doesn't fit me. Years of starvation diet have taken their toll, it really is a superfluous luxury. I will find a good use for it, being a plennie makes one inventive. Nothing is ever wasted and I will turn the suit into roubles.

Corporal Yuri is my best contact and this way we both make a few kopeks. A few days later Yuri arrives and to my delight he brings Hans Schubert with him. The camp elders provide a bed in my billet for him. We are both very pleased to meet up again.

Now to business. I show my suit to Yuri. He is very disappointed when he sees it. Obviously it will not fit him as he is much taller than me. He could keep it for his son but he hasn't even got a girlfriend at the moment and the thought doesn't appeal to him either.

Now the haggling starts in earnest. He realizes that a good deal can be done in the market. But it also means I will have to trust him. Still, the suit as it is is of no practical use to me or any other plennie in the camp. We finally agree on 400 roubles, he takes the suit with him and I just have to gamble on Yuri's honesty.

A recent parcel allows me to treat Hans on his first evening in the new camp.

"I wish I had listened to you all those years ago," he said when I asked him about his escape.

In March 1949 he was sentenced to 25 years. That and a letter from his wife telling him that her parents had died of Typhoid had convinced him that he had to escape.

He had a reasonably easy escape and he had a lot of help from Russian peasants. With the changing seasons he was almost at the end of his tether and in October he ran into a Romanian border patrol.

The patrolmen couldn't believe he had walked most of the way from Kazan. He spent eight weeks with the border guards, they looked after him well, and he cut their winter supply of wood for them. Unfortunately the guard detail from Kazan beat him so badly he spent four weeks in hospital after his return to his old camp. When he came out of hospital he was given another 5 years on top of his 25.

Then he started a familiar journey from camp to camp, his last one being in Vorkuta and now he is in the forest camp.

Then it's my turn. I give him a very brief history and add that I am now waiting for my trial.

We decide to hope for the best and make the most of every day. Yuri has been in the camp a few times to make deliveries, but hasn't tried to contact me so I avoid him. However one day he arrives with a big grin on his face and hands me the agreed roubles and two ice cold bottles of beer as thanks for a good bargain.

It's great to get my money but just as great to see my faith in Yuri justified. I go and see Hans and he too can enjoy a cold beer.

Next day Hans receives his first parcel from home and he is totally confused with excitement. The contents are of very poor quality compared to my West German parcel – one can see that everything is very hard come by.

In future I will only put on the table what we are about to eat, to avoid any unfavourable comparison.

His wife has also sent some pictures and she looks very pretty. I am not surprised Hans longs to be with her. She has changed her job and she no longer works as a cleaner, she is now the housekeeper for a 50 year old widower who has a paper factory.

October 1951

September brings cooler weather, the trees are turning colour and the evenings are longer. Twice a week we get to see East German films with Russian subtitles.

It's the end of October when I am once more called to the MWD office to be met by Captains Hirschfeld and Woronjuk. Their friendly greeting makes me think that all their enquiries have been successful. One of them travelled all the way to Omsk to have my statement confirmed by a witness.

They assure me that I can count on a just and proper trial, but I must not forget the fact that I was a member of the Counter Espionage Corps, however short the time was. Captain Hirschfeld sees that I am beginning to lose hope but comments that apart from the above my trial should be swift and found in my favour. Captain

Woronjuk hands over the official charge sheet which states that I am to be charged by the Socialist Republic of the Ukraine, as our camp is situated in this part of Russia. I have to sign the charge sheet and then await my trial.

It's a strange feeling, the war has been over for six years and I am accused now. I realize that my self-induced illness has not helped one iota. But there is one advantage, had I not been ill I would have got 25 years together with the others in the mass trials of 46 and 47.

This way I am actually to be tried and judged as an individual, whether the outcome will be any different remains to be seen.

I am not able to talk to anyone about this, it's too late in the game and still too dangerous for me.

Hans still hasn't changed his idea, he still dreams of his Hilde and gets very excited when he receives one of her very much improved parcels.

My wife now sends me material things which help to improve my quality of life. In one parcel she sent me a bottle of Eau de Cologne, the corporal who is supervising the opening of parcels is reluctant to hand the bottle over.

"Nix alcohol, alcohol forbidden!"

It took help from Captain Lerner to persuade him to let me have it.

A few drops of this precious liquid made me realize how much we all smelled in spite of our regular laundry and personal washing. She also sends me toothpaste, soap and shaving cream – such unheard luxuries.

I hide these treasures as Hans has become very envious.

"It's all right for those in the West, the Amis throw the stuff at them."

I still share with him when he is in the right mood.

His wife sends him regular photos and he has fashioned an album of pictures and letters. His thoughts about his wife and home are gradually developing into an obsession and I fear for his sanity.

The reality of what it will be like when he actually returns home never seems to enter his mind.

He intends to study at the university. Philosophy is his chosen subject. How he will maintain a home and wife with no salary has not yet entered his calculations.

He is hoping for a grant as a returning PoW, but that these grants will not be available for a former Nazi officer with a Russian war criminal sentence has not entered his theories either.

Hans just doesn't seem to acknowledge the fact that you only have hopes of a decent job in East Germany if you fly the Communist flag. Add to this the fact that his wife has got used to a reasonable standard of living since she got a job as a housekeeper.

Personally I have my own thoughts about her actual living arrangements but maybe I am just too pessimistic.

Hans is convinced his wife will just drop everything the minute he is home, but so many years have passed. People do change and unlike my wife there are no children to keep the memory alive during the waiting years.

After all, they were only married for days when he had to return to the front.

Hans becomes very quiet after our talk, he is obviously trying to come to some decision.

By now it's December. Yuri turns up and asks Hans and I to report to the Budka.

"With all your belongings. Andreitsch is missing you."

He even has his rifle but explains with a big grin that the ammunition is still at home, but it looks good.

Back in the main Prisoner of War Camp
1951

When we return to the main camp Sergeant Wassya is on duty in the guardroom. He looks as if something went a bit wrong with his creation. A big head sits on a plump body, no neck worth mentioning and no forehead either. His one achievement in life is his ability to eat anyone under the table, and Yuri has seen this in action. It's also advisable to keep well out of his way when he has had his fill of vodka. Sadly he has no success with women.

Wassya is wearing a tape measure around his neck. He has been ordered to measure us for coffins or so he was told. After several attempts Yuri takes over and quickly takes our measurements. We are not the only ones being measured, several other plennies arrive to undergo the same thing.

These peculiar goings on are overshadowed by the imminent departure of the Poles and their families. They are all being transported to the North where they will be employed as 'free workers'.

I go through all my things, anything that is not a basic essential in food and clothes I pass onto the women. Even my precious coat is finding a new owner.

When they leave a scream of a thousand voices goes up to heaven.

"Don't forget the Polish Legion – we fought for you!"

When they are outside the camp, they are surrounded by heavily armed guards and their dogs. They are pushed into the waiting lorries. Suddenly the stirring song *'Poland will live forever,'* can be heard.

What a departure, but we have seen and been part of so many in our lives as plennies.

In the morning once order is re-established in the camp Corporal Yuri comes to fetch me. He wants to know the cause of all the commotion about me. Captains Woronjuk and Hirschfeld are waiting for me. The day of my trial has arrived.

I get told to change into civilian clothing. There is a big selection of good clothes the measuring on our arrival was for that purpose. Now I know that and I select an outfit. I keep on my plennie underwear.

A dark blue suit, snow white shirt and grey tie fit perfectly, even braces are provided as well as grey silk socks and black shoes. The whole lot is topped by a beautiful warm navy blue overcoat.

It's twelve years since I wore civilian clothes, and it feels very strange. The translator takes a photo and then I am ready.

I want to take my stick with me but I am advised to leave it behind. I am going by car and suddenly feel like a totally different person with all these beautiful tailored clothes.

A six-seater Zil, parked next to the admin building waits for us, even Corporal Yuri is part of the group. He wears his dress uniform with his Nagant suspended by a blue-white cord.

Woronjuk looks at me and asks how I feel.

"Butterflies," I tell him, so Captain Hirschfeld hands me a bottle of 'medicine', it is a very good vodka. Yuri too is feeling equally nervous in these confined surroundings, but all I can do is wink at him.

It wouldn't do to let on how well we know each other. The vodka has the desired effect and I feel more relaxed and I can enjoy my comfortable ride.

As we arrive in front of the courthouse we feel ourselves surrounded by representatives of the media.

Yuri gets told to stand next to me and to stop looking like a worried nanny. He has to have his Nagant at the ready, but not too ready. You don't want to shoot your business partner. These men know everything, nothing escapes them.

We go up in the lift to the 6th floor and are asked to take a seat. Yuri sits next to me looking and feeling very uncomfortable and wishes he'd had some 'medicine' as well. He feels almost sick with excitement, but he realizes that the photo with me in the papers might do him some good. He would love to find a girl and this might help.

"But," he muses. "What good is a girlfriend to me, I am spending all my time with plennies."

"We hope to go home soon," is my reply.

No worries, in Russia there are always prisoners but Yuri prefers the German plennies they have manners and culture, not like his own people who as a rule have neither.

We sit there for nearly an hour before I get called.

Then Captain Hirschfeld fetches us. He points to the seat in the dock and Yuri is told to sit next to me. He looks more worried than I do! A battery of flashbulbs face us.

I take a seat with a table in front of me. Tonya the translator sits on my other side and in front sits the Clerk of the Court and then the seats of the appointed representatives of the government. My defence, Captain Hirschfeld sits just in front of me.

We all rise as the gentlemen of the court enter. The presiding officer is a Major flanked by two Captains. The filming continues throughout.

Then the major opens the proceedings. I get asked the usual questions: personal life, military life etc. My voice sounds strange as so much depends on the outcome of this day, no wonder I sound odd.

After 45 minutes Captain Woronjuk does his part. His accusation sounds more like a plea by the defence. He tells them that I was unaware of the danger of my position and he continues in this vein and at one point everyone joins in a volley of laughter at my expense no doubt, but who cares.

The prosecution demand four months imprisonment, with the time on remand taken into consideration.

My defence asks for dismissal of the accused due to lack of evidence against me. Then the court withdraw to consider their verdict.

Yuri takes me back into the hall. Captain Hirschfeld keeps the newspaper people away from us, then produces a bottle of Russian cure-all. I have a quick drink and whilst the Captain turns away to speak to the press I hand the vodka to Yuri who opens his mouth and tips the lot down his throat.

Captain H turns around and catches him with the bottle in his hand.

"I didn't know you felt nervous as well. What have you been up to then?"

Yuri goes a funny shade of grey but he realizes the joke was at his expense.

We have to wait a whole hour – it's an hour I don't think I will ever forget, then we get called.

The Chairman of the Court used lots of involved and complicated legal jargon, then said:

"The accused Schmitt, Wilhelm, Max former Major of the fascist oppressor's army..." then I lose the thread. I was so nervous that I was literally shaking in my shoes and felt faint, only to recover my wits just in time to hear the words "Not guilty due to lack of evidence."

Hirschfeld congratulates me, Tonya does the same, then I have to face the press. I feel cold, shaking and empty, all this has just been too much for me. Hirschfeld hands me the dregs of the vodka, if only Yuri had left me a bit more!

Then he too wishes me all the best and hopes we will resume our 'artists' business and make lots of roubles.

Woronjuk joins us now. I had been very lucky the court officials had been very positive. Home was now considerably closer than just a distant dream.

The Captains support me on both sides because of the black ice on the pavement. I always got positive vibes from these two, they had a more humane approach to the aspect of law and justice.

I am under no illusions about the heinous cruelties perpetrated by the German troops, especially the Waffen SS who took it upon themselves to give the word *German* a special meaning of cold blooded murder and cruelty towards a people of simple peasants who initially welcomed them with the traditional gift of salt and bread.

The two Captains had been able to remain objective. They had looked at me not as yet another fascist evil-doer but as a country parson in the wrong place at the wrong time.

My heart is full to bursting point as I gradually recover my equilibrium. We go past a big department store and Capt W invites me to come and take a look round. On the ground floor I notice long queues, a bit embarrassed he concedes that it is the fresh meat delivery, due to the excessive frost and snow there have been no supplies for a few days.

I also get told to watch my wallet, pickpockets abound in the communist paradise. Most of the shop assistants look bored and some could do with a bit of dusting. The people don't buy, they are just window shopping and keeping out of the cold. When I look at the prices I can understand why, they are outrageous and totally beyond the means of the average citizen. I think these people just exist in the hope that one day their children will be able to afford these things.

I know as a Christian we believe that one day we will all live in heaven, but in Soviet Russia, 'Heaven' will be here, not a distant idea of life in heaven.

It's difficult to explain and accept this western logic, but that's how it is and it keeps the average citizen going.

When I ask to see the gents clothing department the Captains oblige. The cheapest suit is 300 roubles but poor design and material, so I figure my suit must have been 1000 to 1200 roubles, so Yuri got himself a very good deal, still I am happy with my 400 roubles.

By now I am tired, the walking about and the excitement are all very different from my normal plennie day.

I need fresh air. The Captains seem to feel the same and they suggest a meal and I am to be their guest.

There is an elegant restaurant in a hotel only a few yards away, few of the tables are occupied. There are snow white table cloths, silver cutlery and crystal glasses. The chairs are pulled out and our coats are carefully hung up in the cloakroom.

We each have an enormous menu which totally bemuses me. Captain Woronjuk offers to order for me. I think of the average Russian like Yuri, he could no more afford to eat there than fly to the moon. I might not be able to read the menu but I can read the price!

Let's talk about something irrelevant, let's just enjoy our meal. I get the message, so walls still have ears even in this restaurant.

What fascinates me is the captains' impeccable behaviour, they act as if they are totally used and familiar in these capitalist surroundings, never a hesitation of which knife to use, which glass to use and such like. We say little, just comment on the food as initially suggested. The mocca is ordered and we sit back and relax. Of course I now wonder what the price for this meal will be for me. I know of Generals who have sold their regiments for a bowl of soup, so what is the price of this sumptuous banquet?

Capt Woronjuk must have been reading my mind.

"You will be going home soon, I hope you will tell them what life is really like in Russia."

I assure him that I will tell the truth, the whole truth and nothing but the truth (whatever that is). That would be a simple price to pay.

It's again very obvious to me that East and West may use the same language but mean different things.

The meal keeps reminding me of Captain Lerner. I have frequently seen him eating his lunch consisting of only dry bread and water.

Our official car takes us back to the camp and it's about 4pm. I get changed into my plennie outfit and after a cigarette with the captains, the two officers say farewell and leave, but not before telling me that should I be asked, that I have been for an interview at the ministry.

Wassya comes to collect me, he looks over the cast off finery, what a load of vodka one could buy for that lot. On our way across camp we meet Juergen who is greatly relieved to see me.

Rumours had been circulating like mad since I left camp this morning, so I tell him the official version about my visit to the ministry.

There has been more measuring and as usual a transport is hoped for.

Hans Wohlgemut comes to wake me about 8pm. Juergen wants to see me and Hans. The news is already over so we just sit and chat, being a plennie one develops a special kind of hearing and understanding.

Christmas is coming up shortly and I would like to hold a special celebration. I go straight to the lions den and ask Andreitsch's permission, but no luck, he throws me out of his office shouting forbidden!

I could of course appeal to Woronjuk or Mirow but someone would have to suffer if I did get permission, so I leave it at that.

Luckily the Germans are getting lots of mail, good news from my wife. She has a flat, kitchen, bathroom, sitting room and bedroom. Independence at last, good people must have helped her with the deposit.

My friend Hans is feeling very low, he too received mail and a parcel. I try not to press him, he will tell me when he is ready.

He finally talks to me on the morning of Christmas Eve. He has given a lot of thought to our conversation and realized that it was unfair to expect his wife to wait for him indefinitely. He had made some enquiries and found out that women in East Germany whose husbands were under sentence in Russia could apply to have their marriages annulled.

That's what he has offered his wife for Christmas. So, it was her decision and Hans is surprised to receive no mail. If he was going to be so magnanimous he should have gone the whole hog and made the decision for her and given her her freedom.

To my mind she has already made plenty of use of her freedom but it's not up to me to judge.

6

January 1952

Somehow we get through Christmas. No festive spirit anywhere with so much uncertainty, and 1952 is with us for another year of imprisonment.

Corporal Yuri comes to pick me up to see the captains. He is a bit annoyed as he has to get three glasses for the occasion.

"It's all right for you Schmitt! You sit there drinking wine with the gentry, while I have to wait in the freezing cold for you."

However, when I offer to exchange places with him he is more than happy to wait outside.

I enter the room and after polite greetings I get asked to take a seat. Captain Woronjuk tells me that I am now officially free for repatriation via Moscow, I just have to sign the official documents of the recent trial.

Captain H assures me of his and especially Capt W's efforts for my individual case. We are all aware of the fate of Russian PoWs in Germany, compared with theirs, our lot in Russia was almost bearable.

Woronjuk for some reason seems to get himself into quite a state, recounting tales of horror of PoW camps in Germany. Captain H tries to calm him down and strangely enough I feel I can talk to them as an equal. We would all like to start again from scratch, but as that is not possible we have to get rid of the ruins.

Only then is it possible to build a world of humanitarian principles where races, faiths and different convictions can live alongside each other. Woronjuk must have had bad experiences in the past with Germans which caused his sudden outburst. Strange, my money would always have been on Hirschfeld but things have calmed down again.

Our dreams of co-existence would no doubt vary greatly, but I am not going to let that come between us.

Woronjuk opens the bottle of wine and we clink glasses.

"To the future, peace and freedom in the world."

His eyes look into the far distance, he really genuinely believes in the communist dream.

I try to bring him back to reality. He sees his utopia brought about by power and subjugation. The most important ingredient is missing I say. Love is my answer.

"Love is something for weaklings," according to Woronjuk. Then he says "Didn't I show love by my efforts for you, just a single individual."

Now it's my turn. In all his positive efforts love never came into it.

"In all our dealings and the kindness you both have shown me, neither of you has ever once shaken my hand."

Both look somewhat embarrassed but they have their instructions on how to relate to a plennie. Any physical contact is not part of the prescribed behaviour.

There is a loud knock on the door. It's Corporal Yuri with a furious look at me, asking to leave in order to go on his rounds at 10pm. He has to do a walk round the camp and Andreitsch is the officer in charge.

The captains apologize to him and hand him a glass of wine, they promise to deliver me safely once they have finished with me.

The room is lovely and warm and Capt W produces another bottle of wine and some cigarettes, but I am on my guard. Some do it the nasty way, some do it the nice way. It would be easy to drop my guard in this pleasant company.

Woronjuk as so often before seems to have a sixth sense.

"No need to worry we are not trying to get you drunk and careless," and with that produces butter, white rolls and sausage.

Now our talk and behaviour gets a bit more relaxed, I open the top button of my jacket and they do the same with their uniform jackets.

They want to know about my most recent news from home. I tell them about my family's new flat. I know accommodation is very hard to come by in Russia and they know my family originally lived in the East. Hirschfeld regrets that I shall be lost to them after my return home, they need people of my calibre for a positive co-operation. An instant wake-up call but no ulterior motives are behind this comment. I tell them about my children, three of them already receiving secondary education.

Woronjuk looks lost in thought.

"Children, we would love to have children but we only live in a tiny one room flat. No space for children there."

Full of longing he studies the photo of my family I carry in my wallet. Bernd the youngest has never seen me, he was a babe in arms when I christened him.

As far as the MGB are concerned my red stamp (not to be repatriated) has been removed from my papers. It's now up to Moscow to let me go.

It's close to midnight when the captains take me back to the Budka. Yuri is sitting behind the table deep in thought. Once the Captains have left with a polite bow and no handshake he drags me to the table and gives me a glass of vodka. Andreitsch has gone to see one of his mistresses and he does not have to do another patrol for two hours.

I have had a healthy swig of firewater and Yuri points to a large piece of white paper obtained from the admin department. I get as far as the date and *Duschinka* (little dove) – a love letter in the making I note.

Love letters and Corporal Yuri just don't go together. Writing is not his forte with his huge paws. He shows me a picture of the object of his desire – a tall slim girl, very attractive and definitely a good catch for Yuri.

She is an apprenticed metal worker and they met at a dance in the local people's hall. She had seen our picture taken outside the courthouse and liked what she saw and recognized him at the dance. He loves dancing but usually because of his height he can rarely find a good partner. This girl was perfect, they danced all evening and when he took her home she kissed him goodnight and also gave him her address.

This is where he was tonight!

He had no idea what to write, would I please help him. It had taken him an hour to write the date and *Duschinka*. So it was my turn to do a kindness for Yuri. He has done lots for me above and beyond the call of duty.

Visibly relieved he hands me the paper and the chewed end of a pencil. I find out some details, such as were there stars when they met, was the moon shining and such like.

When Yuri returns from his rounds I hand him the completed letter. I have used my biro c/o my wife's parcel and then read the letter back to him. I have deliberately written using large letters and then signed with his most aggressive signature.

I also lend him my biro for his next date, just in case she doubts his ability to write such a letter. I even address the letter for him to make sure it gets there. I have a feeling this will not be my last love letter.

When I leave I am full of the joys of spring…whoops sorry vodka and fall flat on my posterior! Thanks to my relaxed state I do not incur any damage.

Next day at lunchtime I meet up with Juergen Bachmann. He has news for me. The East German broadcast he managed to hear on his radio gave a detailed account of my trial. I am grateful to him for not spreading the news. It was a special order by the captains to keep it to myself.

When the broadcast was on the camp radio, he managed to interrupt it due to a 'technical fault'. So nobody, especially Andreitsch is any the wiser.

On the next parcel delivery I do very well with lots of chocolate and other treats. Hans too has received a package from his wife.

Yuri comes to our billet and I give him a bar of chocolate, he is absolutely delighted and can't get over it being a simple gift with no roubles expected. He assures me of his friendship for life. What a lad.

Hans Schubert is once more on an all time high. Hilde is with him every minute of the day and he with her, he thinks.

I wish this was true, but there are a few photos in his pocket that give me cause for concern.

The pictures are from Christmas. Hilde and her employer are shown next to a very festive table, her employer is in his early 50s, well kept and affluent looking. In one picture she is wearing a beautiful diamond ring. The way she is not used to wearing it on her left hand makes me think that she normally wears it on her right hand.

She and Hans come from families who do not own such an expensive ring and if it had been an heirloom she would have had to sell it in times of real hardship.

Hans can't see that and I wouldn't dream of bursting his bubble. In her next letter Hilde explains the ring used to belong to her employer's wife, who passed away some time ago.

When I next meet Yuri he looks very worried, after some prodding he admits that it was a perfect date. The letter was wonderful and the chocolate as well but she wanted to keep the biro!

I can put his mind at rest, I received another one in my last parcel. Now Yuri relaxes and all is well again.

His girlfriend loved his letter and is now waiting for another one, so it's up to me to write another romantic letter. He just has to be careful not to write anything in her presence.

Spring 1952

Winter has passed and once more spring is with us. I had hoped to be home by now, but I know the Russian official mills grind slowly.

Yuri continues to be lucky in love. One day he brings me a beautiful white handkerchief from Sina, she also sends a kiss. With that Yuri gives me a bear hug and gives me a right smoocher on each cheek. I would have preferred a kiss direct from Sina, but I suppose it's the thought that counts. By now there are eleven German officers left and once more rumours about a transport home abound. All the officers get called to the MWD office except for me as I seem to have lost all interest for them.

Yuri tells me there is a transport for 300 the next day. Juergen and I play chess and there is an air of expectancy all around us. Suddenly a big shadow falls across the board.

"Wilhelm, get your gear and report to the Budka."

It's Yuri with this unexpected message. I must have turned a strange colour, the others are concerned and take me back to my barrack to help me pack. I think the homeward bound will be quite glad once I have gone. I seem to be the only one not on the list.

They all try to comfort me and try to hide their own joy, but I am still absolutely shaken. Hans Schubert, and Wohlgemut take me and walk me and my belongings over to the Budka. The others all join us, it's a bit like a funeral march. Juergen too turns up with a box of cigarettes, he shakes my hand and commiserates with me.

Yuri throws my bags on the lorry, helps me to get in and we drive off. One quick wave and we are away.

Yuri is very quiet and for that I'm grateful. I should be used to this it's happened so often.

On our journey we meet two lorries full of singing plennies, its all right for them to sing - they are going home.

The forest camp has already calmed down again, the selection for the transport had been some time ago. There are still ten German plennies and I can take my old bed again.

I feel my trust in humanity is at its lowest ebb, maybe I trusted the two captains too much that January night.

Back to The Forest Prisoner of War Camp

I had barely settled in when I was called to the MWD office and who but the two captains are there. To feed their schadenfreude (pleasure at someone elses misfortune) on my disappointment?

When I ask Woronjuk why I am the only one left behind I find out that all the officers will arrive at the forest camp before long. They only brought me to the forest camp to keep me away from the excitement of a departing transport. Only Wohlgemut who always let me believe he was an officer, but isn't, is going home.

7

The Forest Prisoner of War Camp
Ukraine
1952

Yuri has become a real friend, so I am not surprised when he turns up one day and tells me that Andreitsch is with Lerner and seems to be planning something unpleasant for me. So I am forewarned.

I do not have to wait long. Andreitsch greets me with a slight bow and addresses me as 'Colonel'. I have to put him right. I thank him for the promotion but point out I am still the same grade I was when we last met.

He must have been officially informed of my trial and its conclusions, he cannot get at me with the 'Colonel' bit, but also accuses me of simulating my illness. Now we are on much more dangerous ground.

Before I realize what is going on, he has worked himself into such a state, I have to force myself to remain as calm as possible in spite of all his accusations and colourful language.

When I tell him that I have found out that there is justice and fair play even in his Russia and that I will write a letter of complaint to the MGB he absolutely bristles with fury and makes a very quick about turn. So, it's one up for me Mr Andreitsch.

There are always wheels within wheels. The camp tailor is suddenly getting very friendly. He even gives me a new hat which he has surplus in his store.

This man is very money minded, so why give me something for nothing? My sources tell me he comes from Sudetenland and worked for the German security services during the war. He now wears his Slavic image and to retain and prove it to the Russians he is a very active spy. So I am prepared.

Yuri takes my letter of complaint to the MGB to Mirow. Mirow and Andreitsch are still very much at loggerheads as ever, so this is a safer way. Yuri and I have a secret signal to warn me of Andreitsch's arrival on camp. Whenever he is on Yuri's delivery truck, he will lift his hand to warn me and I can make myself scarce.

Andreitsch always visits the tailor who is making him a new uniform.

The tailor tries to woo me with an extra helping of lunch. Andreitsch has obviously missed his calling and his timing. It's no longer 1945 and our plennie supplies keep us well above starvation standards.

Yuri is aware of what's going on and his warnings keep me one step ahead of Andreitsch. Next time Yuri arrives with him he goes straight to the kitchen and in a very loud voice orders all the extra rations to be taken to the tailor. So that's cooked their goose, now everyone officially knows.

When Yuri goes past the window he lets fly a real mouthful of spit on my window. Andreitsch had arrived just before that and turns to me.

"There you see what an ordinary Soviet man does to show his disgust."

"Why?' I reply. "Did he know you were here?"

Andreitsch goes for me and I grab one of the big wooden paddles they use to turn the laundry in the cauldron, to defend myself.

At this decisive moment Captain Lerner enters. One quick look and he had judged the situation correctly!

"Ah, Andreitsch I have been looking for you. There are some things I would like you to take back to the camp." On his way out he whispers "Just in time wasn't I?"

I will always keep one of the paddles with me when Andreitsch is about, just in case.

I now feel quite ashamed about my feelings and suspicions of the captains, as I am fully aware that it is up to Moscow to fix the date of my departure.

I express my heartfelt apologies to Woronjuk and he accepts them and tells me that he too is only a little wheel in the machinery.

I return to my accommodation strengthened in the faith of my correct judgement. To have moved me in respect of my illness went well above their call of duty.

A couple of days later 50 German plennies arrive led by nine officers, I have been able to reserve a bed for Hans Schubert who is absolutely devastated. I know him so well that I frequently notice he is up to his old tricks again. He is checking the barbed wire for any holes and watches guards and seems to be on a permanent alert.

I make time to speak to him as it is a relatively easy camp. The commandant has given permission for the plennies to go mushroom picking on Sunday. All this would be lost should he try to escape.

I threaten to report him for some minor misdemeanour to effect his removal back to the main camp. He objects by saying the Russians have no right to keep him here, but we have gone over the subject time and again. I am not prepared to go down that road again. I assure him I am a light sleeper and will be keeping an eye on him.

To stop him pacing the camp like a caged lion I get him a job in the laundry to keep him occupied.

He receives his regular cards and parcels, but his cards say little. I show him the cards of my wife so that he can see the difference, every line speaks of love and longing for my return. Hans Wohlgemut has been in contact so she is au fait with the present status.

Hans's wife instead writes how well she is now, how well looked after by her employer and what a good time she is having.

Her 'employer' now gets called Walter, he must hold a high position in the political arena to judge by all the affluence on the frequent photos.

He still chooses to remain blind, he is glad her years of having to do without are over, he just won't listen to any other thought than that his Hilde is waiting for him. Any attempt to bring him back to planet reality has no effect. As far as he is concerned she is waiting to go back to live in poverty with a returning plennie, but no doubt something will provide a wake up call for Hans. Hopefully while he is still here. He can then turn his mind towards a more realistic aim for his own life.

He continues to work in the laundry so at least he is occupied during the day. I also do some light work there, I fold laundry with some Spanish PoWs. I am a welcomed guest there, not least because I always share some of the contents of my parcels with them.

Yuri pops in to see me when he's on a delivery run to the camp. Sina is still the love of his life and I still write to her. He has been introduced to her mother, my occasional spelling mistakes are corrected by Sina and it looks as if this is really serious.

Summer 1952

July and August provide searing heat. The tailor still hasn't given up since losing his contact in the kitchen. I once more note that he invites me for a cup of tea but he is not very clever the way he approaches the subject of my mobility status.

"Disgusting not sending an ill patient home," he proposes, but I laugh.

"The Russians are so fond of me they just can't bear to see me go."

He tries where everyone else has failed to query me about my work in the intelligence corps. Before long he slips up and calls me 'Colonel'.

So I tell him to go back to his employer and tell him to work harder to trip me up. And he if he doesn't want to find himself in the nearest toilet, must give up working for Andreitsch. I suggest he should make a right hash of his uniform blouse and get rid of his dangerous customer that way.

Hans in the meantime seems to have settled down a bit, he continues to receive his fortnightly parcel and card. He is no longer angry with me and proudly shows me a photo which shows quite clearly a breakfast table set for two. I am not judging the woman or anything but why not put him out of his misery? He was sentenced to 25 years, I mean what does she expect?

She would be an old lady after all that time and were the roles reversed would he wait? I don't think so. She wants to make him feel he is not forgotten. They weren't even married in church so it would be quite easy to have the marriage annulled.

Lieutenant Andreitsch visits again and as expected the tailor goes to his office with the new uniform blouse over his arm. Ten minutes later the tailor arrives back the worse for wear.

He has had a massive hiding from Andreitsch for wasting government property! I warned him I was watching him, this time he got away with just a good hiding, but next time…?

Yuri sits in the window so he can keep an eye on the camp street. He looks a bit worried and anxious and keeps moving about and scratching his head and just can't settle. When I push him a bit he tells me Sina is pregnant.

I can't see what the problem is, they love each other, her family approve, so where is the hitch?

He just hasn't the nerve to ask her and he still doesn't know how he got the courage to start this baby. He just took her in his arms and there we were!

I offer to write a letter and in it I ask her to marry him. It will take me an hour to produce my best handiwork for Yuri. This has to be special as Sina will keep it forever. All being well it takes me a while but once in the right frame of mind it flows quite nicely, all ending with the words - until death do us part.

Sounds familiar I know, but the 'person' has to come out somehow.

When Yuri reads the epistle he is moved to tears and I quickly move out of range to avoid another big kiss on my cheek.

He is sad that he cannot invite me to the wedding, but everything else is all laughter and sunshine.

Next morning one of the kitchen helpers is reported to need hospital treatment – he was badly beaten up to such an extent he was moved to the main hospital. One spy less.

Mirow is in the camp to find out what went on, but as no one heard or saw anything except the plennie who found the unconscious man, there is little Mirow can do.

"Nitchewo," and his wounds will heal is his verdict.

My letter to Sina was a 100% success, she has agreed to marry him in November straight after the holidays.

Hans seems to become more and more introvert, he is avoiding all contact with the outside world wherever possible, so a move to the main camp for me is not such a bad thing.

8

Russian Prisoner of War Camp
Late 1952

On my arrival there I run into Andreitsch and I greet him according to the regulations, but he totally ignores me. In future I shall continue to stick to the letter regardless how he responds, he is just waiting to trip me up.

Juergen Bachmann of course has gone home but Dr Giessler is still here and we spend many an interesting evening together. He is a fascinating story teller.

Yuri and I meet up regularly. Sina is busy knitting 'little things' but she is still working.

One day before the big celebrations of the October Revolution the big search is supervised by Andreitsch but undertaken by Yuri.

When it's my turn Andreitsch tells me to strip.

"Well it will be a change to see a naked man! I hope you have had a bath."

Everybody in the barracks laughs but I can see the storm clouds gathering in Andreitsch's face as he yells. "Yuri. Why do you address this man with 'you', instead of 'thou'? You are far too familiar with him, it's a conspiracy with a PoW."

But Yuri just grins innocently and asks what that foreign word means. He has it down to a fine art to play the dope and knows it drives Andreitsch mad.

Andreitsch knows he has drawn the short straw and tries to make a dignified exit.

Behind his back Yuri places my pocket knife clearly visible on my pillow.

"No pointed implements allowed," a volley of laughter follows the officer.

November 1952

The day of Yuri's wedding is here and two days later he arrives a happily married man. He comes to see me to bring his wife's regards and a small package containing bread, ham and cake.

Of course he had to confess who really wrote the letters when she watched him sign on the dotted line in the registry office. She noticed the very obvious difference in signatures.

At first she was a bit sad but then forgave him, she realized it was his spirit but my writing. As soon as the wedding pictures are ready he will bring one or two to show me.

December 1952

Christmas is once more approaching with rapid steps. Andreitsch orders, not requests, a Christmas celebration. I have to prepare it and hand in the outline next day for his approval. So I set to work and as requested hand in the blueprint the following day, but now it's Andreitsch's turn, he rips the paper to shreds.

"Not allowed."

When we are lined up for roll-call on Christmas Eve he calls out "Schmitt, Wilhelm," as if he had no idea who I was and hands me a postcard. It's a photo of my wife used in the accepted form of a plennie card.

I shall never understand this man Andreitsch. First he stops the celebrations, then he keeps this picture of my wife until Christmas Eve.

I spend the evening with Dr Giessler in the Sick Bay. The table is decorated with fir twigs and candles and we spend a quiet thoughtful evening. How many Christmases have we spent behind barbed wire?

We both feel instinctively that this will be our last Christmas in Russia.

New Year's Eve is prepared with the usual performances. The choir is practicing, fireworks are planned as well as various other kinds of entertainment.

On the 30th, just after lights out an unknown to us officer comes to our barracks and calls out my name.

"Oh not again!"

To my mind it's back to prison again and who knows I might meet up with Michail again.

I luckily throw all my written stuff in the stove, unnecessary ballast, no use in prison. Quickly my things are packed, a plennie helps me with my rucksack. Everyone wishes me good luck, I respond by telling them to greet the homeland, they will be home soon.

Sergeant Wassya is on duty in the Budka and takes my name off the register. I look for the prison van, but no sign of it.

The officer tells me to get a move on as we approach the admin building where two men are waiting for me – Woronjuk and Hirschfeld.

Luckily, before I can release my pent up fury and anger, as I am convinced this is a set up, Woronjuk walks towards me with outstretched hands. He grabs both my hands and with absolute delight informs me that I am going home.

He had specifically asked the authorities that he should be the one to inform me of my impending release. But I still don't believe him, I think it's all an evil joke at my expense.

However, Hirschfeld too wishes me good luck and all the best, between them they support me inside the admin block.

To my utter amazement I can see a large number of plennies fast asleep on the floor and there is a distinct smell of alcohol and cigarette smoke. Are they all drunk?

A large ungainly figure weaves around the sleeping plennies. It's Yuri who gives me one almighty bear-hug, the two captains tell me to leave my things and to join them for a drink or two.

In the adjoining room is a big table, around it sits the Camp Major, Mirow and Andreitsch. Mirow laughs and says I look as if I'm going to a funeral, not home to my family.

Andreitsch shakes my hand and calls me "Gospodin (Herr) Schmitt," carefully pronouncing every syllable. "Let's bury ill will and drink to' Druzhba' (friendship)." I happily respond to his handshake and then we all sit down.

As far as alcohol is concerned, I have a lot of making up to do. In our repeated toasts to 'Druzhba' with all the people, I watch with admiration as the Russians tip the whole contents of a glass down their throats. That is totally beyond me, but I will try my best in the name of friendship.

This is a proper night for men. There is laughter, singing and dancing.

I have to pinch myself from time to time to make sure it's all real, whilst I am still reasonably sober. Mirow produces an accordion from one of the cupboards and he plays the first chords of Stenka Rasin's song. Woronjuk has a barrel of a bass voice and the others join in with full force.

Before long they have shed their uniform jackets and gradually the tempo of the music alters. It's enticing, choppy and stirring. Andreitsch jumps in the middle of the room and dances his heart out. His last move is a high jump, legs outstretched accompanied by a loud yell. Everyone cheers and claps as Andreitsch sits down.

When Yuri carefully opens the door to check what's going on Woronjuk sees him and tells him to bring a chair and join the party. Yuri falls in straight away by toasting the officers and gentlemen, again everybody cheers.

Then Mirow starts playing again, it's a soft and gentle song about Moscow I think, and everyone hums along in harmony. I see a wet shine in Woronjuk's eyes.

Before long I can no longer register the proceedings, the alcohol has won.

Next morning I wake up freezing with snoring all around being the order of the day so far. I gradually take note of all the still sleeping plennies. It's Yuri's snoring that woke me and a terrible headache.

I carefully get up and find my way out into the hallway. Outside I stick my head in the snow, what a blessed if temporary relief!

When I return to the room with all the sleeping bodies I open a few windows to dilute the heavy air.

Slowly the others wake, they all have one thing in common, a terrific headache. Yuri is the last one to surface and tells me he rescued me from under the table and carried me in his arms to the other plennies.

Being the last one to join the party it was up to Yuri to get official cars to take the others home, with Wassya as escort.

Andreitsch has been the most difficult to get home, he keeps shouting for his friend "Schmitt."

When we begin to feel a bit more human we check each other out. Who is here and who isn't?

Hans Schubert is there and we both feel a bit awkward. But he laughs a bitter laugh and hands me a card that he received just before Christmas. I do not even have to read it, I can guess its content.

Hilde divorced him a year ago, they married in March and she is pregnant now. The photos were exactly as I thought they were in preparation to make it clear to him what was to come.

He is absolutely heartbroken, big tears run down his face and I try to console him as a mother would. I tell him he is now a free man, life for him begins anew. No more dragging up the past, he is young and able, life is an unwritten book for him. There is always his mother, think how she must feel. Her precious boy is coming home. Mothers never let you down, they stand by you through thick and thin.

After this Hans brightens up visibly and agrees that in all his grief he had quite forgotten his mother. Our lady doctor arrives with a box of headache tablets and she finds many takers.

An MGB officer arrives to inform us that we are waiting for a plennie from Odessa who is being flown in by military aircraft, then we are ready for the way home.

We get supplies of sausage and white bread and a bottle of wine to share between two of us.

No more contact to anyone in the camp is permitted, anyone transgressing will be excluded from the transport.

Yuri takes us to the public baths in town where we all get a piece of soap and new underwear.

He tells me his wife is waiting for me at the baths and I am really looking forward to meeting her.

When we arrive at the banya Yuri takes me aside and whisks me into a side room and I meet Sina.

Large grey eyes examine me carefully before she shakes my hand. She is delighted to meet the writer of the glowing love letters and wants to thank me for the chocolate. She really is quite beautiful with the glowing beauty of pregnancy.

She hands me a small package as a 'thank you'. I tell her that the letters were Yuri's thoughts, my words only. They are a lovely young couple.

When we leave the banya all the citizens who had to clear out while we had our ablutions cheer us and wish us good luck. No hard feelings for having to wait in the freezing cold.

We sing all the way to our temporary quarters and I think many of our group are suddenly grabbed by the reality of our situation. Especially for people under thirty who never had a proper job and went into the armed forces straight from school.

1953

The beginning of a new year gave us all the best present imaginable. Freedom. It's up to us all to make proper use of it. The past is over. Finished.

Shortly after midnight Sergeant Wassya calls and takes me to the commandant's room. Captain Woronjuk is there with his very beautiful wife and they are both there to wish me all the best for 1953.

His wife in particular wants me to convey her personal wishes to my wife, her husband has told her so much about me she feels she almost knows me and my family.

The day after this we get our new padded clothes, once again a very thorough search has to be done, everything on paper, even photos have to be handed in.

Then we are ready.

Andreitsch as well as Mirow are there to see us onto our two lorries.

The guards are strangers and as we are driving along I notice we have an escort. A sleek black limousine drives alongside. Woronjuk sits in the front with the driver. Hirschfeld is in the back.

At the station a whole wagon is reserved for us. There are just a few minutes to go before departure when Woronjuk and Hirschfeld arrive,

I get called to the entrance to the wagon. Behind Hirschfeld's broad back Woronjuk hands me a flacon of Russian perfume. His wife has sent it with a message. I must try and forget about hardships and instead treasure the memory of all the good people who crossed my path.

With a heavy heart I say goodbye to them, when I see Yuri racing up the platform.

"Goodbye my German brother, you were my lucky star," and this time I am quite willing and happy to receive his well aimed kisses and I can see he is crying.

Luckily the two bells sound, the doors are closing and we are really truly off. Everyone is running alongside the train still waving to us. Yuri is the last person I see. He stands still and his hand is up to his fur hat in a salute.

There they stay, eight years of my life. Do I depart full of hatred against this system? The people who wished me well by far outweighed the ones who didn't, and that's the thought I will hang on to.

This is not the time for talking as we are all following our own thoughts. But I am still full of fury against people like Baecker. It is people like him who sold others for a plate of soup and still managed to come out on top.

Russia and Germany seem to breed this particularly loathsome type.

In Brest we change into a German train – I refuse to follow old journeys along the way, but I must look out for two graves. They were always my markers when I was going home on leave during my time in the army.

When we arrive at Terespol, Polish custom officers check our luggage and they are very polite and friendly. I salute the two graves as we pass, wooden crosses topped by steel helmets.

On Sunday 4th January 1953 just around 5pm we arrive in Frankfurt a.d. Oder, many a tear rolls down an ex-plennie's face.

Our wagon gets detached from the main train and we are surrounded by fully armed East German police.

We are allowed to get out and stretch our legs and suddenly we all stand still as we hear our first church bells since 1945. Everyone folds their hands and sends up a silent prayer of gratitude.

The German Red Cross feed us, and our Russian escorts are thoroughly enjoying the German food.

Around midnight we are back in the empty station. Only the fully armed police are there and we are all taken to a big waiting room where we are officially handed over to the DDR (German Democratic Republic). Seventeen of us who are going to the west are separated from the group, who are staying in the east.

I just manage to wish Hans Schubert all the best before the police split us up. A bus takes us through the sleeping town, several security types accompany us and very little conversation takes place. We know the type.

Next morning we arrive at the border station Herleshausen. Big reception, lovely food and of course, speeches.

Once we are in the west, the whole circus starts all over again. Speeches, food and the news media.

In the afternoon we are once more sitting down to coffee and cake when a man announces the next speaker, it is none other than Ministerial Director Dr Baecker.

I still cannot believe it, but yes, it's the man whose confession I heard in the hospital a few years back.

What was it Horst always used to say? 'Fat and filth always rise to the top,' or something along those lines.

Baecker had gained a few pounds and looks very different.

I cannot wait to hear what he has to say.

"Dear homecomers," whether my home will be dear to him remains to be seen.

He congratulates us on our ability to withstand all we have suffered, it's good to hear how brave we have all been and how much he respects us for that.

Baecker is full of enthusiasm, he gets his kicks out of the sound of his own voice. His closing comment is about the two million German PoWs who were lost in Russia. Who will be able to tell us what happened to them?

A deathly quiet follows this when suddenly I hear my own voice breaking into the silence.

You should be more than able to tell us Mr Baecker. You were one of the gang of criminals who created notes of the National Committee, this infamous lot caused the premature death of hundreds of thousands of men.

Once again total silence, a pin could be heard to drop, but two well-dressed gentlemen suddenly stand next to me and invite me to accompany them.

Life in the free world has just begun!

ABOUT THE AUTHOR

WILHELM MAX ROSE

He did not return to his family until January 1953 after the Soviet Union 'found' about thirty German PoWs tucked away in various remote and isolated camps in their vast country.

Wilhelm had to get to know his family again, especially the youngest Bernd, whom he had only seen once on his home leave when he baptized him.

He took up his post in the Lutheran church and was eventually posted to a new modern church in Munich from where he retired in 1971.

Wilhelm and Charlotte retired to a beautiful small village in Bavaria. She died in December 1975 to be followed by Wilhelm in 1980.

ACKNOWLEDGEMENTS

I am the second child of Wilhelm and Charlotte Rose from Silesia.

I left Germany in 1954 when I was 17 to go to Scotland to take up nursing.

In later years when given the chance to read what my father had written of his time as a Russian PoW, it took me just three days to get through it. I simply couldn't put it down.

I decided that my four children had a right to read of their grandfather's experiences as I had done. In order for this to happen, I have translated his written words and hope Sharon, Tanya, Luke and Clive will appreciate reliving his time in Russia as I did when I first read it.

My deepest gratitude goes to Neil Butler, my late husband, who transferred my translation of father's German journal of his 8 years imprisonment in Soviet Russia (1945-1953) onto a computer.

Some years later I met and married Samuel Breadon. Together we attempted to put my father's diary into book form with the assistance, advice and hard work of Cary Smith (an author in his own right) and his wife Grace. At long last we made the publishing of 'Nitschewo' a reality.

I must also include my thanks to my family and many friends and acquaintances. Their interest and encouragement was a great spur to persevere with the change of the raw manuscript into book form.

Thank you and bless you all.

Renate Butler, now Renate Breadon